Real World
QuarkImmedia

Real World QuarkImmedia

David Blatner

Peachpit
Press

A Parallax
Production

To my parents: Barbara, Richard, Adam, and Allee
With my love and appreciation

REAL WORLD QUARKIMMEDIA

By David Blatner

PEACHPIT PRESS

2414 Sixth Street
Berkeley, CA 94710
510/548-4393
510/548-5991 (fax)
Find us on the World Wide Web at:
http://www.peachpit.com

Peachpit Press is a division of Addison Wesley Longman.

Copyright ©1997 by David Blatner
Cover design: Lynn Brofsky
Interior design and production: Parallax Productions
CD-ROM design: David Blatner

ISBN 0-201-88679-0

9 8 7 6 5 4 3 2 1
Printed and bound in the United States of America.

Overview

▼▼▼▼▼▼▼▼▼▼▼▼▼▼▼▼▼▼▼▼▼▼▼▼▼▼▼▼▼▼▼▼▼▼

Contents

▼ ▼

▼ ▼

▼ ▼

Chapter 2   QuarkImmedia Basics 35

▼ ▼

Chapter 3   Building Projects 61

▼ ▼

▼ ▼

▼ ▼

▼ ▼

▼ ▼

▼ ▼

▼ ▼

▼ ▼

Chapter 14 Exporting

▼ ▼

Chapter 15 The Internet and World Wide Web

▼ ▼

Chapter 16 The Real World QuarkImmedia CD-ROM

Foreword

THIS IS THE SECOND TIME DAVID BLATNER HAS asked me to write a foreword for one of his books. I did so enthusiastically for his popular *The QuarkXPress Book*. And I'm just as enthusiastic this time.

When we first began developing QuarkImmedia, our goal was to make it possible for the millions of QuarkXPress users to use their skills and move into the multimedia marketplace. We didn't want to reinvent the wheel, nor did we want to turn designers into programmers in order to enable them to create interactive projects.

What we wanted was a product that would let designers be designers. With QuarkImmedia, our users could build on what they already knew about print publishing and create sophisticated, interactive multimedia projects for entirely new market segments.

Still, as with any tool, the end result of what can be produced using QuarkImmedia depends on the expertise of the people using it. While QuarkImmedia wraps up in one package the authoring tools necessary to create compelling projects, using these tools correctly requires knowledge of animation, sound and video editing, as well as other multimedia skills.

That's why it's so important to understand the issues and technology surrounding multimedia and the design of interactive content. Regardless of how your QuarkImmedia projects are produced – internally or using outside help – the more familiar you are with the technology associated with multimedia, the better off you'll be.

David has a deep understanding of all the issues surrounding multimedia. He is also aware of the concerns that designers have when making a move from prepress to the world of multimedia and the Internet.

Real World QuarkImmedia is also useful for people who are well-founded in multimedia, but who may not be as familiar with QuarkXPress. You'll be introduced to Style Sheets, Master Pages, and other elements that may appear at first to be prepress-related, but are extremely useful in multimedia.

Earlier, I said this isn't the first book David has written about Quark. *The QuarkXPress Book* is still considered to be among the best books written about QuarkXPress. Its easy-to-read style is present in *Real World QuarkImmedia* as well. Best of all, you'll find that this book goes well beyond just explaining the features of Quark-Immedia (after all, that's what we pay our documentation writers to do). Instead, *Real World QuarkImmedia* gives you the foundation you need to create the interactive multimedia projects you want. It tells you how to use QuarkImmedia in a real world setting.

Most important, David never forgets that this stuff is supposed to be fun.

—Tim Gill
Chairman
Chief Technology Officer
Quark Inc.

From Page to Screen

THREE YEARS AGO, TIM GILL* STOOD UP in a small room of QuarkXPress users and asked, casually, "Do you think Quark should develop a multimedia authoring tool?" I wasted no time in expressing my humble opinion: No, Quark should stay focused on producing tools for the page, not the screen.

Actually, Quark had already developed a little-known XTension called QuarkPresents that turned a QuarkXPress document into a slide show. I had once used this XTension to present a talk at a conference, and I found it somewhat effective. Nonetheless, I figured that this was a tiny, niche market and didn't deserve any more thought on Quark's part. And a thousand days ago, in that small group of XPress users, the crowd tended to agree with me.

Clearly, the folks at Quark ignored my skeptical comments.

A year later, when I heard that Quark was developing QuarkImmedia (then code-named Orion), I mused to myself that it'd never fly. But when I was able to lay my hands on an early copy of Orion (after a bizarre series of coincidences that memory only half recalls), I had what some people call an "A-ha!" experience.

I saw, in a flash, that Quark had not entirely ignored us users. In QuarkImmedia, they *had* continued to produce tools for the page...

---

*The founder and Chief Technology Officer at Quark

but they had bridged the gap between the page and the screen, and done so in such a transparent and easy-to-grasp way that I began building multimedia projects almost immediately with glee.

While there are times to be bashful about one's mistakes, there are times to stand proud and shout into the windstorm of life, "I was wrong! I was wrong! Thank goodness, I was wrong." This was not the kind of multimedia that I had envisioned, with a steep learning curve and a separate program that had nothing to do with their flagship product, QuarkXPress. This was a whole new ballgame.

QuarkImmedia and Multimedia

QuarkImmedia is an XTension to QuarkXPress—you can build pages in QuarkXPress that can be used for either print or screen. You use the same set of tools, the same interface, and the same process of laying out text and graphics. On top of that, Immedia offers you many features that only apply when someone is viewing the document on screen—buttons, hot links, movies, sounds, animations, windows, popup menus, and so on.

QuarkImmedia makes building multimedia projects fun because you don't have to learn arcane programming languages or jump through hoops to get your project to perform basic tasks, such as opening a window or playing an animation. In fact, if you already know QuarkXPress, you'll feel right at home most of the time.

I don't want to give you the impression that everything about creating projects with QuarkImmedia is easy. But the majority of troubles that people run into are really problems with multimedia in general. Multimedia is still a new field, and most of us who have spent years at getting files to print find multimedia itself a rocky, confusing, backward place.

▼ ▼

Real World QuarkImmedia

"What do you mean, I should use PICT files? I never use PICT files for print."

"I finally figured out what dots-per-inch means, and now you want me to think about sound-samples-per-second?"

"I've spent thirty thousand dollars on a new scanner that can make beautiful 600 dpi CMYK images... and now you tell me that I only need 72 dpi RGB files?"

"I'm just getting into multimedia, but it seems really complex. Should I just give up now?"

I wrote this book primarily because of these sorts of questions. They're the questions that I kept asking myself when I started working with QuarkImmedia. And now, as more and more people are entering the multimedia and Internet arenas, I'm hearing lots of people ask them.

Real World QuarkImmedia teaches you about how Immedia works. But more than that, the book teaches you how to use the program in a real-world, efficient way. I don't just tell you what a feature does, I discuss why it works and how you might want to use it. I also discuss how to get around some of the more annoying problems with the program (whether they're bugs or just missing features).

How to Use this Book

Although you can use this book as a reference manual, looking up a topic whenever you need it, it's designed to be read from cover to cover. And although you use QuarkImmedia within QuarkXPress, *Real World QuarkImmedia* is not a reference manual for Quark-XPress. In fact, throughout most of the book, I assume that you already know how to use XPress's features.

If you don't know how to use XPress, I've got two suggestions. First, read Chapter 1, *XPress Basics*. This first chapter is for people who haven't used XPress much, but who want to use QuarkImmedia. Second, go buy a book called *The QuarkXPress Book*. This is the book that Quark uses to train their technical support staff; if you ever have a question about XPress, you should probably try to look it up in *The QuarkXPress Book* first.*

---

* Granted, I'm biased about this book because I wrote it. But even advanced QuarkXPress users tell me that they learn something from the book every time they pick it up.

However, if you do know how to use XPress, and you need to learn about QuarkImmedia, skip Chapter 1 and move right on to the heart of the book.

Where to Find More Information

I cover many of the essential bits of information—what I call the conceptual underpinnings—about multimedia that you need to know to get your work done. For example, in Chapter 7, *Sound*, I explore the basics of digital sound before discussing how Immedia uses sound. In Chapter 14, *Exporting*, I talk about what compression is and why you need to know about it before discussing how to do it in your QuarkImmedia projects.

However, there are several books on the market that cover general multimedia and Internet-related topics much better than I can in this book.

▶ *Desktop Video* by Andrew Soderberg and Tom Hudson delves deep into digital video, including methods for getting great QuickTime movies.

▶ *Internet Starter Kit for Macintosh* by Adam Engst is the best all-around book on the Internet and what you can use to explore it.

▶ *The Desktop Multimedia Bible* by Jeff Burger gets into every multimedia nook and cranny.

These books are certainly worth taking a look at in your nearest bookstore, if not adding to your permanent library.

▼ ▼

Thank You!

Everyone jokes about the actors who stand up at the Academy Awards and thank everyone they can think of, from their fellow actors to their family. But the truth is that they're really sincere in their appreciation (at least, most of them are) because even though only one person gets the award, they're always backed up by a team of people who've helped. The same is true with books. My name shows up on the cover of the book, but many (many) people have worked on it behind the scenes.

The folks at Quark were incredibly helpful in the creation of this book. I'd like to especially thank Tim Gill, Fred Ebrahimi, Susie Friedman, Margie Levinson, Terri Ficke, Anke Heckhoff-Wedul, Richard Jones, Jon Maggiora, Dave Knoshaugh, Zach Nies, Paul McLean, Gary Fluitt, Ryan House, Martin Skavish, Trevor Alyn, and Glenn Turpin. Also, Ed Owens and Jonathan Levit of the Quark Evangelist Team; and Kris Petracek, Chris Miles, Steve Spieczny, and the rest of the Multimedia Team at Quark. Thank you to the many helpful folks at Quark's technical support, including Don Williams, Brett Delagrange, Aaron Templer, Deidre Adams, Peter Tögel, and Jason Carncross.

There were many people outside of Quark who taught, advised, and helped in all sorts of ways, including Glenn Fleishman, Adam and Tonya Engst, Geoff Duncan, Leonard Mazerov, Sal Soghoian, Walter Schild, and Josh Bevans, and Steve "it's a squishy" Broback and Steve Roth of Thunder Lizard Productions.

I'd also like to thank my editorial team for their excellent work in making sure I used a noun *and* a verb in each sentence—Jeff "Internet Guy" Carlson, the project's managing editor; Cindy Bell of Design Language and Kris Fulsaas, my eagle-eyed copyeditors; Kim Carlson and Shannon Christenot, who proofed and proofed some more. Everyone at Peachpit Press has been great, including Kaethin Prizer, Mimi Heft, Keasley Jones, Nancy Ruenzel, Victor Gavenda, Roslyn Bullas, Cary Norsworthy, and *peachpit emeritus*, Ted Nace.

Finally, I want to thank Debbie Carlson, whose love and support kept me sane and truly happy throughout the duration of this long, long project.

—David Blatner
Seattle, 1996

QuarkXPress Basics

I F YOU WANT TO LEARN HOW TO COOK tasty Indian dishes, you first have to learn the basics of how a stove works. Immedia sits on top of QuarkXPress like a pan on the stove, ready for you to add your ingredients. But if you don't know QuarkXPress, you'll be out of luck when it comes time to bring it to a boil. In this chapter, we'll take a quick look at the key elements of XPress. This is far from a complete lesson, but once you're done, you'll be able to cook up some exciting multimedia projects.

If you're already a QuarkXPress power user, just skip this and jump to Chapter 2, *QuarkImmedia Basics*. If you're an intermediate XPress user, take a moment and skim through this material—you just might find some jewels you didn't know about. Everyone else: let's jump right in and start cooking!

▼ ▼

Tip: Where to Find More Information. There's only so much about XPress that I can include in this small section. To really get all you can out of QuarkXPress and QuarkImmedia, I recommend taking a look at several other books on the market. The first one is *The QuarkXPress Book*, that 800-page best-selling reference guide. (It's the one that Quark tech support uses to train their new staff.) I'm biased, of course, because I wrote it. If you're an intermediate or

1

advanced user and already own *The QuarkXPress Book,* I suggest another book I co-authored: *QuarkXPress Tips & Tricks.* There are several other XPress books I like, including Nancy McCarthy's *QuarkXPress by Design* (a "here's how other professionals do it" book) and Brad Walrod's *QuarkXPress Unleashed* (he covers things about heavy-duty text manipulation that I don't touch in my books).

▼ ▼

Making a New Document

Here's a quick step-by-step method for creating a new document in QuarkXPress.

1. Select the New popout menu from the File menu.

2. If your document is destined for print, select Document. If you have Immedia and it's a multimedia piece, select Project.

3. Fill in the Page Size, Margin, and other pertinent fields (we'll discuss each of the Immedia project options in Chapter 3, *Building Projects*). I recommend turning off the Automatic Text Box option until you get used to working with XPress.

4. Press OK.

▼ ▼

Boxes and Lines

I hate to break it to you, but QuarkXPress is not as complicated as some people would like you to believe. The fundamentals, certainly, are really easy. First, remember that XPress is designed to do one thing really well: it lets you put pictures and text together on a page. You can do all sorts of other things with the program, but the farther you stray, the harder it gets. Use other programs to generate content whenever possible, then use XPress to pull it all together.

That's not to say you'll never enter text or build a graphic element in XPress. Of course you will. But too many people expect XPress to be the perfect word processor, illustration program, and image editor all in one.

With that in mind, let's look at the basics: boxes and lines.

Text Boxes and Picture Boxes

Every picture and block of text you want on your page must be placed into either a picture box or a text box. You make these boxes using the Text Box tool or one of the several Picture Box tools (see Figure 1–1). Once you create a text box or a picture box, you can fill it with text or a picture in one of several ways, which I'll discuss in a moment. First let's take a look at how you can give these boxes background color, borders, and text runaround attributes.

Background color. Picture and text boxes typically have a background color of White. It's an opaque white, so it hides whatever is behind the box. You can change the background color of picture and text boxes in several ways.

Figure 1-1

Making boxes

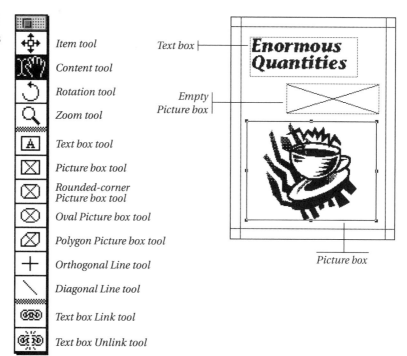

Item tool

Content tool

Rotation tool

Zoom tool

Text box tool

Picture box tool

Rounded-corner Picture box tool

Oval Picture box tool

Polygon Picture box tool

Orthogonal Line tool

Diagonal Line tool

Text box Link tool

Text box Unlink tool

Text box

Empty Picture box

Enormous Quantities

Picture box

▶ Selecting Modify from the Item menu (or pressing Command-M), then selecting the color from the Background popup menu (see Figure 1–2).

▶ Clicking on the Background icon on the Colors palette (see "Palettes," below), then clicking on the color name.

▶ Dragging the little square color swatch out from the Colors palette, and dropping it on top of the box.

You can also make a box transparent by setting the background color to None. In this case, the content of the box isn't transparent, but the background is.

Borders and Frames. Boxes can also have colored frames around them. To apply a frame to a selected box, choose Border from the

Figure 1–2
Modifying a picture
box or text box

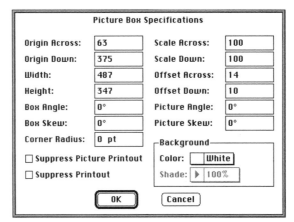

Picture Box Specifications

Origin Across:	63	Scale Across:	100
Origin Down:	375	Scale Down:	100
Width:	487	Offset Across:	14
Height:	347	Offset Down:	10
Box Angle:	0°	Picture Angle:	0°
Box Skew:	0°	Picture Skew:	0°
Corner Radius:	0 pt		

☐ Suppress Picture Printout
☐ Suppress Printout

Background
Color: White
Shade: ▶ 100%

[OK] [Cancel]

Text Box Specifications

Origin Across:	0.5"
Origin Down:	0.5"
Width:	7.5"
Height:	10"
Box Angle:	0°
Box Skew:	0°
Corner Radius:	0"
Columns:	1
Gutter:	0.167"
Text Inset:	1 pt

First Baseline
Offset: 0"
Minimum: Ascent

Vertical Alignment
Type: Top
Inter ¶ Max: 0"

Background
Color: White
Shade: ▶ 100%

☐ Suppress Printout

[OK] [Cancel]

Item menu (or press Command-B; see Figure 1–3). Boxes typically have borders with a width of zero (no border). In the Borders dialog box, select a frame style, give it a width and color, and press OK.

Figure 1–3
Adding a
border to a box

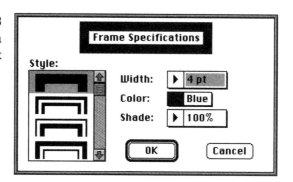

To remove a frame around a box, set the width of the frame back to 0 (zero).

Runaround. Any object that sits on top of a text box may force the text in that box to run around it. This is called *text runaround* or *text wrap*. The way you control this is by selecting the topmost object (the one that's forcing the text underneath it to wrap), and choosing Runaround from the Item menu (or pressing Command-T).

Most boxes in XPress have a runaround set to Item, which means that the underlying text wraps around the edges of the topmost box (see Figure 1–4). There are three other choices.

▶ **None.** If you set the runaround to None, the topmost box has no effect on the text underneath.

▶ **Auto Image.** If the topmost box is a picture box, you can select Auto Image from the Runaround popup menu. This tells QuarkXPress to wrap the text as best it can around the image inside the box.

▶ **Manual Image.** When you choose Manual Image, you get the same text wrap as with Auto Image, but you can then make changes to it by moving corner points and line segments on the *runaround polygon.*

Figure 1–4

Text runaround

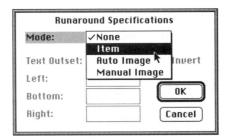

Item runaround applied to the picture

Runaround of None

Auto runaround

Manual runaround

Note that a single column of text cannot wrap on both sides of an object in version 3.32 (or earlier) of XPress. Yes, I know you can do that in PageMaker.

Polygons

Picture boxes and text boxes can be rectangular, or you can make them into polygons. Polygonal picture boxes are easier to make than polygonal text boxes, because you can just create them using the Polygon Picture box tool. Text boxes, however, must start out life as rectangles. To turn a rectangular picture or text box into a polygon, choose the polygon shape from the Box Shape submenu under the Item menu (see Figure 1–5).

To reshape a polygon (to add corner points, move segments, and so on), you have to select Reshape Polygon from the Item menu. To add or delete a corner point in a polygon, Command-click on a point or a line segment. To move a line segment or a corner point,

Figure 1–5
Changing box shape

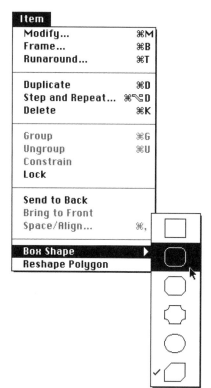

just drag it. When you're finished modifying the polygon, turn off the Reshape Polygon option on the Item menu.

Note that you cannot create polygons with curves, or polygons that don't close (like a three-sided box) in version 3.32 of XPress— you can make polygons only with straight lines that join at the ends.

▼ ▼

Tip: Resizing Boxes. You can change the height and width of a box at any time by dragging one of its corner or side handles. If you resize a picture box while a picture is in it, you'll see less or more of the picture (cropping). To resize a box while you resize the picture or text inside it, hold down the Command key while you drag.

If you hold down the Command and Shift keys while you drag, you force the height and width of the box *and* of its content to be the same (rectangles are turned into squares; ovals are turned into circles). If you hold down Command, Shift, *and* Option, you maintain the ratio of the height and width. That is, you stretch the box and its content proportionally.

▼ ▼

Importing Pictures and Text

Once you've got a picture or a text box, you're ready to put a picture or text into it. This brings us to a crucial (and sometimes confusing) issue in working with XPress: the Item and Content tools.

You must use the Item tool when you want to move a picture box or text box on the page. But you must use the Content tool to affect what's inside a picture or text box. For instance, once you create a text box, you can use the Item tool to move it to where you want it, then switch to the Content tool to type inside it. To select more than one box, you have to use the Item tool. Confusion about the Item and Content tools probably causes more problems than anything else in XPress. If you find you're trying to do something and the program is just beeping at you, make sure you have the right tool for the job. (If this is still confusing, think of it this way: if you only had one tool for both jobs, how would XPress know what you were trying to do when you clicked or dragged inside a box?)

If you have text or a picture saved on disk, you can import it into a selected box by choosing Get Text or Get Picture from the File menu. You can also paste pictures or text from the Clipboard. While it's usually a bad idea to paste pictures into picture boxes when you're creating XPress pages that will be printed, pasting in pictures when you're building multimedia projects is fine (see "Pictures" in Chapter 3, *Building Projects,* for more on graphic file formats and how to import them).

Linking Text Boxes

When you have more text than can fit in a text box, XPress displays a little overset mark in the lower-left corner of the box (see Figure 1–6). You can link two or more text boxes with the Linking tool: click once on the box you want to link *from* (it will start flashing), then click where you want to link *to*. The boxes don't have to be on the same page—if they're not, just click on the first box, then scroll to the other page and click on the next box. Note that you cannot link to a box with text in it; you can only link to empty boxes.

After you link text boxes, the text flows from one to the other—and if you edit the text, it reflows automatically. Some people chop up all their stories into little bite-size pieces because text linking

Figure 1–6
Linking text boxes

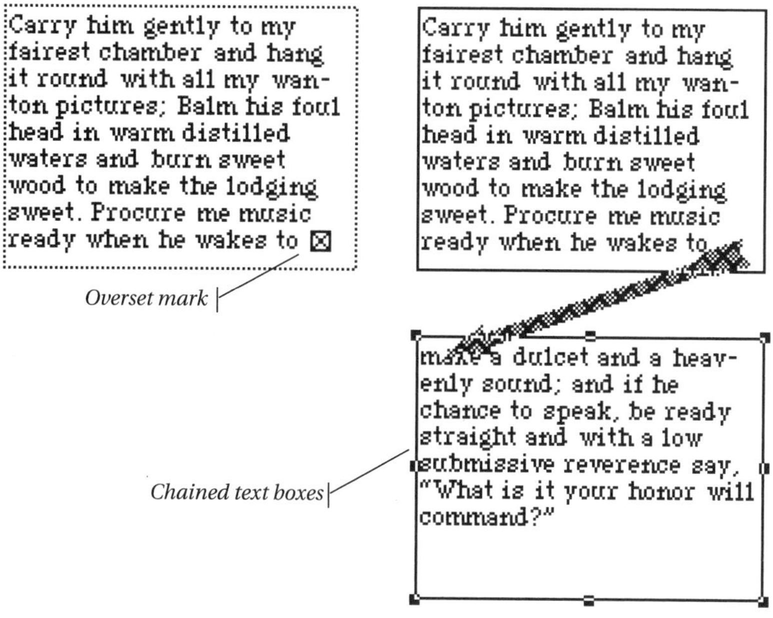

Carry him gently to my fairest chamber and hang it round with all my wanton pictures; Balm his foul head in warm distilled waters and burn sweet wood to make the lodging sweet. Procure me music ready when he wakes to ☒

Overset mark

Carry him gently to my fairest chamber and hang it round with all my wanton pictures; Balm his foul head in warm distilled waters and burn sweet wood to make the lodging sweet. Procure me music ready when he wakes to

make a dulcet and a heavenly sound; and if he chance to speak, be ready straight and with a low submissive reverence say, "What is it your honor will command?"

Chained text boxes

intimidates them (but I know you wouldn't do that). Linking is not really that difficult, and it saves a lot of time.

Unlinking boxes. What if you link a text box you didn't mean to include in the text chain? One option is to delete the box (press Command-K). That takes it out of the text chain, but it doesn't delete the text inside the box (it just reflows to other boxes in the chain).

Another option is to use the Unlinking tool. When you click once with the Unlinking tool on any box in the text chain, XPress shows you how the boxes are linked together by displaying a bunch of plaid arrows. To break a link, you can click on the arrowhead or tailfeather of one of those arrows. One more option: Shift-click anywhere in the box with the Unlinking tool—that removes only that box from the chain.

Lines

Creating a straight line is even easier than making a box. There are two line tools: the first only lets you draw horizontal and vertical lines, and the second lets you draw any kind of line you want. I rarely use the first tool, because I can force the Diagonal Line tool to draw vertical and horizontal (or 45-degree) lines by holding down the Shift key.

Once you create a line, you can give it a width, a color, a style, and end caps (arrows, or whatever). All these options appear in the Line Specifications dialog box you get by choosing Modify from the Item menu (or by pressing Command-M or by double-clicking on the line; see Figure 1–7). You can also make some of these changes in the Measurements palette (see "Pasteboard and Palettes," below).

▼ ▼

Pasteboard and Palettes

Every page in a QuarkXPress document sits on an enormous white area called the *pasteboard* (see Figure 1–8). There's a gray line between each page (or between each spread of pages, if you're

Figure 1–7
Line Specifications
dialog box

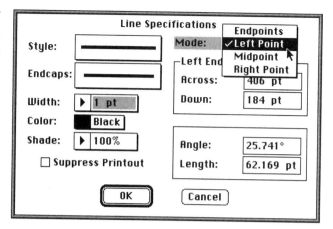

Figure 1–8
The pasteboard

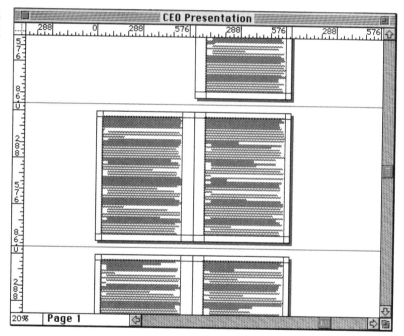

working on a facing-page document like a magazine), and boxes, lines, buttons, and everything else must be on one side of the line or another.

The pasteboard is useful for storing items that you may want to put on a page. But it's also where you'll place your windows and some hidden objects in your Immedia projects.

Note that XPress's pasteboard works differently than Adobe PageMaker's. In PageMaker, the pasteboard is common to each page or spread. So if you put a picture on the pasteboard to the left of page one, then jump to page seven, the picture is still there, off to the left of page seven. In XPress, that picture is still just sitting around next to page one.

▼ ▼

Tip: Adding and Removing Pages. New documents begin with a single page. You can add one or more pages to the document by selecting Insert from the Page menu. To delete a page from a document, select Delete from the Page menu. You can also add or delete pages on the Document Layout palette.

▼ ▼

Tip: What Page Are You On? QuarkXPress has a personality trait that confuses many newcomers, so I'd better explain it right away. When you look at Figure 1–9, at first it seems like you're looking at page five. After all, that's what the page number in the lower-left corner of the document window tells us. However, XPress determines this page number by looking at whatever is in the upper-left corner of the window. Notice that thin gray line at the top? That means the previous page's pasteboard is showing. *That* is page five; we're looking at page six.

Figure 1–9
Page numbering

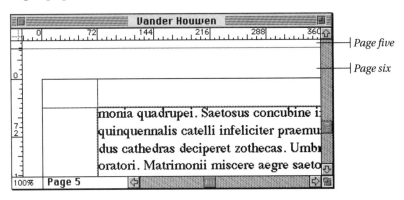

page or spread.

▼ ▼

Guides

By default, QuarkXPress shows you all the guides on a page. This includes both margin guides (around the edge of the page) and guides you've added.

Adding guides. You can add a guide to the page by dragging it out from either the horizontal or vertical ruler around the document page. If you drop the guide on the page, it becomes a page guide (it only goes across the width or height of the page). If you drop it on the pasteboard, it becomes a pasteboard guide (it goes all the way across the pasteboard).

▼ ▼

Tip: Set Guides to Front. For some strange reason, some Quark engineer set the default for guides to sit behind any object on the page. This means that if you have a text box with a white background and pull a guide out on top of it, the guide disappears behind the box as soon as you let go of the mouse button. To fix this strange behavior, go to General Preferences (under the Edit menu, or press Command-Y), and change Guides to In Front. Like almost all the other preferences, if you change this while no document is open, it becomes the default for every new document you create.

▼ ▼

Moving and removing guides. Once you've got a guide on your page, you can move it by clicking on it and dragging it. When you have the Content tool selected, dragging guides is a hassle (you can't click on them while the cursor is over any text or picture boxes), so I like using the Item tool for this kind of work.

If you want to remove a guide, you can drag it out of the document window (doesn't matter which side of the window) or back into the ruler. If you have a lot of guides and you want to delete them all at once, you can Option-click on the rulers. If the page is touching the ruler when you do this, the page guides are removed; if the pasteboard is touching the ruler, just the pasteboard guides are removed.

Hiding and showing guides. When I'm building a page, I have all the guides visible. But occasionally I turn them off so that I can see what the finished exported or printed page will look like. You can hide or show the guides by selecting Hide Guides or Show Guides from the View menu—or (faster) by pressing the F7 key.

Palettes

Palettes seem to be all the rage in computer software these days. These little floating windows are similar to dialog boxes—they tell you about objects on your page, and also let you change them—but you can have them open all the time. QuarkXPress has lots of palettes (though nowhere near as many as some programs), but four of them are particularly useful: Measurements, Document Layout, Colors, and Style Sheets.

You can open or hide each of the palettes by choosing its name from the View menu.

Measurements palette. The Measurements palette is "Control Central" for objects on your page. You must have at least one object selected in order for the Measurements palette to become active. The left side of the palette describes the selected item itself; the right side describes the content of the item (if it's a box) or the line style (if it's a line). See Figure 1–10.

When you change a value on the palette, you affect the item(s) selected. For instance, if you have a picture or text box selected, and you want its left edge to be three-quarters of an inch from the left edge of the page, you can replace the x coordinate in the Measurements palette with .75". If you want to rotate a box 25 degrees, replace the rotation angle with 25 (you don't have to type the degree mark—XPress knows you're talking about degrees here).

Figure 1–10
Measurements palette

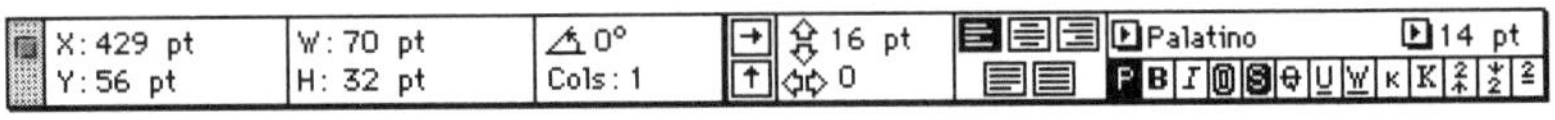

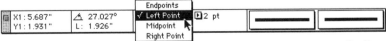

For text boxes

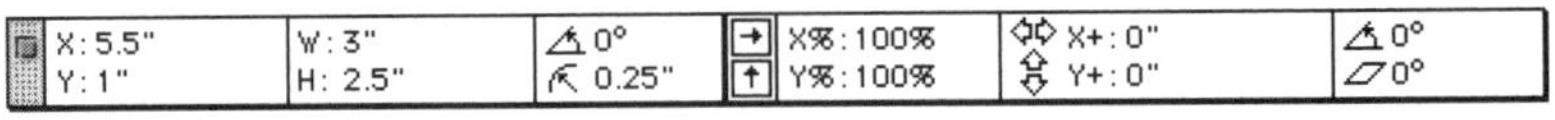

For picture boxes

For lines

▼ ▼

Tip: Measurement Keystrokes. If you like using keystrokes (as I do), you can jump to the first field of the Measurements palette by pressing Command-Option-M. Then you can press Tab to skip forward through the fields, or Shift-Tab to skip backward. If you're in a text box, you can type Command-Option-Shift-M to jump directly to the Font field of the palette. Once you're there, you can type the first few letters of whatever font you want; if XPress can guess the font's name from what you type, it'll fill it in automatically.

▼ ▼

Document Layout palette. The Document Layout palette (press the F10 key) is like an overview of your entire document (see Figure 1–11). It lets you navigate through your document quickly (it's especially useful for jumping between the document pages and the master pages—see "Master Pages," later in this chapter). It also lets you add, delete, or move pages around within your document.

Colors palette. The Colors palette (press the F12 key) displays and lets you apply every available color in an XPress document (see Figure 1–12). There are two ways to apply color from this palette.

Figure 1–11
Document
Layout palette

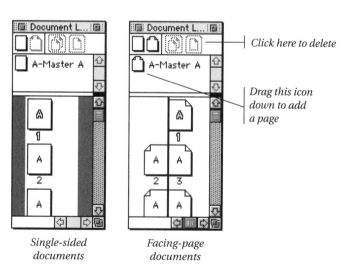

Click here to delete

Drag this icon down to add a page

Single-sided documents   *Facing-page documents*

Figure 1-12
Colors palette

▶ You can click on the color name. But before you do this, you must first select one of the three icons that are displayed across the top of the palette: Border, Content, or Background.

▶ You can drag the color swatch from the palette over the object you want to color (at least one object must be selected in order to do this, but it doesn't have to be the one you want to color). Unfortunately, you can't apply color to the content of a text or picture box this way.

When you choose the Background icon in the palette, XPress lets you choose a solid-color or a blended background. Here's how to make a blend.

1. Choose the Background icon from the palette.

2. Select one of the blend types from the Background popup menu (it's usually set to Solid). If you have the Cool Blends XTension loaded (see "XTensions," later in this chapter), you should have about seven types of blends to choose from.

3. Click on radio button #1.

4. Choose a color and a tint.

5. Click on radio button #2.

6. Choose a color and a tint.

7. If you want the blend to be at any other angle than "left to right," change the angle field in the palette to another value (other than zero degrees).

Note that you cannot see blends in a selected box when the Content tool is selected (XPress only shows you the first color as a solid background). I'll discuss creating new colors in "Other Important Features," later in this chapter.

Style Sheets palette. Style sheets are collections of text-formatting attributes (font, style, size, and so on) with a single name. All the style sheets you create in a document are displayed in the Style Sheets palette (select it from the View menu or press the F11 key), and when a paragraph is selected in a text box, the palette shows you what style sheet is applied to that paragraph. You can also apply a style sheet to text by clicking on its name on the palette.

Sometimes when you select a paragraph, the style sheet name in the palette has a plus sign (+) next to it. This means that the paragraph has *local formatting* which overrides the style sheet (local formatting is different than the formatting called for in the style sheet definition). For instance, if you apply a style sheet that calls for the font Palatino, then apply Helvetica to one word in the paragraph, the Style Sheets palette will show a plus sign whenever your cursor is inside that single word.

▼ ▼

Formatting Text and Graphics

Once you've got text inside a text box or a picture inside a picture box, you can't just let it be . . . . It's time to start formatting and styling. Here's a quick rundown of the sorts of things you can do to text and graphics, and how you can do them. Remember that when you style text or pictures, you almost always need to have the Content tool selected (because you're affecting the content of the box, not the box itself).

Text

It's a tribute to the desktop publishing revolution that most people I meet have a favorite font. Ten years ago, hardly anyone knew what a typeface was; now it's a household word. So although it's often tempting to ignore typography altogether, if you want to communicate or catch someone's attention, you'd better take some time with your type.

You can find almost every XPress feature having to do with typographic control under the Style menu (see Figure 1–13), though many of the features that you need most also appear on the Measurements palette (font, size, leading, kerning, and so on). If you are new to design or desktop publishing, these are some of the more confusing elements of text design in XPress. If you want more information, I strongly recommend two books by Robin Williams: *The Mac is not a typewriter* and *The Non-designer's Design Book* (both published by Peachpit Press).

Figure 1–13
The Style menu
(text block selected)

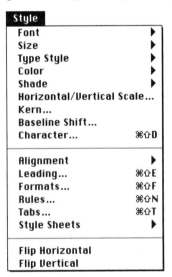

Character versus paragraph formatting. All text formatting features break down into three groups: character, paragraph, and text box formatting. Character formatting affects only the characters that you select. For instance, you can make one word **bold**, or in some other font. Typeface, size, style, baseline shift, color, shade, kerning/tracking, and horizontal/vertical scaling are character attributes. You can control character formats either on the Style menu or in the Character dialog box (Command-Shift-D).

Paragraph formatting affects an entire paragraph, no matter where in the paragraph the cursor is. (It's frustrating to watch people painstakingly select an entire paragraph to apply a paragraph attribute; instead, you can simply place your cursor anywhere in the paragraph, or select one word.) Paragraph attributes include: leading, space before and space after, indents, tabs, and drop caps (I describe some of these below). All the paragraph formats appear in the Formats dialog box (select Formats from the Style menu, or press Command-Shift-F).

The third type of formatting, text box formatting, affects all the text in a text box. This includes text inset (the distance the text sits from the edge of the box), vertical alignment (does the text sit at the top, bottom, or middle of the text box?), and number of columns in the text box. You can control each of these in the Text Box Specifications dialog box (press Command-M, or you can double-click with the Item tool).

Leading. Each character in a line of text sits on a *baseline*. Leading is the amount of vertical space from one baseline to the next. More leading means more space between lines. XPress usually applies an "auto" amount of leading, which is about 20 percent of the type size. It's much more reliable to change this to an absolute number.

Space Before and Space After. It's not a good idea to type two of anything in a row—don't type two tabs, or two spaces after a period, or even two returns between paragraphs. If you want more space between paragraphs, use Space Before or Space After. This not only gives you much more control over how much space to add between the paragraphs, but also saves you from the embarrassment of having an extra empty paragraph appear (when you least expect it) at the top or bottom of a column of text.

Drop Caps. Designers love drop caps. They're certainly good for attracting people's attention. XPress makes drop caps easy for you—just turn on the Drop Caps feature in the Formats dialog box, and specify how many characters you want to drop, plus how many lines you want them to drop. You can still treat the drop cap like text, changing its color or typeface or whatever.

Kerning and Tracking. If you're like most folks, you spend very little time thinking about letterspacing—the amount of space between each character. But the amount of space XPress uses by default is very often less or more than optimal. For instance, if you add an en dash (Option-hyphen) between numbers to indicate a range (*e.g.,* 4–9), the spacing between the numbers and the en dash is often too tight. You can change this value with kerning and tracking.*

To kern two letters together or apart, place the cursor between the letters and choose Kern from the Style menu. To track a range of text, select the text and choose Track from the Style menu.

Pictures

We'll be discussing pictures and what you can do with them in much more depth in "Pictures" in Chapter 3, *Building Projects,* but there are some basic formatting issues that we should cover here. We already talked about how you can crop pictures (just resize the picture box). You can also resize pictures quickly on the Measurements palette, or with a few keystrokes (see Table 1–1).

Other than resizing, you can flip a picture horizontally or vertically, rotate it (either by rotating the picture box, or the picture within the box), change the offset (move the picture within the box), or skew it. The controls for each of these are on the Measurements palette. You can also colorize or tint pictures using the Style menu, but only if they're in TIFF format. TIFF is great for prepress work, but PICT is often better for multimedia projects, so these features may be less relevant here.

Master Pages

When you create a new document and add a bunch of pages, each document page is based on a master page. If you put a big red box

---

Tracking is really the wrong word, but it's the word QuarkXPress uses, so I'll use it, too. A better term would be *range kerning,* as it's really just kerning over a range of text.

Table 1–1
Picture formatting

To do this . . .	Press this . . .
Center a picture in a box	Command-Shift-M
Fit a picture to a box disproportionally	Command-Shift-F
Fit a picture to a box proportionally	Command-Shift-Option-F
Scale up five percent	Command-Shift-Option-period
Scale down five percent	Command-Shift-Option-comma

on the master page, it automatically appears on every document page. Any time a design (whether for print or multimedia) calls for elements that repeat on a number of pages in your project, you should be using master pages.

For instance, page numbers may be in the same place on every page of a book. Or a Next Page button might appear in the same place on 12 screens of a project. Instead of putting that number or button on each and every XPress page, you can put it on only one—the master page. If you later need to change the position of that button, you can change it once on the master page and it will automatically be changed on every document page.

Master Pages versus Document Pages

Master pages are always "behind the scenes." You can see a master page in one of two ways.

▶ You can select the master page from the Display submenu under the Page menu. This is the really slow way to do it.

▶ You can double-click on the master page name or icon on the Document Layout palette. This is much faster.

When you're ready to go back and view your document pages, you can use the same methods (except that you choose or double-click on the document page instead of the master page). You cannot view both the master page and the document page at the same time.

You can have up to 127 different master pages in a single document (though I don't think I've ever used more than six or seven, and many people get by with one or two). That means you can make a master page for each page design that you use more than once or twice throughout your project.

Making a new master page. You can make a new master page by dragging one of the little "blank page" icons from the top-left corner of the Document Layout palette into the master page area of the palette (see Figure 1–14). Or if you're trying to make one master page similar to another, you can duplicate the first by selecting it and clicking on the Duplicate icon on the palette. Then go ahead and make whatever changes you want to the duplicate.

Figure 1-14
Master pages and
the Document
Layout palette

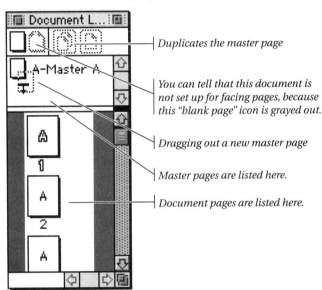

Duplicates the master page

You can tell that this document is not set up for facing pages, because this "blank page" icon is grayed out.

Dragging out a new master page

Master pages are listed here.

Document pages are listed here.

Applying master pages. If you only have one master page in a document, every page in that document is based on the A-Master A page (that's the name of the master page). When you add more master pages, you can apply that master page to existing document pages or create new document pages based on that master page.

> ▶ **Creating new pages.** To add a new page to a document, you can choose Insert from the Page menu. XPress then displays a dialog box asking you how many pages to insert and where to insert them. It also gives you the chance to select which master page the new page(s) should be based on. You can also

create a new page by dragging one of the master page icons on the Document Layout palette down into the document page area of the palette.

▶ **Applying master pages.** To apply a master page to a document page, you can drag the master page icon down over the page on the Document Layout palette. Of course, when you do this, any elements from the last master page (whatever master page the document page *used* to be based on) are deleted and replaced with the elements from the new master page. Be careful—even power users make mistakes when doing this.

▼ ▼

Tip: Applying Master Pages Fast. Dragging icons around is kind of slow if you need to apply a master page to a number of pages, so here's another method.

1. Select all the pages you want to change. You can select a range of pages by clicking on the first page of the range on the Document Layout palette, then Shift-clicking on the last page. Or if the pages are not contiguous, you can Command-click on each one you want selected.

2. Option-click on the master page icon on the palette.

Voilà! Those pages are now based on whatever master page you Option-clicked on.

▼ ▼

Deleting master pages. It's easy to delete a master page: just select it and click the Delete icon on the Document Layout palette. You can delete document pages this way, too. Remember that there may be document pages based on the master pages you delete. If so, all the master page items on those document pages will be deleted when you do this. The document page will be left being based on no master page at all.

Margins

One of the most commonly asked questions about QuarkXPress is "How do I change the margins on my page?" It's not obvious at all, but you can make changes to margins only on a master page (in fact, if you want, each master page can have a different set of margins). For instance, in many of my projects, I have two master pages: one with a big margin (perhaps one inch) around the edge, and another with no margins at all. The first is for titles, introductions, or pages where there's a lot of text. The second is for graphics-heavy pages.

To change the margins, go to the master page you want to affect, then select Margin Guides from the Page menu.

▼ ▼

Style Sheets

A *style sheet* is a collection of text formatting that's given a name. For example, instead of saying "11-point Times italic with 14-point leading and a first-line indent of .5 inch," you could give all of that a name (like "Body Text"). Whenever you want to apply that formatting, you just apply Body Text.

There are three great benefits to using style sheets.

▶ You can apply formatting to a lot of text much more quickly because you only have to apply the single style-sheet name, instead of all the various formats.

▶ Because all the formatting is saved under one name, whenever you use a style sheet you can be assured that paragraph formatting will be consistent. One of the most common (and ugly) mistakes people make is to accidentally apply different text formats to different paragraphs when they want the paragraphs to be the same.

▶ Perhaps the greatest benefit to using style sheets comes when you need to make a change to one of the text formats. For instance, let's say your Heading1 style was formatted in Times Bold, and you used it throughout your 200-page document.

Only then does your art director tell you that she hates Times and wants you to use Univers instead. Instead of having to go back and change every instance of that heading style, you can make one change: to the definition of the Heading1 style sheet. XPress automatically updates every paragraph based on that style sheet name.

Creating a new style sheet. There are various ways to build a new style sheet, but in my opinion, there's really only one good way.

1. Format one paragraph exactly the way you want to define the style sheet.

2. Select Style Sheets from the Edit menu (or take a shortcut: Command-click on any name on the Style Sheets palette).

3. Click the New button.

4. Give the style sheet a name (see Figure 1–15).

5. Press OK, then press Save.

That's all there is to it. Why people say making style sheets is too hard is a mystery to me.

Figure 1–15
Creating a style sheet
by example

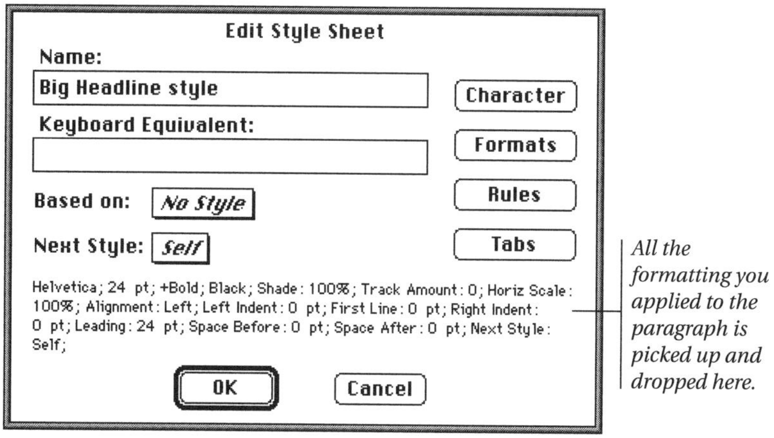

Edit Style Sheet

Name:

`Big Headline style`

Keyboard Equivalent:

Based on: `No Style`

Next Style: `Self`

Character

Formats

Rules

Tabs

Helvetica; 24 pt; +Bold; Black; Shade: 100%; Track Amount: 0; Horiz Scale: 100%; Alignment: Left; Left Indent: 0 pt; First Line: 0 pt; Right Indent: 0 pt; Leading: 24 pt; Space Before: 0 pt; Space After: 0 pt; Next Style: Self;

OK   Cancel

All the formatting you applied to the paragraph is picked up and dropped here.

Applying style sheets. Once you've created a style sheet, you still have to apply it to paragraphs (even the sample paragraph you made first still doesn't have the style sheet applied to it). Applying a style sheet to a paragraph is also called "tagging" a paragraph (I like to picture a little tag hanging off the side of the paragraph with the name of the style sheet written on it).

To apply a style sheet, put the cursor in whatever paragraph you want to tag (you don't have to select the entire paragraph), then click on the style sheet name on the Style Sheets palette. (Or if you want to go the hard way, select the name from the Style Sheets submenu under the Style menu.)

Sometimes the Style Sheets palette displays a plus sign after you've applied the style sheet. This means that local formatting is getting in the way of the style sheet. If you want to override that local formatting, select No Style from the Style Sheets palette, then select the style sheet name again. But be careful: this overrides *all* your local formatting (including words that are bold or italic). You may have to do some fix-up work after you make this move.

Editing style sheets. Later, when you need to edit the style sheet definition (it seems like fate—or your art director—makes this almost always necessary), you can do this by going back to the Style Sheets dialog box (under the Edit menu, or by Command-clicking on the name on the Style Sheets palette), selecting the name from the list, and clicking the Edit button. Again, whatever changes you make here are automatically applied throughout the document.

▼ ▼

Tip: Multidocument Style Sheets. Many people use the same style sheets for multiple documents, but XPress doesn't make this inherently easy to do (at least not in version 3.32 or earlier). Here are a few ways to do it.

▶ **Copy and Paste.** If you want to copy a style sheet from one document to another, you can copy and paste a paragraph tagged with that style sheet. The style sheet comes along with the text. Then you can delete the text, and the style sheet definition stays.

▶ **Append.** The fastest way to copy *all* the style sheets from one document into another is to use the Append button in the

Style Sheets dialog box (select Style Sheets from the Quark-XPress Edit menu).

▶ **Default Styles.** When you build style sheets while no document is open, they appear in every document you create from then on. They aren't added to older documents, but when you create a new document, the style sheets appear automatically. This adds to the default style sheets (usually there's just one default style sheet: Normal).

Note that each of these methods also works for using the same colors in multiple documents!

▼ ▼

Other Important Features

Now that you're able to create new documents complete with master pages, text boxes, and picture boxes, there's still the matter of some nitty-gritty issues like how to navigate around your page, or create new colors. In this last section, we'll explore some features and techniques that you'll surely need for building your projects.

Navigation

Navigating around your page or document isn't one of the more fascinating activities in QuarkXPress, but it *is* the one thing you'll probably do more than anything else, so it's important to get good at it. Here are some techniques you can use to get around (other than clicking in those silly scroll bars).

Scrolling around a page. The best way to scroll around a page is to hold down the Option key to get the Grabber Hand. Then click and drag the mouse until you get where you want to be. This is better than the scroll bars for two reasons.

▶ The Grabber Hand can scroll diagonally.

▶ You can always use the Grabber Hand to scroll, no matter where the cursor is.

Zooming in and out. Next to scrolling around a page, the next most common thing people do is to zoom in and out to get different perspectives of their page. You can do this by selecting view percentages from the View menu, but I find that keystrokes are faster.

- ▶ Command-1 zooms to Actual Size (100 percent).

- ▶ Command-0 zooms to Fit in Window.

- ▶ Command-Option-click toggles between 200 percent and Actual Size.

- ▶ Control-V jumps to the view magnification field in the lower-left corner of the document window. There you can type in whatever view percentage you want (from 10 to 400 percent), then press Enter or Return.

- ▶ Holding down the Control key gives you the Zoom In tool (which typically zooms in by 25 percent each time you click). Control-Option-clicking zooms out by the same amount.

- ▶ If you know where you want to zoom in to, you can drag out a marquee with the Zoom In tool. When you let go of the mouse button, XPress zooms in to that area.

Scrolling around the document. Using the scroll bars to get to other pages in your document can be painfully boring. Instead, you can use the controls on the Page menu (Previous, Next, First, Last). Better yet, use some keyboard shortcuts (you need an extended keyboard to make most of these work).

- ▶ Command-Home brings you to the top of the first page of the document.

- ▶ Command-End brings you to the last page of the document.

- ▶ Command- or Shift-Page Down jumps to the next page.

- ▶ Command- or Shift-Page Up jumps to the previous page.

- ▶ Command-J brings up the Go To dialog box, where you can jump to whatever page you want.

Layering

Every object on a page sits on its own layer, so if you put two objects on a page, one is on top and the other is on the bottom. You can control the layering of objects by choosing Bring to Front or Send to Back from the Item menu. If you hold down the Option key while you click on the Item menu, those features change to Bring Forward and Send Backward (so you can move an object one layer at a time).

When you move objects by a single layer at a time, remember that it's not always apparent which objects are on top of others. A red box may look like it's right on top of a blue box, but if there are any other objects (lines, buttons, or boxes) elsewhere on the page, they might be "between" the red and blue boxes.

New Colors

There's only so far you can get with the eight basic colors Quark-XPress gives you (Red, Green, Blue, Cyan, Magenta, Yellow, Black, and White*). Pretty soon you'll want to start creating new colors. Building colors for prepress applications is a major hassle because you have to concern yourself with spot colors versus process colors, halftone angles, and so on. Fortunately, color in multimedia, while still complicated somewhat by color palettes (which I'll discuss in Chapter 3, *Building Projects*), is comparatively much easier.

Creating a color. To create a new color, select Colors from the Edit menu (or if any object is selected on the page, you can take a shortcut: Command-click on any name on the Colors palette), then press the New button (see Figure 1–16). Because the colors you create here will only be seen on screen (remember, this is a book about Immedia, not prepress), you should create colors in either the RGB or HSB color models. I usually find myself choosing a color in RGB first, then fine-tuning it in HSB (you can switch between the models whenever you want).

However, remember that an Immedia project can only display 256 different colors in a document, so you won't necessarily get

---

*XPress also includes the color *Registration,* which is only relevant in prepress.

Figure 1-16
Creating a color

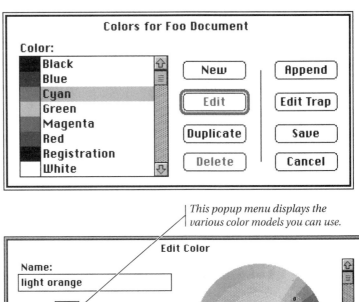

This popup menu displays the
various color models you can use.

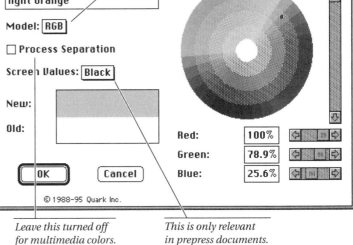

Leave this turned off
for multimedia colors.

This is only relevant
in prepress documents.

every color you want (see the section "Color Palettes" in Chapter 3,
Building Projects).

When you press Save in the Colors dialog box, the color you've
created appears on the Colors palette, ready for you to use.

Step, Repeat, and Duplicate

You can duplicate any item on your page by choosing Duplicate
from the Item menu (or you can press Command-D). Or if you want
more control, you can choose Step and Repeat instead (see Figure
1–17). This way, you can tell XPress how many copies you want, and

where you want them. For instance, you could select a text box, go to Step and Repeat (press Command-Option-D), and tell XPress to make three copies, each with a horizontal offset of two inches and no vertical offset. The first copy will be made two inches over from the original; the second copy will be *another* two inches over (four inches over, in total); and so on.

Figure 1–17
Step and Repeat

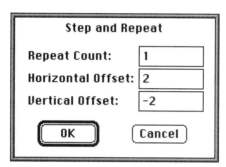

I use Step and Repeat all the time, especially for cloning objects (duplicating an image with zero offset, so the copy is exactly on top of the original). Note that Duplicate uses quarter-inch offsets until you use Step and Repeat; then Duplicate uses whatever offset you last typed in.

Space/Align

Space/Align is one of the most powerful features in XPress, but it has one of the worst interfaces, so many people never even try to use it. Space/Align (on the Item menu, or press Command-comma), lets you control the relationship between two or more objects on your page (see Figure 1–18). For instance, you can use it to align three text boxes along their top edges, or to distribute 10 picture boxes across your page so that there's equal space between all of them. Or you could use it to center two lines on each other.

To use Space/Align, you must have two or more objects selected with the Item tool. Then, in the Space/Align dialog box, you have to tell XPress whether you want to control the objects vertically, horizontally, or both. Finally, you have to tell XPress whether you're trying to align the objects or distribute them. See Figure 1–18 for some common examples.

Figure 1-18
Space/Align

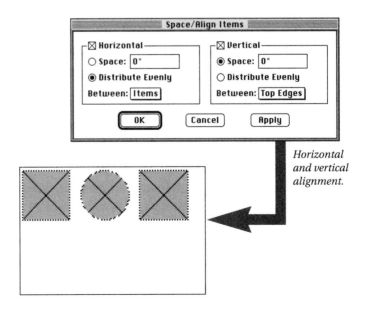

Here, Space/Align is only performing horizontal alignment.

Horizontal and vertical alignment.

By the way, in case it's confusing to you (it is to a lot of people), the word "Items" on the Between popup menu simply refers to the objects themselves (the text box, the picture box, or the line).

What moves? I can hear the question percolating in your brain: which objects move and which ones stay in place? Here's the quick and easy rundown.

▶ When you're aligning objects horizontally, the leftmost object is always the reference point. That is, the leftmost object stays put and the other objects move.

▶ When aligning vertically, the topmost object is the reference point and everything else moves.

▶ When you're distributing objects horizontally, the leftmost and rightmost objects remain in the same place and everything between them moves.

▶ In vertical distribution, the topmost and bottommost objects remain in place.

▼ ▼

Tip: The Apply Button. Because the Space/Align dialog box is so poorly designed, I use the Apply button constantly. The Apply button appears in several dialog boxes in QuarkXPress. When you click it (or press Command-A), the changes you've made to the dialog box are promptly applied to whatever you're working on, but the dialog box doesn't disappear (of course, you need a large enough screen to move the dialog box out of the way).

At this point, you can make another change to the dialog box settings and apply them again, or click Cancel to abort the changes (the objects revert to the way they were, undoing what was applied). I encourage you to use this whenever possible. It certainly saves time and frustration.

▼ ▼

XTensions

Quark XTensions add functionality to QuarkXPress. There are all sorts of XTensions, some simple, some complex, some free, and others very expensive indeed. QuarkImmedia is, in fact, simply an XTension (one of the more complex and expensive ones). Quark-XPress ships with some free XTensions, too, such as Cool Blends and the MS-Word™ Filter (yes, the filters are XTensions, too—without these XTensions, XPress can't read certain file formats).

XTensions should be placed in the XTension folder (inside the folder where your copy of QuarkXPress is located), though you can have them loose in the XPress folder, if you don't care about clutter. When you launch XPress, the program loads any XTensions it can find (that means you must quit and relaunch XPress whenever you add a new XTension).

If you don't use an XTension, I recommend either throwing it away or hiding it in another folder (XPress doesn't look for XTensions inside of nested folders). Throwing the XTension away saves a little disk space, makes XPress launch faster, and requires that much less RAM.

▼ ▼

Many More Miles to Go . . .

If there's one thing I've learned about QuarkXPress, it's that there's always more to learn. In this chapter, we've covered most of the basics—plus a few important intermediate topics, like master pages and style sheets—in preparation for the rest of this book. Now we're ready to jump in and start cooking up some real live multimedia projects, using QuarkImmedia along with QuarkXPress.

QuarkImmedia Basics

EVERY STORY MUST HAVE A BEGINNING, middle, and end, right? And if you think of the previous chapter as a prologue (many of you experienced XPress users probably skipped right over it), our story really begins here. If you're like most people learning QuarkImmedia, your head is full of questions but your fingers are itching to go make something. In this chapter and the next, I'll try to answer most of your more basic questions, explaining how Immedia works and how you should go about building a project. Along the way, however, I will explore some issues that you may not know are important, as well as offer some clues to the riches we'll find in the rest of the book.

I promise you that if you take the time now to learn how to set up Immedia and your projects, you'll save time later not banging your head against a wall.

Getting Ready, Getting Set

The first step in working with QuarkImmedia is to install it. I won't bore you with the details here—Quark has laid out the installation procedure pretty clearly for you. However, there are a few things to note about the installation.

▶ Some people get this far without realizing that QuarkImmedia is actually an XTension to QuarkXPress. That is, you must have QuarkXPress on your hard drive to run Immedia.

▶ To be more specific, you must have QuarkXPress version 3.32r5 or later. If you're not sure what version you have, hold down the Option key while selecting About QuarkXPress from the Apple menu (see Figure 2–1).

▶ Because Immedia is an XTension, it must sit in either the QuarkXPress folder or the XTension folder. Unlike most other XTensions, this one has a QuarkImmedia Data file that must accompany it.

If you don't own QuarkImmedia, you can use the demo version on the CD-ROM in the back of this book; you just have to put the right files in the right place (see Chapter 16, *The Real World Quark-Immedia CD-ROM).*

Memory Management

One of the most important steps you can take before launching QuarkXPress—after installing Immedia—is to increase the amount of RAM allocated to XPress. The RAM in your computer is like the office in which you work; even if you work in a large office building, you're allocated only a certain amount of space for your office or

Figure 2–1
The QuarkXPress
Environment
dialog box

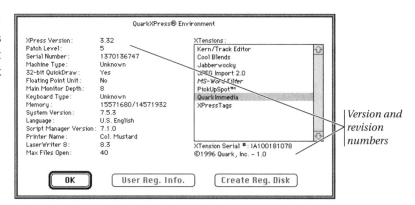

cubicle. If your particular office is really small, you'll be able to type just fine, but if your boss asks you to design the annual report or collate 50 pages of investment records . . . no way! You just won't have the room.

When you launch QuarkXPress, the program asks the operating system for a certain amount of RAM in which to work. It asks for an amount that varies according to your configuration. However, this is *all* the space it has to work within, even if you have gobs of RAM in your machine. If you're just typing a letter, it hardly matters how much RAM it gets (how large a "cubicle" it's got). But if you're trying to build a complex multimedia project, you must ensure that it gets more than the default amount.

You can allocate more RAM to XPress by selecting the program's icon in the Finder (XPress can't be running when you do this), and choosing Get Info from the File menu (or press Command-I; see Figure 2–2). The number in the Preferred Size field is the amount of RAM XPress will ask for; the number in the Minimum Size field is the amount it'll settle for.

I recommend that you set the Minimum Size to no less than 8000 (about 8 Mb), and the Preferred Size to no less than 15000 or 18000 (about 15 to 18 Mb). Of course, this means you must have at least that amount of RAM in the first place, but multimedia is not for the faint of heart or the poor of RAM. If you don't have at least 24 Mb, I suggest you go and buy some today.

Figure 2–2
Allocating more
RAM to XPress

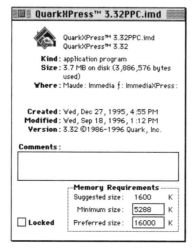

If you have RAM Doubler, it may appear that you have lots of RAM, but it's important that you not allocate to any one program more RAM than you physically have. For instance, if you have 16 Mb of RAM in your machine and use RAM Doubler, it looks like you have 32 Mb of RAM; however, you should not allocate more than 16 Mb to Immedia (or any other program). In fact, it's probably a good idea to save a few megabytes for the system software, so make that 13 or 14 Mb.

What takes RAM? Note that certain functions in Immedia take up more RAM than others. For instance, building animations can take up a lot of RAM because every animation frame is kept in memory (see Chapter 8, *Animation*), plus a few extra frames for an Undo buffer and so on. The larger (in frame dimensions or length) an animation, the more RAM you'd better have allocated to XPress.

In general, Immedia projects are significantly larger than for-print documents, and you need to allocate RAM accordingly. On the other hand, QuarkImmedia hungers for RAM most when working with QuickTime movies and animations. When it can, Immedia holds an entire animation or movie in memory before playing it. That means you may want to allocate several additional megabytes of RAM to XPress when working with these kinds of files.

In general, the consensus appears to be: the more RAM you give XPress, the better.

▼ ▼

How QuarkImmedia Works

You know how QuarkXPress works, and you've allocated enough RAM to the program. Now it's time to learn how Immedia works, and how you can make it do your bidding.

QuarkImmedia adds a new palette to the screen and a new menu to the menu bar (see Figure 2–3). You can hide or show the QuarkImmedia palette from the View menu, but I find it faster to simply press Shift-F10 (once to hide, again to show). These two items—along with the QuarkImmedia Preferences dialog box, and a few other minor features—let you control every aspect of your multimedia project.

Let's take a look at the four most important building blocks of Immedia: projects, objects, events, and actions.

Projects. Every multimedia authoring program uses a different model for building a project. Some make you build a flow chart that shows how each screen connects to the next. Others work on a time line, letting you specify what happens 10 seconds into the project, then what happens 45 seconds in, and so on. Immedia takes an approach that I find particularly intuitive: it's a page-layout authoring tool. That is, whatever you put on a page shows up on screen. If you want another screenful of text, you just add a new page to the project (we'll see how to jump from one page to the next in Chapter 3, *Building Projects*).

Objects. You can place *objects* on each page. An object can be a text box, a picture box, a line, or a button (buttons are a new type of object in XPress; I talk about them in Chapter 6, *Buttons*). A picture box might contain a picture, but it just as well might contain an animation or a QuickTime movie. Nonetheless, it's still an object.

Figure 2–3
QuarkImmedia's
interface

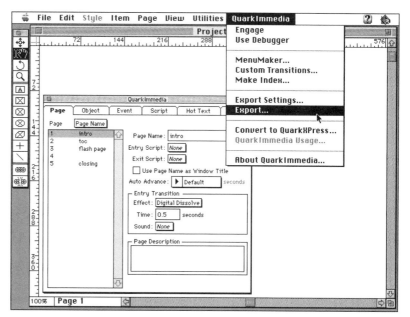

Events. *Events* can happen to these objects. For example, your user might click on a button, move the cursor over a picture, or double-click on a word. Each of these is a separate event. Anything that can happen while your project is running is an event.

Actions. Each event can trigger an *action*. A click on a button might play a sound; moving the mouse over a picture might start a movie; double-clicking on a word might jump to a different page. You can also trigger actions when you first start up a project, when you jump to a new page, or even when your user selects an item from a menu. There are over 100 different actions you can trigger in Immedia and, in fact, I spend much of the rest of the book describing these.

Engage versus Export

You can view your Immedia projects in one of three modes. First, there's the authoring stage, where you put objects on your pages and assign actions to various events. When you're ready to test your project, you can "start it up" by selecting Engage from the QuarkImmedia menu* (or even better, just press F15 once to engage it, and F15 again to disengage). You can test almost every aspect of a project while it's engaged, but because XPress is only simulating how the final exported project will act, some things (the Internet controls and the Open Project action, specifically) don't work.

▼ ▼

Tip: QPS Keystrokes. If you use the Quark Publishing System, you'll have to press Shift-F15 to engage or disengage your projects, because QPS reserves the F15 key for logging on to the network.

▼ ▼

Finally, you can export your project and open it with the Quark-Immedia Viewer. The Viewer was installed on your hard drive when you installed QuarkImmedia; it's free and you can give it to anyone you want so that they can run your exported projects, too. Every action works in an exported project, including the Internet-related

---

*If you're a Star Trek fan, you know very well the origin of this term. If you avoid commercial television, just smile and nod and pretend you care.

actions (see Chapter 14, *Exporting*, and Chapter 15, *The Internet and World Wide Web* for more information about exporting your files).

▼ ▼

The QuarkImmedia Palette

The QuarkImmedia palette is Immedia's "control center." You will become exceedingly familiar with this palette in the days to come, for this is where you specify every object, event, and action in your project. The QuarkImmedia palette is tabbed; that is, there are actually six palettes in one, and you choose the one you want by clicking on its tab (see Figure 2–4). Let's take a look at each tab, what it contains, and how you will find yourself using it.

Page

The Page tab lists each page in your project. It also lets you give each page a name, a description, and particular attributes, such as the transition effect you should see when you enter the page. I talk much more about pages and the Page tab in "Turning the Page" in Chapter 3, *Building a Project*. Don't worry; you don't need to know too much about it yet.

Figure 2–4
QuarkImmedia palette

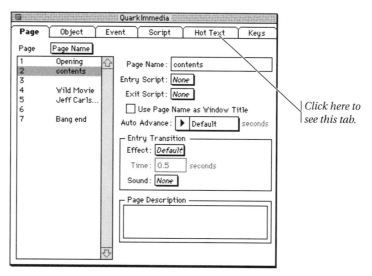

Click here to see this tab.

Object

As I mentioned above, an object is a text box, a picture box, a line, or a button. What I didn't tell you was that every object that does something (triggers an action or slides across the page or whatever) must have a name. The Object tab of the QuarkImmedia palette is where you can give an object a name and set attributes specific to that object (see Figure 2–5).

Every object starts out as a Basic object (the Object Type popup menu is set to Basic). That means what you see is just what you'll get in the final project. But the Object tab lets you make a text box editable or not, or give it scrollbars or turn it into a list. The Object tab is what lets you specify that a plain ol' picture box should actually contain a movie or an animation, or should, perhaps, be a dialog box or a palette.

There are four options from which you can choose for every object you create. You can find the first three (Initially Hidden, Initially Disabled, and Keep Status on Page Entry) on the Options popup menu on the Object tab, and the last option (Initially at) has its own popup menu (see Figure 2–6). You can choose one or more options (they're not exclusive of each other).

Note that if you have not given an object a name, when you choose from any of the popup menus on the Object tab, Immedia

Figure 2–5
The Object tab

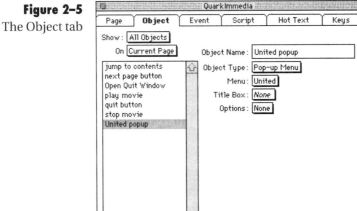

Figure 2-6

Options for objects

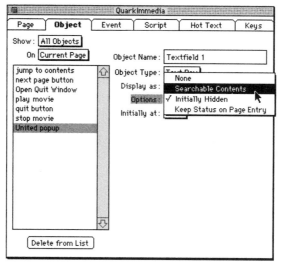

assigns a name for you (usually something really boring, like "Standard 1"). I encourage you to change this name (in the Name field) to something more descriptive. The more objects you have on your page, the more necessary it is to discriminate among them by name.

Initially Hidden. If you choose Initially Hidden from the Options popup menu, you won't be able to see the object when you first enter the page it's on. Because it's hidden, you also can't click on it. In Chapter 3, *Building Projects*, we'll take a look at how to make an invisible object visible again. You might use this feature to hide some text on your page that you later make visible.

Initially Disabled. As I said, you can trigger actions by assigning them to an event on an object—for instance, a click event on a box object, or an Option-click event on a line object. If you turn on Initially Disabled, Immedia disables all the object's user events and actions, so that clicking on the object has no effect (nor does double-clicking, Option-clicking, or anything else you can think of). You can enable it again with the Enable Object action (see Chapter 3, *Building Projects*).

Let's say you are designing a game in which there is a door to a secret passageway. To open the door, the user has to click on it. However, you want the door to open only if the user has already done something else. You could set the door object to Initially Disabled, and then enable it at the proper time.

Keep Status on Page Entry. The *initial state* of an object is how it first appears when you display the page it's on. For example, the initial state of an Editable text box is whatever text is in the box at first. If you change the state of an object while the project is running—hide or move the box, or change the text, for example—and then display a different page, when you return to the changed page, every object returns to its initial state (the box is hidden again, and so on).

If you select the Keep Status on Page Entry option for an object, that object "remembers" its state whenever you leave the page, and will not revert to its initial state when you return.

Initially at. An object's initial state also includes where it is on the page. The popup menu labeled "Initially at" defaults to Home, meaning the object should appear on the page exactly where you put it. However, you can also choose Left, Right, Top, or Bottom from the Initially at popup menu. These let you tell Immedia to place the object off the page. I discuss why you might want to do this when I talk about the Slide Object action in Chapter 8, *Animation*. The only important thing to remember here is that "Home" means "where you've put the object on the page."

▼ ▼

Tip: Selecting Objects on a Page. Once you have named an object, there's no reason to select it on your page when you want to make changes on the QuarkImmedia palette. You can simply select the object's name from the Object tab's list (or the Event tab's object list) and then make the change.

However, if you want to select a named object on the page, you can either click on it with the Item or Content tools (the way you'd normally select anything in your document), or double-click on the object's name on the Object tab of the QuarkImmedia palette.

▼ ▼

Event

The Event tab lets you assign actions to objects (see Figure 2–7). Below is the basic procedure for making an object *hot* (an object is hot if it does something in response to a user event).

1. Select the object and make sure it has a name (you can name objects on the Event tab, too).

2. From the User Event popup menu on the Event tab, choose the event that should trigger the action. Your choices here depend on what the object is, but typically include Click Up, Click Down,* Double-click, Mouse Enter, and so on.

3. Choose the action from the Action popup menu (also on the Event tab).

That's it! Note that you can assign more than one action to an object. For instance, the Mouse Enter user event (when you move

Figure 2–7
The Event tab

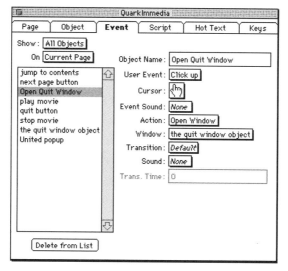

---

*Many newcomers to multimedia get confused by these terms because they think the phrases are more complex than they really are. When you press the mouse button, first you "click down" and then—when you release the button—you "click up." We usually think of this as one act, but in fact there are times when it's useful to have different things happen for each event. By the way, Mouse Enter is the designation for when the user puts the cursor over an object; Mouse Exit is the designation for when the user takes the cursor off an object.

the cursor over an object) might trigger one action. Click Up on the object might trigger another action. On the User Event popup menu, Immedia puts a checkmark next to each event that has an action associated with it (see Figure 2–8).

Cursor and Event Sound. There are also two other popup menus on the Event tab: Cursor and Event Sound. While I discuss these in depth in Chapter 10, *Cursors*, and Chapter 7, *Sound*, here's the quick lowdown: these two popup menus let you choose a different cursor and sound for each user event. For instance, you might want one "click" sound to play when the user clicks down, and a different one to play when the user clicks up (releases the button). When it comes to cursors, however, there's really no reason to assign a cursor to anything other than the Mouse Down and Mouse Enter user events, because the other events happen so quickly that you never actually see the cursor change.

Strange choices. I have a bone to pick with the engineers at Quark, and who knows? . . . maybe someday they'll listen to me. My beef has to do with the User Event popup menu and how it changes depending on what type of object you've selected. For example, if you have a Window object selected (we'll learn more about these in Chapter 5, *Windows*), you cannot choose any of the standard user events (Click Down, and so on). The only user events to which you can assign actions are Window Open and Window Close—and Window Open isn't even a user event! (Window Open is when a window gets opened; Window Close is when the window is closed.) I think it's just silly.

▼ ▼

Tip: What Objects to List. The larger your project, the more objects you have to keep track of. In a moderate-sized project, you might have as many as 20 objects per page; when you multiply that by 50 pages, you've got a handful. That's when you want to remember the Show and On popup menus (these appear on both the Object and Event tabs). The Show popup menu lets you choose what kind of objects to display on the palette's object list (see Figure 2–9). You can choose from any of the following.

▶ All Objects (this is the default setting)

▶ Basic Objects (all the objects that are named but still have "Basic" chosen on the Object tab's Object Type popup menu)

▶ Animations

▶ Buttons

Figure 2–8
Assigning an action
to a user event

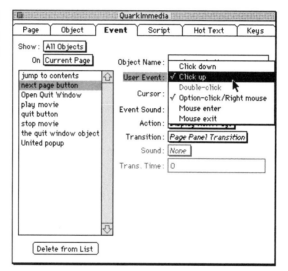

Figure 2–9
Displaying objects

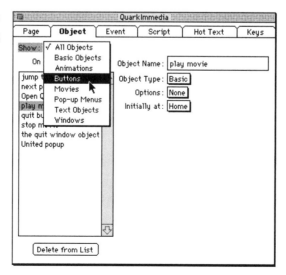

- ▶ Movies

- ▶ Popup menus

- ▶ Text objects

- ▶ Windows

Once you've made a choice from the Show popup menu, you can specify a page range to view from the On popup menu. Your choices here are slim: you can pick Current Page or Entire Project.

For instance, when you want to pick out a particular button on some other page, instead of searching for it, you can set the Show popup menu to Buttons and the On popup menu to Entire Project.

▼ ▼

Script

Whereas the Event tab lets you assign a single action to an event, the Script tab gives you the tools to trigger a series of actions with one event. The more you work with QuarkImmedia, the more you will find yourself building scripts; it's just an integral part of making a project. I cover scripting and the Script tab in significantly greater detail in Chapter 13, *Scripting*.

Hot Text

As I said earlier, any text box, picture box, line, or button can trigger an action. But a range of text can trigger an action, too. You can specify a word or a phrase (or even a single character) to be "hot" on the Hot Text tab. I discuss exactly how to do this in Chapter 4, *Text*.

Keys

I love keyboard shortcuts because they're so dang efficient. Why take the time to select a menu item if you can press a key instead? The Keys tab of the QuarkImmedia palette lets you assign keyboard shortcuts to any script or button in your project (see Figure 2–10). The nice thing is that you can assign any keystroke, no matter how obscure or mundane. (As you'll see in Chapter 12, *Menus*, you can assign keystrokes to menu items, but you can only make keystrokes that use the Command key.)

Figure 2-10

The Keys tab

Select the page or master page that contains the button to which you want to assign a keystroke.

Select Global to create a projectwide keystroke for a script.

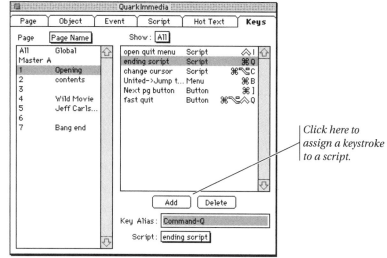

Click here to assign a keystroke to a script.

Buttons. Let's say you have a button labeled "Home" that, when pressed, takes the user to a specific page. You could assign a keystroke to do the same thing, like this.

1. First, open the Keys tab of the QuarkImmedia palette, and select the button's page from the page list.

2. Select the button name in the list on the right of the palette.

3. Click in the Key Alias text field and type the keystroke you want to use (you don't have to press the Add button or anything like that).

When the user presses the keyboard shortcut, the button won't look like it's being pressed, but the action assigned to the button will get triggered. Note that you cannot assign more than one keyboard shortcut to the same button. You can, however, assign a keystroke to a button on the Object tab (probably even more easily than doing it here).

Scripts. Generally scripts have to be triggered by some object, or by the turning of a page or something of the sort. However, you can also assign a keystroke to a script you've created. When the user presses the keystroke, the script runs.

▼ ▼

The One-Minute Immedia Tutorial

Everyone learns differently. Some people can learn a program by reading the documentation that came with it. Others learn by watching someone else use it. And some folks even learn by ditching all the printed materials and just playing around. With that in mind, I have put a little Immedia project, called the One-Minute Immedia Tutorial, on the disc in the back of the book that walks you through the basics of making a project interactive.

I encourage you to go look at that project, then come back and read the following script. Then (and here's the most important part) go try it yourself before continuing on with the book. I've found, when teaching this stuff, that if you just get your hands on it for about four minutes, somehow the brain kicks in and is better able to understand everything else that I write about after this. Note that some of the things I go over here aren't covered in depth until Chapter 3, *Building Projects.*

New Project. The first step is to create a new project by selecting Project from the New submenu (under the File menu). My suggestion for now is to just use the default values that appear in the New Project dialog box (see Figure 2–11).

Add objects. Now it's time to place some objects on your page. My suggestion is to put a picture box and a text box anywhere on the

Figure 2–11
New Project
dialog box

page. You can put a picture in the picture box, or just fill it with a color. Go ahead and type some random text in the text box and format it anyway you'd like.

Add actions. Next, we want to make this project *do* something. Select the picture box, click on the Event tab of the QuarkImmedia palette, and type a name in the Object name field (like "my picture box"). Let's leave the User Event popup menu at its default setting (Click Up). Now, pick an action from the Action popup menu: scroll down the list until you see the Sound popout menu, and choose Beep from that popout (see Figure 2–12).

Engage! Finally, it's time to run the project to see it in action. Select Engage from the QuarkImmedia menu (up on the menu bar). Your screen should go blank for a moment, then the page, however you designed it, should appear. Click on the picture. Did your computer beep? If not, go back and make sure you followed all my steps. If it did: congratulations, you've just entered the world of multimedia. Remember, you can type Command-Q or press F15 to disengage the project and go back to authoring.

Figure 2–12
Adding an action

1. Select the page on which you want the keystroke to be functional from the page list on the left side of the palette. If you want the keyboard shortcut to be functional throughout the entire project, select Global from the list.

2. Click the Add button on the Keys tab.

3. Choose a script from the Script popup menu.

4. Finally, type a keystroke in the Key Alias field.

Unlike buttons, more than one keystroke can trigger the same script; just press Add again, select the same script, but assign a different keystroke.

▼ ▼

Tip: Multiple Keystrokes for Buttons. It's annoying not being able to assign more than one keystroke to a button, because I often want to give maximum flexibility to my audience. For example, when I make an OK button, I like to let people press it with either Enter or Return. In Immedia, you have to choose one or the other. Or do you? Here's a way you can use multiple keystrokes for the same button.

1. Build a script with one action in it—the same action which the button triggers (again, see Chapter 13, *Scripting*).

2. Set the action for the button to Run Script, and specify the script you just made.

3. On the Keys tab, press the Add button to create as many keyboard shortcuts as you want for that same script.

▼ ▼

Menus. We'll see exactly how to assign keystrokes to custom menu items in Chapter 12, *Menus*, but for now just trust me that it's easy to do. These menus can appear either on the menu bar or on popup menus on your page. If you assign a keyboard shortcut to a menu item and then put that menu on your project's page (as a popup menu), that item and keystroke appear on the Keys tab of the QuarkImmedia palette, alongside the other keystrokes you've set up.

Quark's documentation says you can change the keystroke here, but I've never figured out how to do it. I tend to think they changed their minds at the last minute and left that feature out.

▼ ▼

Repurposing XPress Documents

As I said in the introduction, one of the best uses for QuarkImmedia is to repurpose for-print documents that you created in Quark-XPress. But before you get too excited about this, I need to include some heavy-duty caveats.

▶ Designs for the printed page are rarely appropriate for the screen. The fonts are often too small, even the pictures are sometimes too small, and—here's the kicker—the page is usually too big! An 8.5-by-11-inch page just doesn't fit on a 640-by-480-pixel screen (that's the standard size of a 14-inch monitor).

▶ Graphics for print are usually saved in TIFF or EPS format, and you usually don't care much about how they look on screen (which is good, because they usually look lousy). However, you care a *lot* about the screen quality of pictures when making Immedia projects, because what you see on screen is what you're going to get. Therefore, you often need to make some significant adjustments to your images. This may mean different resolution, tonal correction, color correction, sharpening, and changing the file format (see "Pictures" in Chapter 3, *Building Projects*).

▶ For-print documents are often text-heavy. Not a bad thing . . . until it comes to displaying all that text on screen. Few people want to sit and read a lot of text on a computer monitor. That means that you may have to do some major editing and convey your ideas graphically rather than with text.

There are other problems with converting something you've already got into a multimedia project, but I think you get the idea.

On the other hand, many of these problems will concern you less if you've taken a few practical steps beforehand.

▶ Save all your original scans in RGB format. That way you can adjust them for the screen much more easily than if you only saved your for-print CMYK versions.

▶ Use style sheets religiously. If you want to change all your body text from 11-point Goudy to 18-point Verdana, it's a snap with style sheets.

▶ Put repeating items on master pages. I've seen documents that converted from full-page size to screen size in a matter of moments just by changing settings and objects on two or three master pages. Of course, some documents are so customized, page by page, that changes to the master page won't help much.

If you don't know much about master pages and style sheets, check out those sections in Chapter 1, *QuarkXPress Basics*; then, if you need to know more, you might try another book on XPress, like *The QuarkXPress Book* from Peachpit Press.

Convert to QuarkImmedia. If, after all that, you still want to convert your QuarkXPress documents into QuarkImmedia documents, you have to recite an incantation, click your heels together three times, and select Convert to QuarkImmedia from the QuarkImmedia menu (see Figure 2–13). When you do this, Immedia brings up the Project Setup dialog box, which lets you choose various options for your document (I discuss these in the next chapter).

Note that Immedia will not let you proceed if you've got objects on your page outside the bounds of the project dimensions. That is, if you've got a picture box way down in the lower-right corner of your page, and you try to resize your document down to a 640-by-480-pixel project, Immedia won't let you. You have to move that box before converting the project.

Names and actions. Note that you can actually name objects and set up actions and scripts even before converting the document to an

Figure 2–13
Convert to
QuarkImmedia

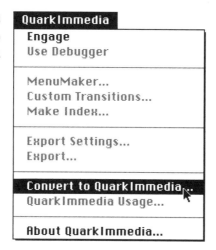

Immedia project. However, you can't engage or export the document until you convert it. The only reason I can think of for assigning names and actions to a regular XPress document is when you're building a document that you know will be used for both print and multimedia. If you give objects names as you create the document, the conversion process will be much faster down the road.

Troubleshooting Techniques

There is a school of thought that says all design is a process of problem solving. Perhaps the problem you need to solve is how to communicate a message in a single image; perhaps it's how to fit seven paragraphs in two languages in a single advertisement. If you're the kind of person who enjoys problem solving, you're really going to love multimedia.

Building a project in QuarkImmedia (or any multimedia authoring program) is a lesson in patience and problem solving. We already looked at one problem that needs to be solved: converting designs for the page into designs appropriate for the screen. But that's only where the process starts—after you've found a suitable design, you've got to implement it. And while implementing, you're going to run into troubles.

I'm not trying to say you're a bad or stupid person; everyone runs into troubles when building multimedia projects, no matter how long they've been doing it. What comes with experience is the speed with which you solve these problems.

The documentation. The section on troubleshooting in the Quark-Immedia documentation should be required reading for budding multimedia authors. It's not very long, covers the ground well, and provides explanations of all Immedia's error messages. Nonetheless, here are a few of my favorite troubleshooting techniques.

Bugs

One of the benefits of being an independent writer is that I'm allowed to point out all sorts of things they can't say in the manuals. For example: There are bugs in QuarkImmedia. No, I don't mean little creepy-crawly things; I mean there are problems in the software that Quark's engineers have not fixed yet.* This is pretty common in software products, and it's a sure bet that the folks at Quark are working on eradicating these bugs as quickly as they can.

Fortunately, these bugs are relatively rare compared to all the things that do work in Immedia. However, you will probably run into them occasionally. Where possible, I try to warn you about particular problems in each chapter, but sometimes weirdness just happens out of the blue. For example, I recently had a problem where my scripts didn't appear properly on the Script tab—they all appeared as a bunch of ellipses. It was very odd. I quit the program and restarted it, and the problem went away. I don't know why. I hardly want to know why. What's important is that I got my job done and the bug hasn't reappeared.

Media Files

One of the most common problems that people encounter when building Immedia projects has little to do with Immedia and a lot to do with the media files they're using. Fonts, pictures, animations,

---

*Some people refer to these as *software anomalies, functional blemishes,* or *life-degrading features.*

QuickTime movies, buttons, cursors, and sounds all have one thing in common: they can become mysteriously corrupted and cause strange things to happen in your projects.

No one knows why a file becomes corrupted—perhaps there was a glitch in the cables when you transferred the file from one hard drive to another, or maybe gremlins sneaked in at night with their black-magic destructo-dust. But if a file becomes corrupted, you might experience unexpected crashes or odd alert messages.

Use Debugger

One of the most useful features when attempting to solve a problem in QuarkImmedia is Use Debugger. When you turn on Use Debugger (on the QuarkImmedia menu) and engage your project, Immedia lists out every action as it occurs (see Figure 2–13). Use Debugger rarely helps when you run into a bug, but it's very useful for ferreting out design or logic flaws (which are much more common).

For instance, I often find myself making scripts and then trying to figure out why the script doesn't do anything in the engaged project. As soon as I turn the debugger on, I can see that (once again) I've forgotten to trigger the script with the Run Script action.

Figure 2–13
Use Debugger

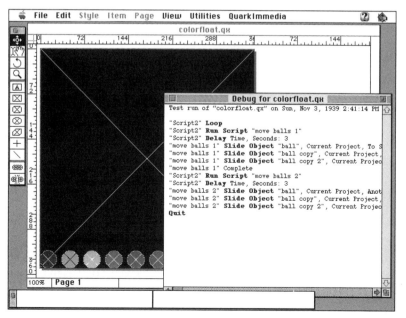

Trying Everything

There just isn't enough room in one chapter (much less a whole book) to discuss all the things that can go worng (sic) and methods you can use to troubleshoot your problems away. So here are just a few of my favorite techniques, the ones that I find help most often.

Quitting and restarting. You know how sometimes just walking outside to get some fresh air can clear your muddled head? Well, I find quitting QuarkXPress and relaunching it can sometimes clear up even the strangest problems you'll encounter. Even better, quit, restart your computer, and then relaunch XPress.

XPress Preferences. QuarkXPress and QuarkImmedia rely on the XPress Preferences file (this file is usually in the same folder as QuarkXPress, but some people move it to the Preferences file in the System Folder). And, just as with media files, this file occasionally becomes corrupted. When quitting and restarting doesn't clear up some problem, and I'm pretty sure it's not a design or logic flaw on my part, I try running XPress with a clean XPress Preferences file.

1. Quit QuarkXPress.

2. Drag the XPress Preferences file (wherever it is) out onto your desktop or into some other folder.

3. Restart QuarkXPress. The program won't be able to find the XPress Preferences file, so it'll create a new one.

If the problems go away, then throw away the old Preferences file and just keep using this new one. Note that settings in any of the Preferences dialog boxes (like General Preferences, Typographic Preferences, QuarkImmedia Preferences, and so on) are saved in this file, so you'll have to set them again if you do this.

▼ ▼

Tip: Back Up Your Preferences Files. Other settings are stored in XPress Preferences as well, such as hyphenation exceptions and custom tracking and kerning values. If you've built these sorts of things, make sure you keep a backup of your XPress Preferences file somewhere safe. That way, if your original is lost or corrupted, you can replace it with your backup copy.

By the way, if you're in charge of a number of copies of Quark-XPress, you can copy all the preferences from one computer to another by copying the XPress Preferences file. Just replace everyone else's file with yours.

▼ ▼

Keeping a clean system. Remember how I talked about RAM being like the office space in which you work? Well, the files in your Extensions and Control Panels folder (in your System Folder) are like clutter on your desk—the more you have around, the more likely you are to knock something off your desk and cause havoc (okay, so it's a lousy analogy—but you know what I'm trying to say: wacky extensions that you think are fun may drag down your efficiency).

Quark XTensions can contribute to problems, too. The more XTensions you have loaded, the more RAM they take and the more likely you'll have conflicts among them. There are XTensions (and system extensions and control panels) that I just won't do without, but I try to maintain a critical eye and weed out those I don't really need in order to keep my system a lean, mean production machine.

QuarkImmedia Preferences. The QuarkImmedia Viewer also has its own Preferences file, saved in the Preferences folder inside the System Folder. While it's rare for this file to become corrupted, every now and again something odd happens in the Viewer itself (sometimes the Viewer thinks that it doesn't have enough memory to run, for instance). In these cases, the first thing I try is to move the Quark-Immedia Preferences into some other folder and then launch the Viewer again. If the problem goes away, go ahead and throw away the original. Again, you'll have to reset each of the Preferences dialog boxes if you do this.

▼ ▼

Ready to Roll

Here we are, perched on the crest of building QuarkImmedia projects. In this chapter, we've looked at the essentials of Immedia: the QuarkImmedia palette and menu, how objects can trigger actions via user events, and how you can troubleshoot the problems you're bound to encounter along your way. In the next chapter I take us deeper, exploring how to use all these tools in nuts-and-bolts techniques for creating solid projects. By the time you're done with that chapter, you'll really be ready to roll.

Building Projects

As far as I can tell, the main things they teach you in engineering school are patience and how to put one foot in front of the other. I'd make a lousy engineer. If I were contracted to construct a building, I'd be tempted to just jump in and start hammering pieces of wood together. What I *should* do is—before even breaking ground—hire an architect, get a solid plan going, and make sure that I've got all the materials on hand. Next, I should prepare the ground, build a firm foundation, and finally start piecing the materials together to form the building.

Your job, as a multimedia author, is no less stringent than the engineer's. True, your projects may not be life-threatening if they fall down, but more than one author has felt the weight of a project collapsing on them when it comes time to demo it in front of their boss. There are many things that can go wrong with a project, from crashing to inconsistent text or graphics, but you can solve many of them with clear thinking, careful construction, and common sense.

In this chapter, I talk about infrastructure and how you can lay down a firm foundation on which to build your projects. I also discuss many of the core actions that you'll use repeatedly in your projects: displaying pages, moving and hiding objects, and jumping from one project to another. If we take it logically, step by step, it's not only safer, but also more fun.

▼ ▼

Project Design

You wouldn't hike into the backcountry without a map and compass, would you? You wouldn't buy a car without taking it for a test drive, would you? You wouldn't go grocery shopping on an empty stomach without a shopping list, would you? (No, me neither.) Then, can you tell me why so many people get the itch and just jump in, making their multimedia project before they sit down and plan *what* the project is going to do and *how* it's going to do it?

Don't get me wrong—I have nothing against spontaneity and impulse. It's just that ninety-nine times out of a hundred you'll be sorry if you don't design your project before you start building it. Designing a multimedia project doesn't have to be a big deal— though the more complex the project, the more you'll have to work on the design beforehand. Here are just a few things to keep in mind when designing your project. This list is far from complete, but it should get you started.

Who's your audience? You're probably using a Macintosh to build your project, but what will your users be using to look at it? A Macintosh? A Windows-based PC? Both? How big will their screens probably be? Will they be able to view more than 8-bit color on those screens? A project built for viewing on a fast Mac may not run as you'd expect on a slower Windows machine, so you may need to test it along the way (see "Tip: Testing with Base Camps," on page 64).

What's your distribution channel? If you're under 30, you probably still think you're invincible, but unfortunately you have to play by the same laws of physics that we all do. (As the Tick says, "Gravity is a harsh mistress.") One of these laws says that you can't pump out the same awesome, butt-kicking movies, sound, animations, and general mayhem over the Internet that you can when running a project off a hard drive. So the question of how you are going to deliver your stuff becomes really important.

Two of the key issues regarding distribution are compression and file size. You can put some really cool stuff on the Internet, but unless the files are really small, only people with expensive T1 connections to the Internet will look at it. You can put more stuff on CD-ROMs, but even then there may be concerns. For instance, it's not a great idea to play music off a CD-ROM while you're also playing a QuickTime movie, because the two files are written on two different parts of the disc; some CD drives aren't fast enough to skip back and forth, so you get jerky sound or jerky movies.

Compression of sound, pictures, movies, and so on is discussed throughout the book, and especially in Chapter 14, *Exporting.*

What are you including? Although the best thing I make for dinner is "reservations," I know enough about cooking to be sure I get all my ingredients together *before* I start burning my meal. I think you'll find that laying out your project's elements (movies, sound, buttons, text, and so on) on your XPress pages takes much less time than actually designing and making those elements. In a recent project, it took me about half the time to lay out my project in Immedia than it did to just make the buttons.

How will the project work? Sitting down to design a multimedia project is like going to the gym. You know you should do it. You know that you'll feel better after doing it. You know that it doesn't take *that* much time out of your day. It's a hassle, but it's worth it. You know those really buff designers who make projects as cool as they look? They work out *and* they take the time to design their projects before jumping in.

One of the best ways to design the project is—gasp!—a pencil and paper. Even a quick sketch on the back of an envelope is better than nothing. Here's a few more questions for you to think about while sketching.

▶ How will your users navigate through the project? Buttons? Menu items? Keystrokes?

► Consistency is key. What elements should be consistent throughout the project?

► How will your users know how to use your project? You'll know how to use it because you're designing it, but if the users have to sit and figure out how stuff works, they're probably not going to use it for very long.

▼ ▼

Tip: Testing with Base Camps. I know of at least one company that asked all the right questions, designed carefully, and then built a large and complex Immedia project—only to find, when they were almost finished, that Immedia was missing a crucial ingredient to their plans. They knew what they wanted, but had never checked to see if Immedia could really give it to them. While I felt badly for them, I knew exactly where they had gone wrong: they hadn't tested each of the various elements in their project.

QuarkImmedia is a new product. The engineers at Quark still haven't gotten rid of all the bugs. They're working as hard as they can to fix the bugs, plus they're building many new features for the product. And, there are some things that you might think would work, but just won't (like the sound and movie example I used earlier). So you've got to take some responsibility for figuring out what will work and what won't.

I like Greg Vander Houwen's concept of building "base camps." Every now and again, it's a good idea to stop, save your work, and test out what you've built. This is a base camp. Next time you start working, save the project under a different name; that way your base camp is safe and secure, and you can return to it if something you do later doesn't work out the way you'd planned.

When you're testing, make sure you test how the project will work when it's done, too. That means if your audience has a Windows machine, test it on Windows. If you're going to ship the product on a CD-ROM, test it on a disc. And so on, and so on.

▼ ▼

▼ ▼

A Strong Infrastructure

QuarkXPress is a page-layout application. That means its job is to make it easier for you to put stuff on your pages: text, graphics, lines, and—when you have QuarkImmedia installed—buttons, animations, movies, and other interactive elements. XPress and Immedia excel at this part of the job, but they're not necessarily the best tools for creating those items in the first place. Throughout this book I discuss just about every feature in Immedia, but while you're reading, keep in mind that it's often easier to use Photoshop or FreeHand to build graphics, or to use a word processor like Microsoft Word to write and edit text.

Once you've got all your materials together, it's time to launch QuarkXPress. But before you begin building your project, let's take a quick look at a few ways to make the process a little easier.

QuarkXPress Preferences. As I mentioned back in Chapter 1, *Quark-XPress Basics*, you can—and should—customize XPress in all sorts of ways. The program gives you a number of tools for this, mostly on the Preferences submenu (under the Edit menu).

Working on a multimedia project requires preference settings different from those for working on a piece for print. For example, I always open the General Preferences dialog box (press Command-Y) and change the Horizontal and Vertical Measurement popup menus to Points. Unless you change the Points/Inch setting in this same dialog box (you *don't* want to in multimedia, and you rarely should even in prepress work), one point will equal one screen pixel—they're both $1/72$ of an inch. That means when you choose Points from these popup menus, the Measurement palette and most dialog boxes in the program display numbers of pixels. Very useful indeed.

Remember that if you set up this preference in XPress while no documents are open, it becomes the default for all new documents you create.

Later in this chapter, in "Pictures," you'll see that multimedia requires you to think very differently about pictures. One example of this is the Color TIFFs and Gray TIFFs settings in the Application Preferences dialog box (Command-Option-Shift-Y; see Figure 3–1). These control the way XPress displays TIFF images on screen.

For years I've been recommending that people leave Color TIFFs set to "8 bit" and Gray TIFFs set to "16 levels." The screen preview isn't as good, but it keeps file size down considerably and it prints just as well. However, when it comes to multimedia, having a good screen image is usually of the utmost importance. Remember: what you see on screen is what you'll get in your final project. So before you start importing TIFFs into your multimedia projects, change Color TIFFs to "32 bit" and Gray TIFFs to "256 levels."

Note that if you already have images imported at the lower settings, you will have to re-import them (using Get Picture under the File menu) in order to get the better screen image.

Figure 3–1
Application
Preferences
dialog box

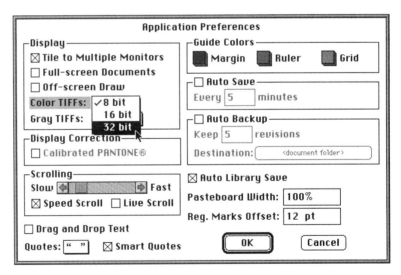

Making a New Project

Okay, it's time to create a project. As I pointed out in the last chapter, you can make a new project by selecting Project from the New submenu (under the File menu; or press Command-Option-Shift-N). When you choose this, Immedia opens the New Project dialog box (see Figure 3–2).

Figure 3–2

New projects

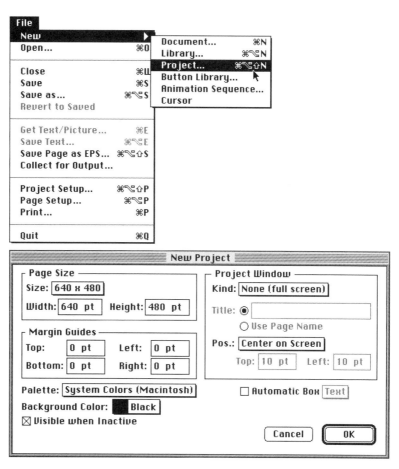

The New Project dialog box is reminiscent of QuarkXPress's New Document dialog box, and in fact many of the features are identical in form and function. For instance, the Margin Guides feature works just the same—the values you type in determine how far the margin guides are placed from the sides of the page. Most people don't use margin guides for multimedia projects, so these default to zero. We'll talk about how to use other guides later in this section.

There are several other features in this dialog box that require some explanation. Remember that even after clicking OK, these values aren't set in stone; you can always go back and change them once you've built the project.

Page Size. When you create documents for print, the Page Size area of the New Document dialog box provides you with several standard page sizes (like US Letter, Tabloid, and so on). In the New Project dialog box, you get similar choices from the Size popup menu; however, now they're typical screen dimensions. The default, 640 x 480, has become the *de facto* standard of the multimedia industry because so many people have screens with these pixel dimensions.

Nonetheless, you can always override these settings and type in whatever pixel dimensions you want. Note that Immedia remembers what you typed; next time you open this dialog box, the same settings are present.

Project Window. What happens when your project doesn't fill the entire screen? You can tell Immedia how you'd like to handle this by choosing from the Kind and Pos. popup menus in the Project Window section of the New Project dialog box. You've got three choices on the Kind popup menu (see Figure 3–3).

▶ **None (full screen).** The default setting, None (full screen), tells Immedia to cover the entire screen with the project. If the project isn't big enough, Immedia fills the surrounding space with a color (see "Background Color," below).

▶ **Page Size.** If you choose Page Size from the Kind popup menu, Immedia simply puts the project in its own window on screen. The window has a one-point black border, and acts just like any other Immedia window. You'll see what I mean and how you can take advantage of this in Chapter 5, *Windows*.

▶ **Page Size with Title.** The Page Size with Title option also puts the project in its own window, but this time it adds a title bar across the top. When you select this option, Immedia lets you choose what name you'd like displayed in the title bar. If you don't want any title, just leave the Title field blank.

▼ ▼

Tip: Titling Using Page Names. When building a project, I periodically stop and test it out using Engage (under the QuarkImmedia menu). The problem is that sometimes I get confused about what page I'm looking at. One solution is to name each of the project's

Figure 3–3

Project
window types

None (full screen)

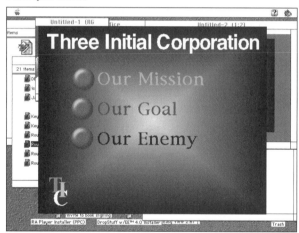

Page Size

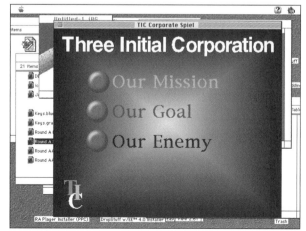

Page Size with Title

pages (I discuss how to do this later in this chapter), and then tell Immedia to display that page name in the project's title bar. You can do this by first choosing Page Size with Title from either the New Project or Project Setup dialog box, and then choosing the Use Page Name option.

▼ ▼

The last option in the Project Window section is the Pos. popup menu. This defaults to Center on Screen (which, believe it or not, centers the project on the screen). However, you can specify exactly where on screen you want the project to appear by choosing Other from this popup menu. For instance, if you want to make sure the project appears in the upper left corner of the screen, you can type 0 (zero) into both the Top and Left fields of this section.

Palette. QuarkImmedia lets you display up to 256 colors in your project. But which 256 colors? Immedia, like most multimedia programs, uses a color lookup table (CLUT) made up of 256 colors, also called a *palette*. I talk about color palettes, how to use them, and why you need to carefully think about them, in "Color Palettes," later in this chapter. For now, suffice it to say that the Palette popup menu in the New Project dialog box is where you first decide which palette your project will use.

Background Color. The color you choose from the Background Color popup menu is placed behind the project window just before Immedia displays the first page. For example, if you set this to Red, then engage the project, Immedia fills the project window with red, then puts the project window over this field of red.

The result: If you selected the None (full screen) option (see "Project Window," above), Immedia fills the whole screen with red and places the project in the middle of it. If you selected either Page Size or Page Size with Title, Immedia fills just that area with red, then immediately transitions into the first page (which will completely cover up the color).

▼ ▼

Tip: Adding Default Colors. The Background Color popup menu in the New Project dialog box only displays QuarkXPress's default colors: Red, Green, Blue, Cyan, Magenta, and so on. If you want to select a different color, you have to add it to the default color list first. You can do this by creating the color while no documents are open (see "New Colors," in Chapter 1, *QuarkXPress Basics)*.

▼ ▼

Visible when Inactive. Programs are *active* when you're in them, and *inactive* when you're in some other program (but they're still running in the background). For instance, when you're in QuarkXPress, it's active. When you switch to the Finder without quitting XPress, XPress becomes inactive. However, you can usually still see it. Immedia gives you the choice of whether to make projects visible or invisible when they are inactive. I can't think of any good reason to turn off the Visible when Inactive option, but it's always nice to have another option.

Automatic Box. If you turn on the Automatic Box option in the New Project dialog box, Immedia puts a picture box or text box on the project's master page for you (you can choose which type from the popup menu next to this option). The box fills the page to the page margins. I leave this option turned off. If I want a box on the master page, I'll put it there myself.

Project Setup

As I said earlier, your choices in the New Project dialog box are not permanent and binding. Once you click on OK, you can go back and change most of the options in the Project Setup dialog box (choose Project Setup from the File menu, or press Command-Option-Shift-P; see Figure 3–4). Note that you cannot change your margin guides here; you can only change margin guides on a master page (see "Master Pages" in Chapter 1, *QuarkXPress Basics)*.

Figure 3–4

Project Setup
dialog box

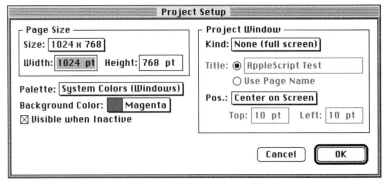

Style Sheets and Master Pages

QuarkXPress has two features that are almost unheard of in other multimedia authoring tools, but are actually incredibly useful: style sheets and master pages. For some reason, many experienced XPress users seem to forget about these two features when it comes to building QuarkImmedia projects. It's as though they can't find any use for them. However, both features help ensure consistency in your projects.

Style sheets. Inconsistent text formatting is common in print, but it's almost epidemic in multimedia projects. You'd think it'd be easy to set each of the headlines and blocks of body text to the same font, size, leading, color, and so on. Apparently not. The result is a shoddy-looking project that appears as though it was not well thought-out. You can avoid this by using style sheets religiously. As you know, style sheets are great for two reasons.

► They let you apply the same group of text-formatting to a number of paragraphs quickly and painlessly.

► They let you change that formatting even faster when your art director tells you to change the color, the size, the font, or whatever.

As you saw back in Chapter 1, *QuarkXPress Basics*, making style sheets is easy, and using them is even easier (if you aren't familiar with style sheets yet, you should check out the "Style Sheets" section in that chapter).

Master pages. Master pages also speed up production and help you stay consistent. Anything you put on a master page appears on all the project pages based on that master page. For instance, if all your pages are based on A-Master Page A (they will be until you assign a different master page to them), and you put a background picture on that master page, that picture appears on all your pages.

Many projects include buttons that appear on a number of pages. You can build a master page with these buttons on it, then assign this master page to the pages on which you want the buttons. That's much easier than having to place the buttons one page at a time. Plus, you can be sure that the buttons appear at the *same place* on every page.

I also often include guides on my master pages so that they appear on my project pages. This helps me place text boxes, picture boxes, animations, and other items consistently across a number of pages.

▼ ▼
Color Palettes

While I'm sure that someday QuarkImmedia will accommodate full 24-bit color graphics, right now all it can handle is 8-bit indexed color. What that means in English is you can use up to 256 different colors in a project. While that may seem like a lot, you'll soon find that it can be a severe limitation, especially when you're working with blends, scanned images, or any other kind of fancy graphics.

8-bit monitors. Computer environments like the Macintosh and Windows have been using color palettes for years for two reasons. First, many (if not most) computers can only display 256 colors at any given time. The computer screens can display many more than that, but the hardware that drives the monitor can't dish that many out. Most of the newer computers on the market can handle 16-bit color ("thousands of colors") or 24-bit color ("millions of colors"), and they give you a choice of how many colors you want to use (you can control this on the Macintosh in the Monitors control panel).

The second reason operating systems use color palettes is that displaying only 256 colors is very fast, and takes up very little memory. The reason has to do with how 8-bit color works. Eight-bit color is called *indexed color* because each color in the palette is given a number. For instance, color number 1 might be white, number 2 could be orange, number 3 could be light blue, and so on all the way up to number 256. When the computer wants to make something blue, it just asks for color number 3; it doesn't have to actually describe the color using RGB or any other color model.

If you're in 8-bit color mode, and you ask for a color that isn't in the palette, the computer has to simulate it using the colors that are in the palette. The computer can do this in a number of ways, but it generally uses some sort of patterning or dithering, mixing two colors together to get close to the color you want (see Figure 3–5).

System and custom palettes. Both the Macintosh and Windows operating systems have their own standard color palettes. When your computer is set to display 8-bit color (256 colors), it uses the standard *system palette*. However, many programs, including QuarkImmedia and Photoshop, can temporarily override the system palette, imposing a different set of 256 indexed colors.

There's a project on the *Real World QuarkImmedia* CD-ROM called "Zap!" that uses white, black, and about a hundred different blues. The standard system palette has white and black, but it has only a handful of different blue colors. The result is that the computer has to simulate all the extra blues by dithering. I was able to get around this problem by creating a custom palette that contained all the blues I needed for the project (I'll explore how to create and use custom palettes in the next section).

Of course, if I had wanted a bright red square in the middle of one of my "Zap!" pages, I couldn't get it because there were no reds in the palette at all. The computer would try to simulate the red, but would fail and just make it blue.

Palette Problems

Having a limited color palette can be as frustrating as a broken water cooler on a hot day in Texas . . . or it can be a creative challenge.

Figure 3–5
Simulating a color
in an 8-bit palette

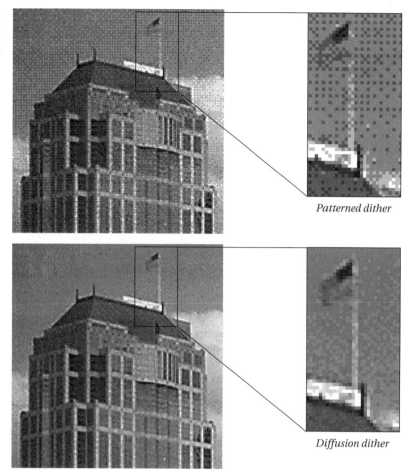

Patterned dither

Diffusion dither

Before I get into the intricacies of building and using palettes in your Immedia projects, here are just a few things you'll run into.

Palette flash. One of the biggest problems with indexed color palettes is that of *palette flash*. Palette flash occurs when your computer is set up to display only 256 colors, and you switch from one color palette to another. In the example above, I said that color number 1 was white; what happens if a program comes in and imposes a custom palette that makes color number 1 green? The system keeps asking for "color number 1" expecting it to be white, but it comes up green instead.

When you quit an Immedia project that uses a custom palette, there's often a quick flash when all the colors on the screen freak out for a moment (that's the technical term, of course). This is just the computer switching back to the system palette. You can get palette flash when you move from one project to another (if one or both use custom palettes), or when you move between programs.

Again, palette flash typically happens only when a computer display is set up to display only 256 colors.

Blends. Blends are notoriously difficult in indexed color situations. Blends usually require a lot of similar colors in order to appear smooth, and because most color palettes don't contain them all, the blends look really weird—dithered or patterned (see Figure 3–6). One solution is to make a custom palette that includes many of the colors the blend requires. However, if you have one blend from black to white (which needs a lot of grays), and another blend that goes from red to blue (which requires purples), one of them is probably going to suffer.

Scanned images. Natural images—like photographs that you've scanned—can look great in indexed color. It's surprising how few colors you really need to make an image look good. But they have to be the *right* colors. If you're using a standard system palette when trying to display a picture of a person, your subject will not be flattered by the result. The system palette just doesn't include many flesh tones. However, if you use a custom palette full of flesh tones,

Figure 3–6
Blends

System palette *Custom palette*

that picture might look great, but a picture of a house in the same project may look really odd.

Using the Palette in Immedia

Okay, enough already with the theory! Let's get down to brass tacks and see how to use palettes in QuarkImmedia. You've seen the first use of palettes earlier in this chapter, when I talked about the New Project dialog box. If you've built a custom color palette before you started constructing your project (I recommend this, whenever possible; making palettes in Photoshop is covered in the next section), you can assign this palette to your project in this dialog box.

Of course, after the project is already open you can always change palettes in the Project Setup dialog box.

Your options in the Project Setup and New Project dialog boxes are slim.

▶ System colors (Macintosh)

▶ System colors (Windows)

▶ System grays (Macintosh)

▶ Other (custom palette)

If you want to use a custom color palette, you have to first save one out of Photoshop (see "The Color Table," later in this chapter). Then you can import it into your project by selecting Other from the Palette popup menu in either the New Project or Project Setup dialog box.

Some people believe that if you expect anyone to look at your project on a Windows machine, you should select the Windows system palette. The reason is that, for technical reasons, Windows only really lets you use 236 colors (see "Tip: Windows Palettes," later in this chapter), and 216 of them actually overlap with the Macintosh color palette. In other words, if you can make the project look good in a Windows palette, there's a pretty good chance it'll look good on a Macintosh, too.

What gets converted? No matter how many colors your screen (or your user's screen) can display, when you engage or export your project, Immedia converts every color you used to the nearest color in the palette. That includes colors in your pictures, animations, and buttons. The only exception is QuickTime movies, which can display in out-of-palette colors if your monitor is displaying 16- or 24-bit color (see Chapter 9, *QuickTime Movies).*

With this in mind, it's a good idea to ensure that the colors you used to build the animations, buttons, and pictures are already in the palette you're going to use. If not, they they'll get mapped to other colors and your images may not appear exactly as you'd expect.

Simulating colors. When your monitor is set to display 8-bit color (256 colors), QuarkImmedia actually uses the color palette while you're authoring. This means that what you see on screen while you're authoring is what you'll get when you engage or export the project. Plus, Immedia does *not* try to simulate the requested color with dithering; it just snaps to the nearest color in the palette. For instance, if you set the Background Color of a picture box to 10-percent blue in a project based on the Macintosh system palette, it appears white. That's because white is the nearest color in the palette to this light blue.

While some people think this feature is odd, I use it to my advantage. Even though my computer can display full 24-bit color, I often change it to 256 colors (in the Monitors control panel) so that I don't have to engage my project just to see what a color will look like in the final piece.

▼ ▼

Tip: Getting Colors from Photoshop into XPress. The best way to match a color in a Photoshop image is to write down Photoshop's RGB values, then type those into XPress's Edit Color dialog box. The problem is that Photoshop and XPress specify RGB in different ways. Photoshop thinks in terms of numbers between zero and 256. XPress thinks in terms of percentages between zero and 100. Here's what you do.

1. Find the RGB values for the color in Photoshop (you can see them on the Info and Picker palettes). Write them down.

2. In XPress, create a new RGB color.

3. For each of the RGB values, type the value from Photoshop, divided by 2.55. For example, let's say the RGB values are 51/153/102. In the Red field of the Edit Color dialog box, type "51/2.55"; in the Green field type "153/2.55" and so on. XPress does the math for you, resulting in 20%, 60%, and 40%.

Of cource, this math is for the birds. That's why I use an XTension called PickUp Spot. It's on the *Real World QuarkImmedia* CD-ROM (see Chapter 16, *The Real World QuarkImmedia CD-ROM*).

▼ ▼

Adobe Photoshop's Color Palettes

There are a lot of image-editing programs on the market, but I must admit that I (and the majority of professional multimedia authors) use Adobe Photoshop. I even take images that I build in other programs (like Fractal Painter or Strata Studio Pro) into Photoshop to prepare them for Immedia. The number-one thing I'm concerned about in preparing these images is creating, adjusting, and assigning color palettes. And though this really isn't a book on Photoshop, let's just take a quick look at how this is done.

Converting to Indexed Color mode. You can convert any RGB or grayscale image to indexed color mode by selecting Indexed from Photoshop's Mode menu. If the image is in RGB mode, Photoshop opens the Indexed Color dialog box (see Figure 3–7). If the image is already in Grayscale mode, Photoshop just assumes you want the standard grayscale color palette (where each of the 256 "colors" is a gray value), so it skips this dialog box.

You can make three choices in the Indexed Color dialog box.

▶ **Resolution.** The Resolution setting lets you choose how many colors you want in the palette. For instance, 8 bits per pixel results in a full 256 colors. Four bits per pixel results in Photoshop reducing the entire image to 16 colors. The fewer the colors, the more an image will compress (I discuss the topic

Figure 3-7

Converting to indexed color

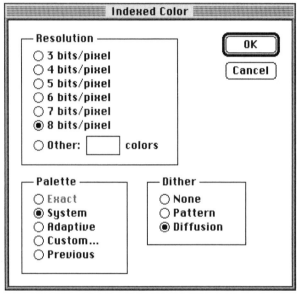

of compressing file sizes and why it's so important in Chapter 14, *Exporting)*. As I said earlier, what's amazing is how few colors you can get away with and still retain the essence of an image (see the project "NecessaryColors" on the *Real World QuarkImmedia* CD-ROM).

▶ **Palette.** The Palette section offers several options for palettes. If you're converting to the standard Macintosh system palette, choose eight bits per pixel in the Resolution section, and then choose the System option from this section. If you want to create a new color palette that's optimized for a particular image, select Adaptive or Exact. Or, if you've already created an indexed color palette that you want to apply to this image, select Custom.

▶ **Dither.** Reducing the number of colors in an image to an indexed color palette is a tricky business no matter how you slice it. The biggest problem is what to do with colors that don't fit into the color palette. Photoshop gives you the option of simulating colors using dithering (or patterning, if you're converting to the System palette). Most of the time, you should choose Diffusion from the Dither section. However, for line-art images or pictures of text, you may get a better result by turning off dithering (select the None option).

I rarely use the Pattern dither option, as I think it usually looks really ugly. However, when you're converting large areas of flat color, Pattern can actually look better than Diffusion. It's worth a try, at least.

The Color Table. Once you've converted an image into Indexed color mode, you can see the color palette by selecting Color Table from the Mode menu (see Figure 3–8). You can then save the color palette to your hard drive by clicking on the Save button (as I said earlier,

Figure 3–8
Viewing the
color palette

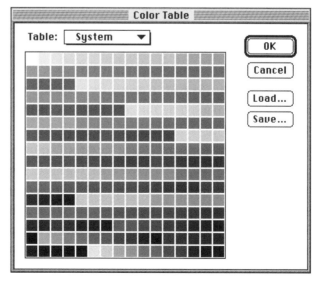

you need to do this if you want to use the color palette in your Immedia project).

Note that you can also edit any color in the color palette by clicking on the color in the Color Table dialog box. For example, let's say I was working on the "Zap!" project that I discussed earlier; the color palette is made up entirely of white, black, and a number of shades of blue. As it stands, I wouldn't be able to color some text red because there is no red in the palette. Here's how I could do it.

1. Open any indexed color image (or create a new one). You have to have any indexed color document open in order to edit a palette.

2. Select Color Table from the Mode menu. Then open the color palette that you want to edit from your hard drive by clicking on the Load button.

3. Find a color that isn't used much in the project. For instance, if there are two colors that look almost identical, choose one of them.

4. Click on that color to edit it, and choose the color that you want to use (in this case, a bright red).

5. Save the color palette out to disk again, and import the new one into your Immedia project.

Now Immedia will let you use that color in your project.

▼ ▼

Tip: Ganging up Pictures. You know how to get a custom color palette based on the colors in a single image. But how can you get a palette representative of a number of different pictures? One method you can use is to gang up a bunch of images in one big Photoshop file. Then convert that big file to indexed color, choosing an adaptive palette. Photoshop does its best to build a color palette for all the images at once. You can then save this file to disk and close the ganged-up image without saving it (once you've got the palette made, there's probably no reason to keep this big file).

▼ ▼

Tip: White and Black in Palettes. When you're building custom palettes in Photoshop, note that Immedia expects that the first color will be white and the last color will be black. If you don't do this, your projects might work, or odd things might occur.

▼ ▼

Tip: Windows Palettes. The Windows operating system reserves the first 10 and the last 10 color palette positions for system-level things. Immedia adjusts your custom palettes internally so that, when you run a project on the Windows platform, only the first 236 colors of the project's palette are saved; the last 20 are remapped to the remaining colors. Therefore, if you know your project will be viewed on a Windows-based machine, you should not put any really important colors in the last 20 places of the palette. Otherwise, they may not appear exactly as you expect.

▼ ▼

Tip: Debabelizer. No discussion of color palettes would be complete without a mention of Equilibrium's Debabelizer software. Debabelizer is the world's best color-palette manipulator. You can use it to do all sorts of things.

- ▸ Build a "super palette" that represents the colors in 50 different images, but with five of the images weighted as "most important."

- ▸ Batch-convert QuickTime movies to custom palettes.

- ▸ Batch-convert TIFFs to PICTs, PICTs to BMPs, and many other common file type conversions.

- ▸ Build color palettes that will work great on Windows and Macintosh (and the Internet, and other platforms).

It does a whole lot more than this. So much, in fact, that its interface is almost totally incomprehensible. In fact, I know several people who have proclaimed it the "worst interface of any software program." High praise. Nonetheless, they insist they wouldn't do multimedia without it.

Fortunately, I've got good news and more good news. First, there's a "Lite" version of Debabelizer on the *Real World QuarkImmedia* CD-ROM at the back of the book (see Chapter 16 for more information about that). Second, Equilibrium is in the process of revamping their interface. The next version of it will be much, much easier to use. In the meantime, the best consolation is a cup of hot chocolate and the program's documentation.

▼ ▼
Pictures

After I'd worked in the prepress industry for years, it was with great chagrin that I learned that everything I knew about pictures was either wrong or inconsequential in the world of multimedia. So, while I hate to be the one breaking the bad news to you, in this section, I'm going to run down a few rules for working with pictures in your QuarkImmedia projects.

Image resolution. One of the hardest lessons when switching from prepress to multimedia is using low-resolution images. While there are all these rules about image resolution when going to print (you need at least one and a half times your halftone screen frequency, and so on), in multimedia there's pretty much only one thing to keep in mind: what you see on screen at Actual Size view is what you're going to get in your final project. That means you generally want 72 dpi images (because most screens are 72 pixels per inch).

Some people insist that they'll get better images in Immedia if they import them at 300 or 400 dpi. Not so. You may get better quality images if you *scan* at 300 or 400 dpi, but you should quickly downsample them to 72 dpi in Photoshop before bringing them into an XPress picture box.

Preparing images. When preparing images for Immedia projects, it's a good idea to do as much work on them in Photoshop as you can before importing them into your picture box. That means sizing, cropping, rotating, correcting tone and color, and sharpening. This almost always results in a better image than when you scale or rotate on your QuarkXPress page.

File types. I've spent half my professional life telling people not to use PICT images. "PICT images are bad!" I'd yell at them. However, while PICT images are inappropriate for prepress work (when it comes to printing, they're nothing but trouble), they're perfect for multimedia. In fact, most multimedia authoring programs insist that you use PICT images.

QuarkImmedia lets you use PICT, TIFF, EPS, BMP, JPEG, and several other file types. However, the only file types I ever use for multimedia projects are PICT, TIFF, and occasionally EPS with a JPEG preview (see the next tip). As I noted earlier in this chapter, if you use TIFF files, make sure you set the Color TIFFs setting (in Application Preferences) to 32 bit. Again, I'd never do this for prepress work, but it's necessary to get good quality images from TIFFs when doing multimedia.

▼ ▼

Tip: JPEG Previews. Whenever possible, do all your image editing while your image is in RGB mode, and only convert to indexed color as the last step in the process. In fact, even if you're using a custom palette, you may not want to convert to indexed color mode at all. You can import RGB images into your XPress picture box, and Immedia will convert them to whatever color palette you're using. This is great if the color palette is likely to change at any time while you're building the project.

I used to convert RGB images to indexed color mode because I thought I was saving hard disk space. Then I realized that I could stay in RGB and save even more space by saving my pictures as EPS files with a JPEG preview.

1. Open the image in Photoshop and select Save As.

2. Select EPS from the Save As dialog box's Format popup menu and give the file a name. Don't copy over the original RGB file.

3. Select JPEG from the Preview popup menu in Photoshop's Save as EPS dialog box (see Figure 3–9). Note that this won't

work if the image is in indexed color mode or if QuickTime is not loaded.

4. Select JPEG (low quality) from the Encoding popup menu. Selecting this actually damages the high-resolution data part of the image (that's why you're not saving over your original), but we don't care because we're not printing this image . . . we just care about the preview image that we'll get on screen.

5. Save the image and import it into your project.

This gives you a great preview to see on screen (the JPEG preview is as good as you'll get), and reduces the file's size to a fraction of the original RGB image. Remember to keep the original RGB version as

Figure 3–9
Saving a JPEG
preview in an EPS
from Photoshop

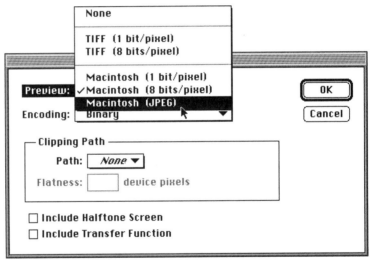

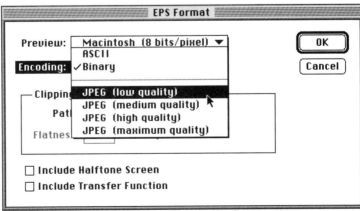

a backup, just in case you need to resize the graphic or make other edits to the picture.

▾ ▾

Trashing the original. QuarkXPress only saves a link to the high-resolution data in EPS and TIFF files. When you go to print, XPress chucks the on-screen preview and uses the high-res data instead. But, if you're building a multimedia project, you don't care about the high-res data, do you? That means you don't have to worry about maintaining links to those EPS and TIFF files after you import them into your document.

Of course, you should always keep backups of the files. You never know when you'll have to make a change to one of them.

Aligning graphics. Because I'm using high-resolution graphics in my prepress work, what I see on screen is almost never what's really going to print out. That makes it nearly impossible to align two graphics together, or some type with an element in a picture, or whatever. No matter how hard I try, when I print the piece out, it's not quite right.

However, this problem goes away in Immedia because every element is 72 dpi, and what you see on screen is what you'll get in the final project. You've got to admit that while some parts of multimedia are a pain, there's some stuff that is just so easy!

▾ ▾

Tip: Importing versus Pasting. I never paste images in to picture boxes when doing prepress work because they rarely print the way I expect—it's just really unreliable. But pasting is perfectly reasonable in a multimedia project; you get about the same quality as if you imported a PICT image with Get Picture.

The first problem with pasting is that you lose any link to a file on disk. For example, if you import a PICT into a project, then later change that PICT file on disk, it's easy to re-import it (either automatically, using Auto Picture Import in the General Preferences dialog box, or manually in the Picture Usage dialog box).

The second problem with pasting is that it can slow down the time it takes to draw the image on screen, especially with larger graphics. On a fast enough computer, however, you may not notice the slowdown.

▼ ▼

Turning the Page

It's time to put all these "conceptual underpinnings" to work, and start building your project. You've already seen how to create a new project, how to assign a color palette, and how to prepare images to put on your pages. But as soon as you have more than one page in your project, the question immediately arises of how to move from one page to the next.

Once you engage or export the project, you can only have one page visible at a time, so how you move among the pages in your document is very important. Let's first take a look at the Page tab of the QuarkImmedia palette, and then delve into the various actions that you can use to control pages in Immedia.

The Page Tab

When it comes to thinking about the pages in your document, the first place you need to look is on the Page tab of the QuarkImmedia palette (see Figure 3–10). The Page tab lets you name pages and apply a number of different controls to them.

Page. The first section of the Page tab displays all the pages in your document in a column on the left side of the palette. This control simply lets you specify the page to which to apply the rest of the tab's settings. To name a page, for instance, select the page in the Page column, then enter a name in the Page Name field. While it's true that double-clicking on the page name in the list actually takes you to that page, you don't have to have the page visible in order to make changes to it on the Page tab.

If you choose Master Page from the Page popup menu (just above the Page list), Immedia displays not the page's name but

Figure 3–10

The Page tab

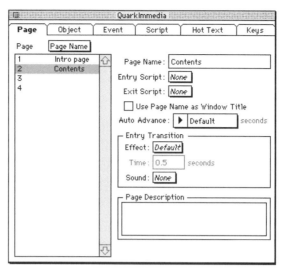

which master page is assigned to each page. This is useful when you are working with a number of master pages: rather than having to skip back and forth between this palette and the Document Layout palette, you can find most of the information you need here.

Note that the page numbers in the Page list are absolute numbers. If you've used the Section feature to change the page numbers to roman numerals or something like that, the Page list ignores that. The first page is always "1," the second is "2," and so on.

Page Names and Descriptions. As I said above, you can name a page by selecting it from the Page list and typing into the Page Name field. You can also type a description of the page into the Page Description field. Giving a page a name and description can be very useful for a number of reasons.

▶ You can display a particular page by its name rather than number (see "Page Actions," below). If you later rearrange your project's pages, or add or remove a page, your page numbering will change, but the page name never does (until you change it yourself).

▶ There are some cool tricks you can use to display a page based on a page name that your user has selected from a pop-up menu or list.

▶ Later, in Chapter 4, *Text*, you'll see how you can search for particular words or phrases from the list of page names and descriptions. For instance, "find me all the pages that have the word 'requirements' in their description."

▶ Last, but certainly not least, I find naming and describing each page in my document to be incredibly useful while authoring and debugging my projects. You can control an item on a different page from the one you're on (in an engaged or exported project), but you have to tell Immedia *which* object on *which* page. It's much easier to remember "the red ball on the page named 'Karaoke Page'" than "object number 3 on page number 8."

Script. The Entry Script and Exit Script popup menus on the Page tab let you trigger a script when you enter or leave a page. Scripting sounds like a big, ugly, hairy mess, but you'll see in Chapter 13, *Scripting*, that building scripts is just as easy as anything else in Immedia. Once you've made a script, you can select it from one of these two popup menus.

Use Page Name as Window Title. As you saw earlier, in "Making a New Project," you can place the page name in a title bar above the project (when the project doesn't fill the entire screen). You can find this option in the New Project and Project Setup dialog boxes. Why, then, is there an option on the Page tab titled Use Page Name as Window Title?

In rare instances (at least, rare to me), you'll want to place one title in the project's title bar for the majority of pages, but then use a different title for a small number of pages. That's what this feature does. When you turn on Use Page Name as Window Title, the page name overrides the title you've specified in the New Project or Project Setup dialog boxes—just while you display that page, of course.

Auto Advance. If you're familiar with presentation software, such as Microsoft Powerpoint or Adobe Persuasion, you undoubtedly have seen Auto Advance before. This feature lets you automatically move from one page to the next, like a slide show on autopilot.

When you first open the Page tab of the QuarkImmedia palette, every page's Auto Advance setting is Default. This means "use the Auto Advance setting in the QuarkImmedia Preferences dialog box" (see Figure 3–11). Your pages won't auto-advance at first because that setting is usually turned off. If you want your pages to auto-advance, you've got two choices.

▶ If you want all of your pages to advance automatically, turn on the Auto Advance checkbox in the QuarkImmedia Preferences dialog box.

Figure 3–11
Auto Advance

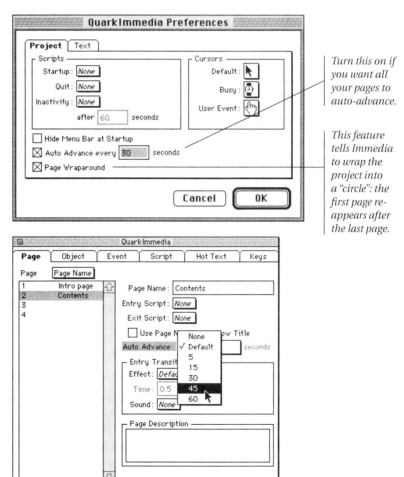

Turn this on if you want all your pages to auto-advance.

This feature tells Immedia to wrap the project into a "circle": the first page reappears after the last page.

▶ If you want just a few pages to advance automatically, leave the Preferences dialog box out of it, and just specify an Auto Advance setting on the Page tab.

Of course, if you want all but a few pages to advance automatically, you can also turn on the setting in Preferences, then set the Page tab's Auto Advance value to None.

When the project comes to the last page, Auto Advance stops . . . unless you have turned on the Page Wraparound option in the QuarkImmedia Preferences dialog box. If you have, then the "next page" after the last page is page 1 again.

Entry Transition. The last section of the Page tab, Entry Transition, lets you set a default transition effect between any other page and the page you've selected from the Page list. In other words, how do you want this page to appear on screen? I discuss all the various transition types in "Transitions," later in this chapter.

Page Actions

In the last chapter, I included a "One-Minute Tutorial" that showed how to assign a single action—a Beep action—to a user event: clicking on a box. I then claimed that almost every other action in QuarkImmedia worked just the same way. Now it's time to see how true that is. In this section, I discuss eight different actions that control pages. Each one of these can be tied to any user event. As I noted before, the best way to learn each of these is to try them out.

1. Create a new document and add several pages to it.

2. Put different objects on each page (like a blue box on page 1, a red box on page 2, and so on).

3. Select the box on page 1, and assign one of the following actions to the box's Click Up user event (on the Event tab of the QuarkImmedia palette).

4. Engage the project and click on the object. If the action worked, pat yourself on the back. If not, disengage the project and try to find what went wrong.

Display Next Page. The Display Next Page action (select Display Next from the Page popout menu on the Action popup menu on the Event tab; see Figure 3–12) simply jumps to the next page in the project—like from page 1 to page 2. Your only option, when choosing this action, is what transition effect to use when moving from one page to the next.

Like all Page actions, the default transition—Page Panel Transition—tells Immedia to use whatever transition you've set up on the Page tab of the QuarkImmedia palette. You can override that by selecting a different effect from the Transition popup menu (I explore transitions more fully in the next section).

Figure 3–12

Page actions

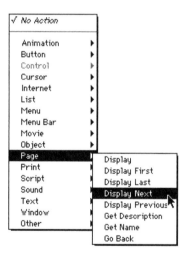

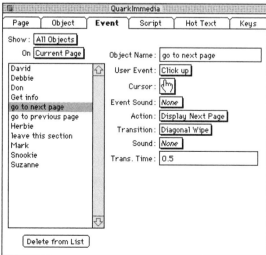

Unless you have turned on the Page Wraparound feature in the QuarkImmedia Preferences dialog box, Immedia just ignores the Display Next Page action when it's on the last page of your project.

Display Previous Page. The Display Previous Page action does just the opposite of the last action: it jumps to the previous page in your project. If you trigger the Display Previous Page action on the first page of your document, Immedia just ignores it (unless you have turned on the Page Wraparound feature; then, the page "before" page 1 is the final page of your project). Once again, your only option in this feature is what kind of transition you want from one page to the next.

Display First Page/Display Last Page. The Display First Page and Display Last Page actions take you to the first page or the last page of your project. I rarely use these, only because I find that they don't suit my authoring style. That is, I may use a Display First Page action one day, then the next day I'll think "Oh, I need to add a new introduction page to the beginning of the project." All of a sudden, the Display First Page action doesn't take me where I expected it to anymore. Nonetheless, you might find it useful in your projects.

Display Page. I use the Display Page action constantly because it lets me specify exactly which page I want to jump to. This is the most powerful and flexible of all the page actions, but it also appears more complex (see Figure 3–13). It really isn't. As you'll read throughout this book, the actions often look complicated, but if you read the action's options one at a time, they make a lot of sense.

The Display Page action really has only two options: Method and Transition. The Method popup menu lets you choose *how* you want to specify which page to display. You've got three choices.

> ▶ **Page Number.** If you choose the Page Number option from the Method popup menu, Immedia lets you type in the page number you want to display. To display the fourth page of the project, type "4" into the Page field (under the popup menu). As I said earlier, this method is fragile, and I don't use it

Figure 3-13
Display Page

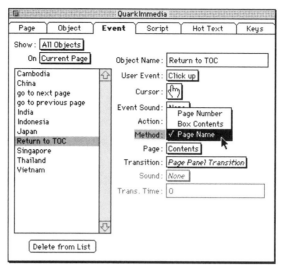

much—if you rearrange the pages in your project, or add or delete a page, the action may display the wrong page.

▶ **Box Contents.** The second choice in the Method popup menu, Box Contents, tells Immedia to display whatever page is written in a text box object somewhere in your project. (I discuss how to turn a regular text box into a "text box object" in the next chapter.*) Select the text box object from the Text Box popup menu under the Method popup menu.

If that text box object has a number in it, Immedia displays that page number. If the text box object has a word in it, Immedia displays the page whose name matches that word.

The text box object doesn't have to be on your page; it can be on the pasteboard, or on another page. To choose a text box object on a page other than the one you're currently on, select Other from the Text Object popup menu (see Figure 3–14).

▶ **Page Name.** The Page Name option lets you choose a page to display by its name. Once you've named a page (on the Page tab), you can choose it from the Page popup menu (under the

---

*I know it's frustrating learning about features that you can't use until you learn something in a later chapter, but it's the nature of multimedia—everything is interrelated to everything else. I can only ask for your patience; the puzzles will all unfold in time.

Figure 3–14

Choosing an object on
a different page

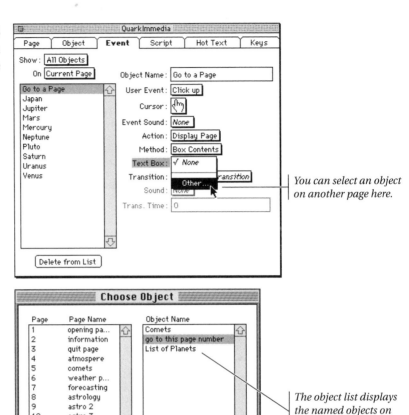

*You can select an object
on another page here.*

*The object list displays
the named objects on
each page.*

Method popup menu in this action; see Figure 3–15). I like
naming my pages and then using this method to display
them because I frequently add and remove pages, or reorder
the pages in the project. Specifying a name is robust—it
always takes me to the correct page.

Get Page Name/ Get Page Description. The Get Page Name and Get
Page Description actions are both really text actions—that is, they
add text to text box objects—but because they appear on the Page
popout menu (on the Action popup menu), I'll quickly discuss

Figure 3-15

Displaying a page by name

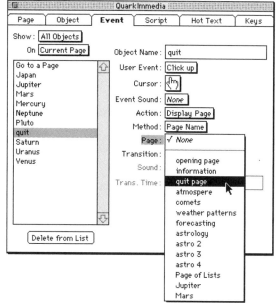

them here. Both actions retrieve information and put it in a text box object. Both actions work in the same way, though they provide slightly different results. The Get Page Name action grabs a page's name; Get Page Description grabs the page's description.

Let's say you've named and inserted detailed descriptions for each page in your project. You could build a window in your project (see Chapter 5, *Windows)* that displays the name and description of each new page you enter. Actually, even this example is stretching these actions' usefulness. To be honest, I haven't found a really good use for them yet; though I'm sure I will, sooner or later.

You've got three options in each of these actions.

▶ **Select.** First, you've got to select which page you want the name or description from. You can do this by choosing Current Page, Page Number, or Page Name from the Select popup menu. For example, you could say, "Get the page name of whatever page the user is currently on."

▶ **Text Object.** The next step is to select the text box object you want the name or description dropped into. You can select this from the Text Object popup menu. Again, if you want to select a text box object on a different page, choose Other.

▶ **Placement.** The last choice you have to make here is from the Placement popup menu: where in the text box object do you want the name or description to go? You've got several options: Add to Beginning, Add to End, Replace All, and Replace Selection. I discuss each of these in detail when exploring the various text actions in Chapter 4, *Text.*

Go Back. The last action on the Page popout menu (on the Action popup menu) is Go Back. When you trigger this action, Immedia returns to the last page you were on. If you jumped from page 1 to page 6, and then triggered a Go Back action, the project would return to the first page. I use this constantly in my projects because it's just so dang convenient—much easier than having to use one Display Page action to go to some page, and then *another* to return to where you were.

▼ ▼

Tip: Opening on a Different Page. Occasionally, you don't want your user to see page 1 of your project first. Perhaps when they first start up your project, you want to jump immediately to page 12. Unfortunately, Immedia doesn't let you do this. Here's one quick workaround, though.

1. Add a new page at the beginning of your project. Either leave it blank, or cover it with a box with some background color.

2. Build a script with a single action: Display Page 12 (or whatever page you want to display; see Chapter 13, *Scripting).*

3. On the Page tab, select your new page 1 and choose this script from the Entry Script popup menu.

The result: when the project first opens, your blank page 1 appears for just a moment, then the script kicks in and takes you to the page you really want your user to see first.

▼ ▼

▼ ▼

Transitions

Just watch the evening news on television and you'll see a bevy of wild transitions from one scene to the next. Cutting from one picture to the next seems so abrupt in these days of high-tech video. Whether you call them digital fades, wipes, or crossovers, transitions lend a hand in creating an atmosphere in your project.

Immedia uses transitions for three different things: moving between pages, hiding and showing objects on the page, and opening and closing windows. You can specify one of 18 default transitions, or customize them to fit your needs. For each transition, you can also specify the length of the transition (in seconds), and a sound to go with the transition (see Chapter 7, *Sound*).

I'm not poet enough to describe each of the transitions in writing, so I've put a small project—cleverly called "Transitions"—on the *Real World QuarkImmedia* CD-ROM. This project shows you every default transition . . . check it out.

Pages

Every time you display a page, a transition happens. The default transition—the one you get if you don't select any other type—is a normal transition that simply switches from one page to the next. You can use a different transition effect, like Digital Dissolve or Reveal, in one of three ways.

▶ **Page tab.** You can set an entry transition for any page on the Page tab of the QuarkImmedia palette—choose one from the Effect popup menu (see Figure 3–16). Some people seem to overlook the fact that the label above the Effect popup menu says "Entry Transition." This is the transition effect that you'll see when you display this page, not when you exit it.

▶ **Page actions.** As I noted in "Page Actions," above, each of the actions that display a page lets you choose a transition effect.

Figure 3-16
Default page
transitions

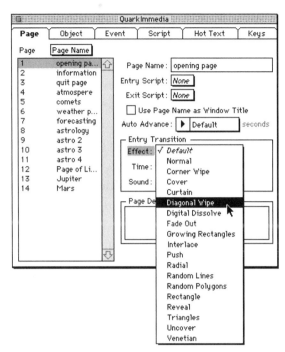

If you opt for one of these, it overrides any transition effect you may have specified on the Page tab.

▶ **Default transition.** You can also change the default transition, so that the default always gives you something other than a normal, boring switch from one page to the other. I'll discuss this in "Custom Transitions," below.

Objects

In the next section, I discuss how to make objects on your page (such as picture boxes, text boxes, lines, buttons, and so on) disappear and reappear using the Show Object and Hide Object actions. Each of these actions lets you specify the transition between seeing the object and not seeing it. Again, the default setting is that the object simply pops in on or out of your page. You can make it slowly fade in or appear with any one of the various wipes on the Transition popup menu. (This is how I created the effects in the Transition project on the *Real World QuarkImmedia* CD-ROM.)

Windows

In Chapter 5, *Windows*, I discuss how to create, open, and close windows on your screen (such as dialog boxes, alert boxes, palettes, and so on). Immedia lets you specify a transition whenever you open a window. Curiously enough, the program does not let you choose one when you close the window again.

I rarely use anything other than the default, normal transition when opening windows because the others look kind of strange. The problem is that Immedia first always draws a black rule around the area on the page that contains the window, *then* uses the transition effect to "fill in" the window. It just never appears as you'd expect.

Custom Transitions

Sometimes the 18 transitions Immedia provides aren't quite what you wanted—perhaps this one could go from left to right instead of right to left, or that one transitioned more smoothly. While you can't build your own fanciful transitions in QuarkImmedia, you can edit any of the default transitions, or create new transitions based on the defaults, but with different settings.

The key to building your own transitions is the Custom Transitions feature (under the QuarkImmedia menu; see Figure 3–17). Note that if a project is open when you make a change in this dialog

Figure 3–17
Custom Transitions

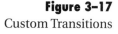

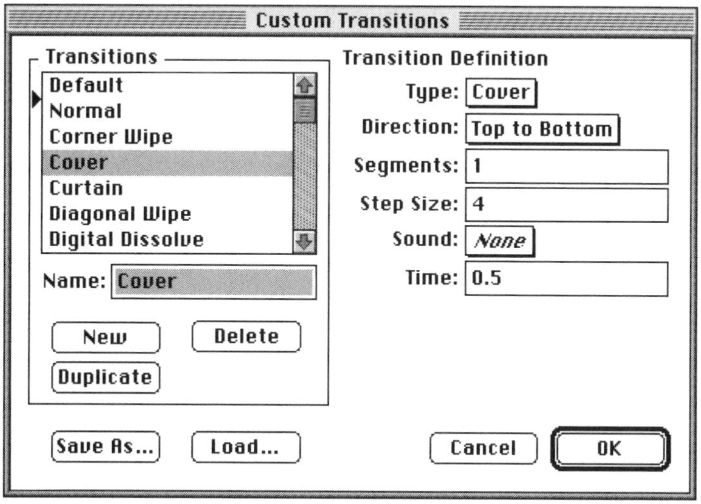

box, the change only affects that project. If no projects are open, then the change affects all the projects you create from then on.*

Editing transitions. The left side of the Custom Transitions dialog box displays the list of transitions—this list is the same as the one you see whenever you specify a transition somewhere. You can edit any of these transitions by selecting it from the list and changing the options Immedia displays on the right side of the dialog box.

Every transition lets you choose the length (in seconds) of the transition and a sound that begins playing when the transition starts (see Chapter 7, *Sound)*. For some transitions, like Digital Dissolve, these are all the options you get. However, some transitions like Push or Interlace have options such as Direction, Segments, Step Size, and Steps.

> ▶ **Direction.** The Direction popup menu contains choices like Top to Bottom, Left to Right, Bottom Left to Top Right, and so on. Different transitions offer different choices here.

> ▶ **Segments.** Immedia breaks some transitions into pieces, called *segments*. To be honest, I've never come up with a good way to describe this. The best way to understand segments is to try changing the value and see how the transition changes.

> ▶ **Step Size.** The smaller the step size, the smoother the transition. A step size of 10 allows Immedia to jump up to 10 pixels at a time. If the step size is too high, the transition becomes jerky. On the other hand, low step sizes (like 1) can make the transition slower than you might expect, especially on slower computers.

> ▶ **Steps.** Some transitions have an option called Steps, which lets you control how many discrete steps the transition will go through before it's done. For instance, the Interlace transition usually has four steps. First a quarter of the transition occurs,

---

*When you make a change to Custom Transitions while no documents are open, it's saved in your XPress Preferences file. If this file becomes corrupted or you lose it for some reason, you'll have to re-create those transitions.

then Immedia pauses for just a moment; then the second quarter occurs, followed by another short pause, and so on.

▼ ▼

Tip: Changing the Default Transition. You can change the default transition—the one that Immedia uses in all transitions unless you specify a different one—by selecting Default from the top of the Transition list and choosing a different transition from the Type popup menu.

▼ ▼

Tip: Deleting Unused Transitions. If you're going to use only a few transitions in your project, go ahead and delete all the others. That way, you don't have to scroll through a long list of transitions every time you want to pick one. You can delete a transition by selecting it from the Transitions list and pressing Delete. You can delete more than one if you select more than one: Shift-click to select contiguous items in the list; Command-click to select discontiguous items. Remember, as long as a project is open when you delete from this list, you're only affecting that single project.

▼ ▼

Creating new transitions. You can create a new transition in the Transition list by clicking on the New button in the Custom Transitions dialog box. Then you must choose a name, the transition type on which to base your new transition, and the various options that the type offers. To be honest, I usually skip the New button entirely; instead, I select a transition similar to the one I want, and click on the Duplicate button. That way, all I have to do is give it a new name and choose different options.

Moving transitions. What to do if you've built a transition in one project and want to use it in another? It's not that hard to re-create these transitions, but it's even easier and faster to simply save them to disk and then load them again. You can save transitions to your hard drive by selecting one or more (again, you can use the Shift or

Command keys to select more than one transition) and then clicking on the Save button. When you want to import a transition, click on the Load button and locate the saved file on your hard drive.

▼ ▼

Objects

Back in Chapter 2, *QuarkImmedia Basics*, I discussed the concepts of objects in Immedia: an object is any text box, picture box, line, or button that you give a name (on the Object or Event tab of the QuarkImmedia palette). As soon as you give an object a name, you can do things to it—you can move it, hide it, animate it, and make it "hot" (assign actions to it, so Immedia does something when you click on the object).

In this section, I discuss two issues that are essential to building projects in QuarkImmedia: object actions (actions that target objects on your pages) and object layering.

▼ ▼

Tip: Using Libraries. If you're going to use the same object in multiple projects, consider putting it in a QuarkXPress library. Every Immedia object (windows, animations, movies, text box objects, and so on) retains its settings when you put it in a library, so when you pull it out of the library again, it's all set to go. In fact, if one object controls another object (like a button that starts a movie), those relationships are also maintained.

▼ ▼

Object Actions

Most of the time, you'll rely on objects to trigger other actions—such as click on a button to make a movie play, or move the mouse over a picture box to play a sound. However, you can also make an object itself the target of an action. For example, you can hide a text box, show it again, move it around the project, and then reset it back to where it was originally.

Note that these object actions each let you target a single object on a single page. For instance, let's say you've got a picture box on a master page, and you want to use the Set Object Position action to move that picture box on every document page that's based on the master page. Well, you can't; Immedia won't currently let you target an object on a master page (master pages are really just for authoring, and have no place once you've engaged or exported the project). The only solution is to use a series of Set Object Position actions, each one moving a picture box on a page.

There are nine actions in QuarkImmedia that target objects, and they're all found on the Object popout menu under the Action pop-up menu (see Figure 3–18).

Disable Object/ Enable Object. Any object that has an action assigned to it is "hot." You can disable a hot object with the Disable Object action, so that nothing happens when the user clicks on it (or whatever user event you've chosen). The same thing goes for popup menus, buttons, and text box objects (such as Lists, Editable text box objects, and Scrollable text box objects; see Chapter 4, *Text).* When you disable any of these objects, the user cannot click on them to select an item from a list or popup menu, press the button, edit, or even scroll the text box.

You can then later enable the object again by triggering the Enable Object action.

Figure 3–18
Object actions

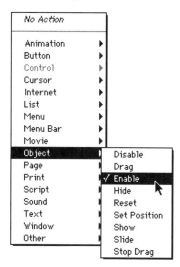

Show Object/Hide Object. You can hide or show any named object with the Hide Object and Show Object actions. Your only options with each of these actions are the object you want to hide or show, and the transition effect you want to use (see "Transitions," earlier in this chapter).

Obviously, these two features are very simple. And yet, they turn out to be two of the most useful features in QuarkImmedia. For example, in one Immedia-built Myst-like game, the user is confronted with a set of stairs leading up to a landing. Later, after the user has solved a puzzle, the stairs "magically" switch to lead down into a lower level (see Figure 3–19). The "magic" is perfomed by simply hiding one picture (a picture of stairs leading up) and revealing the picture underneath (a set of stairs leading down). A simple trick and yet very effective.

Drag Object/Stop Drag Object. The Drag Object action lets your user click on an object and drag it someplace else on the screen. For example, in a game you might hide a secret treasure under a picture of a rock. The user would have to drag the rock picture out of the way to see the object underneath. For a while, Quark hid secret buttons on their Immedia-built World Wide Web site so that you could get to some interesting information only when you dragged other items out of the way.

There are many other, non-game uses for the Drag Object action, too. In one "electronic book" I've worked on, the user can drag special markers, akin to paper clips, next to particular text passages.

Generally, you assign the Drag Object and Stop Drag Object actions to the object you want to move. For instance, you might assign a Drag Object action to a picture box's Click Down user event, and a Stop Drag Object to its Click Up user event. That way, as long as the user held the mouse button down, they could drag the picture around the screen (or even right out of the project; there's no limit to where they get to drag).

You can also build a script that lets the user click once to "pick up" an object and drag it around. Then, when they click again, Immedia would "drop it down" again with a Stop Drag Object action (see Chapter 13, *Scripting*).

Figure 3-19
Hiding and
Showing an Object

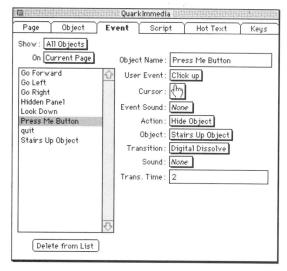

*Before hiding
the picture object*

*After hiding the
picture object*

▼ ▼

Tip: Dragging Multiple Objects. At the beginning of this section, I said that you could only apply object actions to a single object on a single page. However, there's always a workaround. You can create a script (see Chapter 13, *Scripting)* that contains multiple Drag Object actions in a row. If you set up a Click Down user event to trigger this script, all those objects get dragged at the same time. Then, Click Up could trigger another script full of Stop Drag Object actions.

▼ ▼

Set Object Position. Instead of letting a user drag an object from one position on the screen to another, you can tell Immedia to move an object to a particular spot on screen with the Set Object Position action (see Figure 3–20). When you choose this action, you must also choose from three popup menus.

1. First, from the Object popup menu you have to select which object to move.

2. Next, you have to use the In Window popup menu to tell Immedia whether to put the object in your project's window or into another window that you've created (see Chapter 5, *Windows)*. Generally, you'll just leave this set to the default setting (Current Project).

Figure 3–20
Set Object Position

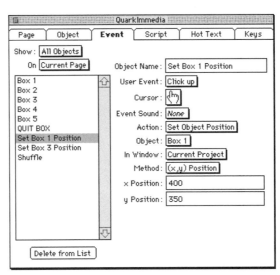

3. Finally, the Method popup menu lets you specify where to move the object. You've got five options in this popup menu.

▶ **(x,y) Position.** The most straightforward method of setting the object's position is to select (x,y) Position from the Method popup menu. Immedia lets you type in x,y coordinates for the object. The "x" value is the number of pixels from the left edge of the project (or window), the "y" value is the number of pixels from the top.

▶ **(x,y) Offset.** Instead of typing in an absolute coordinate, you can tell Immedia to move the object based on where it currently is. For instance, if you choose (x,y) Offset, you can tell Immedia to "move the object 36 pixels over to the right" or "move it 120 pixels down."

Note that positive numbers mean "move it to the right" or "move it down," and negative numbers mean "move it to the left" or "move it up"—it's easy to remember because it's just how the rulers work in XPress.

▶ **Another Object.** Instead of working with all those numbers, you can make life easy for yourself by selecting Another Object from the Method popup menu. This tells Immedia to move the upper-left corner of the object you're moving to the same point as any other object's upper-left corner. I sometimes make a little picture box on the page, name it on the Object tab of the QuarkImmedia palette, and then set its Background Color and Runaround to None. That way, I can put it anywhere on my page and it's invisible in the final project. However, I can use that picture box as a "dummy" and move my other object to it. Again, that way I just don't have to worry about figuring out the coordinates.

▶ **Home.** I mentioned the concept of "Home" in Chapter 2, *QuarkImmedia Basics*—it's where you actually place an object on the page (before you engage or export the object). If the user drags the object around the screen, or if you've used the Set Object Position action to put it somewhere else, you can reset the object's position by selecting Home from the Method popup menu.

► **To Sides.** The last option in the Method popup menu is To Sides. This places the object outside the project boundaries, to the left, right, top, or bottom (you get to choose, of course). The only good reason to use this, as far as I'm concerned, is if later you're going to use the Slide Object action to animate the object back on to the page.

Slide Object. The Slide Object action is one method of animating objects in QuarkImmedia. It lets you move an object around your screen in various ways. I discuss the Slide Object option in Chapter 8, *Animation*.

Reset Object. I mentioned earlier that you could reset an object's position to its "home" state by using the Set Object Position action and selecting Home from the Method popup menu. There's one other option, too. The Reset Object action sets an object back to its home position *and* original state. For example, let's say you've got a box with the Initially Hidden option turned on, and while the project is engaged, you use a Show Object action to make it visible and then a Drag Object action to drag it elsewhere on the screen. If you then trigger a Reset Object action, the box moves back to the original position and becomes hidden again.

Object Layering

You already know that every picture box, text box, and line is on its own layer in QuarkXPress (see "Layering" in Chapter 1, *Quark-XPress Basics)*. QuarkImmedia takes this concept one step further: many Immedia objects sit on a layer on top of normal QuarkXPress items when you engage or export the project.

For example, if you put a QuickTime movie on your page (you'll see how to do this in Chapter 9, *QuickTime Movies)*, and then put a big blue picture box on top of it, it looks like the movie is covered by the blue box. However, when you engage or export the project, the movie always appears on top of the blue box—it's an Immedia object, so it's on a higher layer (see Figure 3–21).

What's literally going on is that when you engage or export the project, Immedia fuses together the regular XPress items into a single background image. Then Immedia puts some of the Immedia objects on top of that background image.

Which objects are in the background layer, and which are in the higher, Immedia object layer? An object is on the higher Immedia layer if it satisfies either of the following conditions.

▶ If you've selected anything other than Basic from the Object Type popup menu (on the Object tab of the QuarkImmedia palette), that object will be on the higher layer. This includes animations, QuickTime movies, buttons, popup menus, windows, and text box objects.

▶ If the object is the target of any object action, it'll be on the higher layer. For instance, if you use Disable Object, Show

Figure 3–21
Immedia layering

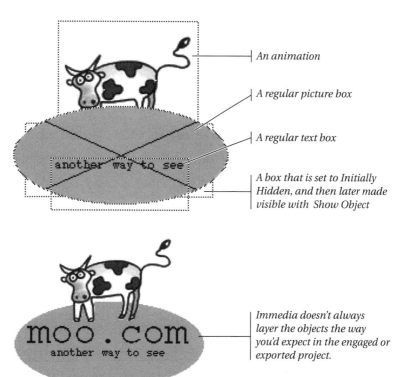

An animation

A regular picture box

A regular text box

A box that is set to Initially Hidden, and then later made visible with Show Object

Immedia doesn't always layer the objects the way you'd expect in the engaged or exported project.

Object, Reset Object, or any of the other object actions on an object, it immediately is set to the higher layer.

If you've got two objects that are in the higher, Immedia object layer, and one is on top of the other, they will appear like that in the final project.

▼ ▼

Tip: Controlling Layering. You can force a box or line to be on top of an animation, button, or any other Immedia object in the higher layer by giving it a name and making it the target of an object action anywhere in your project. You don't actually have to ever trigger that action! You can even make a script (see Chapter 13, *Scripting)* with an Enable Object action in it, target the object, and then never call that script. The fact that you've made that action is enough to flag the object to be put on the "higher layer."

▼ ▼

Other Actions

I have a confession to make: in this section, I explore nine actions that I simply couldn't figure out where else to put in the book. Clearly, Quark didn't know what to do with them either, because they all appear on a popout menu called Other (on the Actions pop-up menu; see Figure 3–22). It's important to know one of them now (the Quit action), but the others become important in time.

Three of the actions on the Other popout menu—Allow User Interactions, Flush User Events, and Delay—are really only relevant when building scripts, so I discuss them in Chapter 13, *Scripting*. Here, let's cover the other six quickly so you can get on with what you most want to do: make multimedia projects.

Quit. You (or your user) can almost always quit your project by pressing Command-Q (or Control-Q on Windows). In order to get your project to quit on *your* demand, however, you have to trigger the Quit action.

Figure 3–22
Other Actions

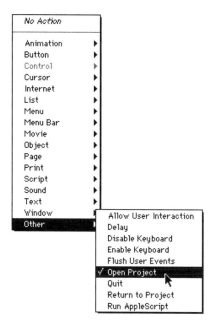

Open Project/Return to Project. In Chapter 15, *The Internet and the World Wide Web,* I discuss how to jump from your project to another Immedia project on the Internet. But what if you want to simply jump from this project to another project on your hard drive or a CD-ROM? That's where the Open Project and Return to Project actions come in. Triggering an Open Project action is like quitting the current project and opening the new one, with three exceptions.

▶ Open Project lets you jump directly to a specific page in another project. You can tell Immedia what page to jump to by typing the number in the Page field (see Figure 3–23).

▶ You can use the Return to Project action to automatically return to the current project later.

▶ Open Project lets you specify which page of the current project should display if—or when—the user comes back (if a Return to Project action is triggered). You've got two choices on the Return To popup menu. The first, Current Page, returns right back to the page where the user was when the Open Project action was triggered. The second, Start of Project, returns the user to the first page of the project.

Figure 3-23
Open Project

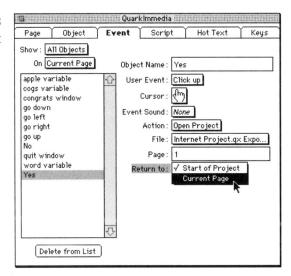

One of the problems with the Open Project and Return to Project actions is that Immedia does not keep track of any changes the user may have made in the first project. If the user typed in his or her name, made choices from a row of buttons, or moved objects around using Drag Object, those settings are wiped out as soon as the new project appears.

However, there are many times when this isn't a problem at all. For example, you may have 50 different QuarkImmedia projects on a server, and use a single project to choose among them.

Disable Keyboard/Enable Keyboard. One of the biggest problems when running a project on a kiosk or a demonstration station is that people walking by may be able to get access to the computer's keyboard and type things you don't want them to type. QuarkImmedia takes a step toward a solution with the Disable Keyboard and Enable Keyboard actions. When you trigger the Disable Keyboard action, Immedia blocks almost everything a rogue user could type. They can't type into Editable text boxes and they can't press any keystrokes you've set up on the Keys tab.

I say "almost everything" because Immedia does not block Command-Q (or Control-Q on Windows). This keystroke still quits the project, no matter what. I suppose Quark threw that in for safety, but it does seem to defeat the purpose, doesn't it?

Of course, when you want to "turn on" the keyboard again, you have to use the Enable Keyboard action (or quit the project).

Run AppleScript. The Run AppleScript option is one of the coolest features in the program, in my humble opinion. However, there is one major catch: it doesn't do anything when you run the program on a Windows computer. AppleScript is a Macintosh-only feature that lets you control one program from within another.

For example, you could have an Immedia project that controls QuarkXPress (putting pictures on a page, formatting text, and so on), even a copy of QuarkXPress on another computer on your network. You could also run AppleScripts that would retrieve information from a FileMaker Pro database and drop it into various text box objects in your Immedia project. The possibilities are endless.

AppleScript is actually a computer programming language, but it's really easy to program and understand because its syntax is based on natural language (see Figure 3–24). How to program in AppleScript is beyond the scope of this book, but how to run the scripts from within QuarkImmedia is not.

The Run AppleScript action lets you play any AppleScript that has been saved in a "compiled" format. To tell Immedia which file you want to run, you must choose Other on the AppleScript popup menu, and then direct Immedia to the file on your hard drive.

For a small example of what AppleScript can do, check out the AppleScript project on the *Real World QuarkImmedia* CD-ROM.

Figure 3–24
An AppleScript program in the Script Editor

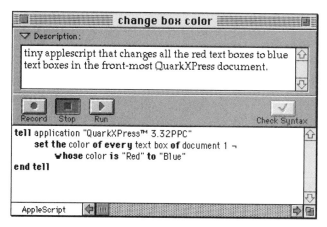

▼ ▼

Putting It Together

Your job, as multimedia designer/author/engineer, is beginning to take shape. In this chapter, you've learned the basics of building a project, including how to build a firm infrastructure, prepare your images, manage custom color palettes, and construct documents that will be flexible and robust. You also learned many of the actions that you will repeatedly use while constructing projects, including actions that display your pages and control your objects.

Coming up in the next chapter is a topic crucial to most people's multimedia projects: text. But with the lessons learned from this chapter, you should have no problems breezing through the next.

Text

THERE IS A SCHOOL OF THOUGHT that says written language will become obsolete (any day now), replaced by multimedia, visual symbols, and sound bites. While I have no doubt that these kinds of visual tools can be more effective when conveying some types of information, it's also clear that written language isn't losing any market share in the global communication biz. Nonetheless, if you're one of those forward-looking thinkers and have no need for the written word, go ahead and skip this chapter. As for the rest of you: come along and see what textual goodies QuarkImmedia has in store.

▼
Text Box Objects

You know how to make a text box in QuarkXPress; it's easy as pie. QuarkImmedia, however, makes a distinction between text boxes and text box objects (and it's important that you do, too). When you draw out a text box and put some text in it, you've got a basic text box, and it works the way you'd expect. You can turn it into a text box object by selecting the Object tab of the Immedia palette, giving the text box a name, then selecting Text Box from the Object Type pop-up menu (see Figure 4–1).

Text boxes and text box objects look the same and, in fact, you won't notice any difference between them until you engage or export your project. Then you'll notice, to your horror, that there are all sorts of things you cannot do when using text box objects.

▶ You can't link boxes.

▶ You can't use multiple columns.

▶ You can't use paragraph formatting—such as Leading, Space Before, Drop Caps, First Line Indents—or character formatting—such as kerning, tracking, horizontal scaling, and so on.

▶ You can't anti-alias text in text box objects (I'll discuss anti-aliasing later in this chapter).

If text box objects are so limited, why would anyone want to use them? Because they're very flexible, and there are all sorts of things you can do with them that you cannot do with basic text boxes.

▶ You can make text box objects editable, so that your users can type in them. (You can even make sure they type the right kind of text into a box, such as typing a numeral instead of a spelled-out number.)

Figure 4–1
Making a
text box object

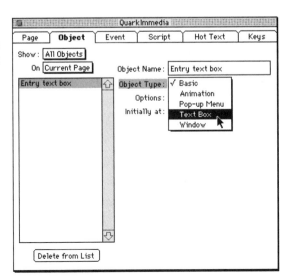

- ▶ You can make text box objects into lists.

- ▶ You can make text box objects scrollable, so if there's more text than what fits in the box, your user can scroll through it.

- ▶ You can import text from the Internet or from your hard drive into a text box object while a project is running.

- ▶ You can search for text within text box objects.

You can do even more, but I don't want to give away all the cool things too soon. The key is to remember the difference between the two: to make a text box object, you first have to set the Object Type popup menu to Text Box.

▼ ▼

Tip: Breaking Apart Text Boxes. It's unfortunate, but linked text boxes cannot be turned into text box objects. There are several XTensions that will unlink boxes from each other while leaving each box's text in the proper place. For instance, XPert TextLink (part of a lowly apprentice production's XPert Tools Volume 2) and Missing Link from Vision's Edge both do this quickly and painlessly.

▼ ▼

Fractional Character Widths

Before any further discussion of text, you should know about an issue that concerns text in both basic text boxes and text box objects: fractional character widths. In order for QuarkXPress (or any text program) to figure out how to lay out a line of text, it has to know how wide each character is. This information is stored in the font file on your hard drive.

The problem is that most fonts were designed to look good when printed on laser printers rather than to look good on screen. A laser printer (or imagesetter) can make very fine adjustments between characters (so small that you'd hardly notice them). Computer screens, however, are significantly coarser: you can't move a character by half a pixel; it's got to be a whole pixel or nothing. So when the font file says the letter "e" should be 36.4 units wide, XPress has to make a decision about where to put it on screen.

QuarkImmedia Preferences. When you're designing a document for print, you want XPress to use that fractional character width, rather than rounding it off to the nearest point. Fortunately, that's what it usually does. However, when you're designing for the screen, you almost always want XPress to round the character widths off to the nearest pixel. That's where the Fractional Character Widths checkbox comes in (under the Edit menu, go to the Preferences submenu and select QuarkImmedia; see Figure 4–2).

When you create a new Immedia project, the Fractional Character Widths checkbox is turned off by default. However, if you convert an XPress document to an Immedia project (see "Repurposing XPress Documents" in Chapter 2, *QuarkImmedia Basics*), the checkbox is turned on by default; if the text doesn't look right on screen, turn off this option.

Figure 4–2
Fractional
character widths

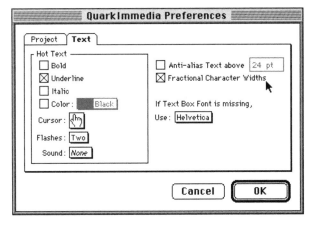

Text on screen – Fractional Character Widths turned off

The quick brown fox jumped over the lazy dog.

How the above text prints. Note the looser letterspacing.

When Fractional Character Widths is on, letters bump into each other more.

The quick brown fox jumped over the lazy dog.

How the text prints – Fractional Character Widths turned on

Your decision. Ultimately, the decision whether to turn on Fractional Character Widths is an aesthetic one. You'll find some fonts look better when it's turned on, and others look worse. Some fonts don't change at all on screen whether you have it on or off—notably, fonts that were designed to be viewed on screen, such as New York, Geneva, and so on. Unfortunately, this feature is projectwide; you have to turn it on for all the fonts in your project, or leave it off.

Printing. Remember that if you print your document on a laser printer while the Fractional Character Widths checkbox is turned off, the spacing between characters may look odd. Yes, you can turn it on to print and then off to view on screen, but your line breaks may change. There's always a compromise, isn't there?

Formatting

QuarkXPress has some very powerful text-formatting tools, and you can use them all when building Immedia projects. However, remember two things.

▶ What you see on screen is just about what you're going to get in the final exported project. That means that zooming in to 400 percent to perform minor tweaking of the text won't help at all. You know that if you set the kerning between two characters to -5 units and then print, you'll see a difference. But if nothing changes on screen, it's meaningless in your multimedia project.

▶ You can format text all day, but if the text box is actually a text box *object*, little of that formatting survives after you engage or export the project (see Figure 4–3).

The fundamental difference between basic text boxes and text box objects is this: when you engage or export your project, Immedia turns text boxes into pictures and saves the text in the text box objects as text. Therefore, you never lose formatting in a basic text box (because the whole thing is a picture). However, the text formatting within a text box object depends on the limitations of the

AND IT CAME TO PASS that we were about to be swallowed up in the *depths of the sea*. And after we had been driven back upon the waters for the space of four days, my brethren began to see that the judgements of God were upon them, and that they **must perish** save that they should repent of their iniquities.

You can format the text in a text box object any way you want . . .

And it came to pass that we were about to be swallowed up in the *depths of the sea*. And after we had been driven back upon the waters for the space of four days, my brethren began to see that the judgements of God were upon them, and that they **must perish** save that they should repent of their iniquities.

. . . but when you engage or export the project, only a few attributes are saved.

Immedia Viewer. Unfortunately, the Viewer is pretty limited when it comes to text formatting.

▶ **Font.** The proper font gets used if your audience has it installed. If not, the Viewer replaces it with another font (see "Unavailable Fonts," below).

▶ **Size.** The project always remembers and uses the size of the text you specified.

▶ **Leading.** The Immedia Viewer has no clue when it comes to leading. All text in text box objects is set to the leading value specified in the font itself (this is up to the font designer). This might be tighter than you'd want, but unfortunately the only way to change it is to change the font itself (with a font-editing program like Fontographer).

▶ **Paragraph formatting.** Nothing in the Paragraph Formats dialog box (Drop Caps, Left Indent, Space Before, and so on) is saved, except Left aligned, Right aligned, and Center aligned. If you need space between paragraphs, you've got to type two carriage returns.

▶ **Color and Shade.** The color and the shade of the text are always saved (of course, they may get mapped to the nearest color on the color palette).

▶ **Style.** The Immedia Viewer can handle bold, italic, bold italic, and underlined text. It drops any other styling.

▶ **Character formatting.** Kerning, tracking, horizontal scaling, and baseline shift are ignored entirely in text box objects.

▶ **Text Inset.** Curiously enough, Text Inset does work (in the Text Box Specifications dialog box—select Modify from the Item menu, or press Command-M; see Figure 4–4).

Figure 4–4
Text Inset

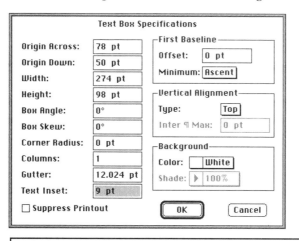

This Scrollable text box object has a Text Inset of 0 (zero).

Increasing the Text Inset value increases the space between the text and the edge of the box.

▼ ▼

Tip: Variable Text Inset. There are XTensions that let you specify different Text Inset values for each side of a text box, including SetInset by XTend (if you're not sure where to buy XTensions, check out my Web site; see page 430). For example, I often use this feature to set up Scrollable text box objects (like the one in Figure 4–4). I like to specify no inset for the top and bottom, and perhaps six points inset on the left and right. It's a minor detail, but I think it looks better.

▼ ▼

Unavailable fonts. As I mentioned above, you can specify a font in a text box object, but if the font isn't around when the Viewer needs it, the Viewer uses a different font. You can tell it which font to use by selecting the Text tab of the QuarkImmedia Preferences dialog box (see Figure 4–5). Choose any other font from the popup menu labeled If Text Box Font is missing, Use. Now, if *that* font is missing when the Viewer displays the text, it just uses system font—on the Macintosh, that's usually Geneva; in Windows, it's Ariel.

Aliased versus Anti-aliased

As you've no doubt noticed, on-screen text often looks jaggy and is hard to read. One solution for this is anti-aliasing the text. Anti-aliasing is the process of blurring hard black-and-white edges slightly so that you get a smoother transition from black to white. Because

Figure 4–5
In case of
missing fonts

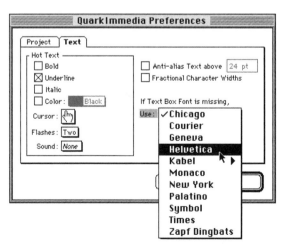

basic text boxes are rasterized (turned into bitmapped pictures) and text box objects are not, Immedia can only anti-alias basic text boxes. Text box objects never get anti-aliased.

You can tell Immedia that it should anti-alias text in the Quark-Immedia Preferences dialog box. First, turn on the Anti-alias Text Above checkbox; then set the minimum point size for which you want the program to anti-alias the text.

While it's true that some fonts look better on screen when anti-aliased, there are three reasons why you shouldn't anti-alias all your text (or even any of it).

▶ Not all fonts look better when anti-aliased. You just have to check and see.

▶ Fonts at small sizes usually fall apart or blur to illegibility when anti-aliased. That's why Immedia gives you the option to select minimum point size. I find that text above 12 or 14 points usually looks okay, unless it's a very thin typeface (see "Tip: Use Photoshop for Anti-aliasing," below).

▶ Anti-aliased text doesn't compress as well. If you're concerned about the size of your exported file (let's say you're putting the project on a floppy disk or on the Internet), you'll see that anti-aliasing the text increases the file size noticeably, though not necessarily significantly (it all depends on how much text is anti-aliased, what else is on the page, and so on).

Boxes that don't anti-alias. Anti-aliasing basic text boxes that have a transparent background (background selection of None) works just fine, unless you apply one of the following actions to that text box: Drag Object, Slide Object, Set Object Position, Hide Object, or Show Object (see "Object Actions" in Chapter 3, *Building Projects*). As soon as you do any of these things to the text box, Immedia won't even try to anti-alias it. The reason: proper anti-aliasing requires knowing what color is behind the text; if you move anti-aliased text on top of a different color, the anti-aliasing would have to be done all over again (and the Viewer can't handle that).

▼ ▼

Tip: Use Photoshop for Anti-aliasing. QuarkImmedia just can't handle anti-aliasing small text. If you want to anti-alias text under 14 points, it's usually better to do it in a program like Photoshop. I don't know why Photoshop's anti-aliasing is better, but it is. Of course, it's much harder to go back and edit the text later because Photoshop doesn't let you change text after you've rasterized it. Immedia anti-aliases type over 16 or 18 points reasonably well, however.

▼ ▼

Tip: Keep Those Small Font Sizes. When you install a font on your hard drive, you usually get a bunch of pre-made sizes, like 10, 12, 14, 18, and 24 points. The font designers spent a lot of time building these to look good on screen. Before I started doing multimedia, I would immediately open the font's suitcase on my hard drive and throw away all but one of the font sizes. The reason: I cared more about saving disk space than how good the font looked on screen. Now, of course, I hold on to all of them. Remember: if the font looks better on screen, it'll look better in your final project.

▼ ▼

Searchable Text Boxes

Later in this chapter there is a discussion of how you can search for text in the text boxes, but right up front here I want to point out an important difference between basic text boxes and text box objects. The Add List Items Using Search action can work on both basic text boxes and text box objects; however, the Find action can only be used on text box objects (see "Searching for Text," later in this chapter). In order for a text box to be searchable using Add List Items Using Search, you must give it a name and, on the Object tab of the Immedia palette, choose Searchable Contents.

▼ ▼

Textual Trimmings

Now that you know something about text box objects, let's explore the five different types, plus all the things you can do with them.

Once again, you can create a text box object by selecting any text box, giving it a name on the Object tab of the Immedia palette, then setting the Object Type popup menu to Text Box. You can then choose one of the five types from the Display As popup menu.

► Simple

► Editable

► Scrollable

► Editable and Scrollable

► List

The final step is to select the various options for each type. You've seen some of these options before; for instance, the Initially At popup menu works the same for all Immedia object types. Other options, however, may be quite specific.

Note that text box objects, like all Immedia objects, sit on a layer above non-Immedia objects when you engage the project (see "Object Actions" in Chapter 3, *Building Projects*).

Simple Text Box Objects

Text box objects always start out life with the Display As popup menu set to Simple (see Figure 4–6). While the other four types each have particular attributes, the Simple text box object is like a stripped-down version of the others. You can't edit the text (when the project is engaged), the box has no scrollbars; in fact, there's only three reasons (as far as I'm concerned) that you'd want to use a Simple text box object.

► You can search for text in Simple text box objects by using the Find action (see "Searching for Text," later in this chapter).

► Your exported project is much smaller when you use text box objects rather than basic text boxes, because the text can be compressed more.

► Many actions in QuarkImmedia require a text box object to either read or write information. For instance, you can set up

Figure 4-6
Simple text
box objects

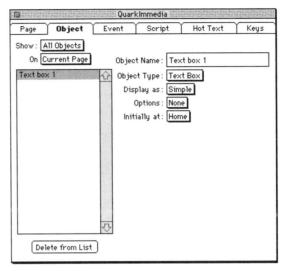

the Display Page action so that it displays the page name or number that is written in a text box object. I often put these sorts of simple text box objects on the pasteboard so that I don't have to see them in the final project.

If you don't care about any of these reasons, you might as well just use a basic text box.

After choosing Simple from the Display As popup menu, you can choose among three features from the Options popup menu.

Searchable Contents. All text boxes and text box objects let you select Searchable Contents on the Options popup menu. You don't have to turn this on for the Find action to work; you do, however, have to turn Searchable Contents on if you want the Add List Items Using Search action to search a text box.

Initially Hidden. The Initially Hidden feature works just as it does for all other Immedia objects: when it's on, the object is invisible until you select the Show Object action for it (see "Object Actions" in Chapter 3, *Building Projects*).

Keep Status on Page Entry. Later in this chapter, you'll see how to change what's in a text box object or select portions of the text. If you don't select the Keep Status on Page Entry option, all those changes are lost as soon as you move to a new page. For example, in an engaged project, you use the Set Text action to place a word in a text box object on page one. You then move to the second page, and back to page one again. If you have selected the Keep Status on Page Entry option, the word will still be there. If the option is not select-ed, Immedia resets the text box to its state before the Set Text action was made.

I almost always turn on this option. That way I don't have any nasty surprises.

By the way, this option saves the position of the text box object if you use Set Object Position, Drag Object, or any other action that can move objects on your page. Of course, if you jump to a differ-ent project (or quit and then start the project again), Keep Status on Page Entry won't make a bit of difference.

Editable Text Box Objects

You're in the business of creating interactive multimedia, right? And when it comes to text, the best way to get interactive is to make a text box editable. Editable text box objects (choose Editable from the Display as popup menu) let you build forms into which your audience can type text. For example, you might have a text box object for people to input a search word; then, when they click on a button, your project could build a list of where that word occurs throughout the document.

▼ ▼

Tip: Formatting Editable Text. People are used to seeing ugly, plain text—like 12-point Geneva or Helvetica—in editable text fields. But it doesn't have to be that way. Remember that you can specify some formatting in text box objects, including font, size, Text Inset, color, and so on. If you set the formatting for an Editable text box object that formatting is what appears when your audience types in the exported project.

▼ ▼

Editable text box objects offer five choices on the Options pop-up menu (see Figure 4–7). Two of them—Initially Hidden and Keep

Figure 4-7
Editable text boxes

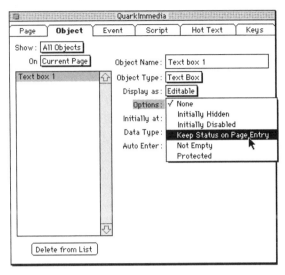

Figure 4-7

Status on Page Entry—work the same as for Simple text box objects. Let's look at the other three.

Initially Disabled. Some people get confused with the Initially Disabled selection on the Options popup menu because, intuitively, it seems as though it means "when you first engage the project, make this Editable text box object non-editable." While that was Quark's intention, it doesn't quite work like that. Initially Disabled stops you from clicking in or on the text box object. For example, if you assign a Play Sound action to the box's Click Up user event, the action will be disabled until you enable the text box object (with an Enable Object action). Similarly, you cannot click inside the text box object to add or edit text.

Where this feature fails is that, if you move more than one Editable text box object on the page, the user can press the Tab Key to jump from one text box object right into the disabled one! Oh well, maybe they'll fix it in a later version.

Not Empty. The Not Empty option also occasionally trips up the literal-minded, who think it means "this box isn't empty." Actually, it means "don't let the user leave this box empty." For instance, you may want those who use your product to fill out an on-screen form (name, address, phone number, and so on). When setting up the form, if you set one of the Editable text box objects to Not Empty, the user *has* to put something in it before the Immedia Viewer lets them select a new field.

Unfortunately, in version 1.0 the feature isn't as robust as it might be. It still lets the user jump to a new page or perform other acts that relieve them of filling in the form properly. This may have been fixed in version 1.0.1 (which should be shipping by the time you read this).

Protected. Everybody has their little secrets, and you wouldn't want to force someone to divulge one of theirs, would you? You can protect any secret information that users might type into an Editable text field (like a password) by selecting the Protected option. When this feature is on, Immedia turns anything you type into asterisks (see Figure 4–8).

Figure 4-8
Protected text boxes

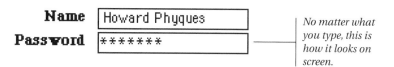

Name | Howard Phyques |

Password | ******* |

No matter what you type, this is how it looks on screen.

Data Type. You can usually type anything you want into an Editable text box object, from your name to the number of miles to Saskatoon. However, you—as multimedia author—may wish to limit the scope of a user's entry, and that's where the Data Type popup menu comes in handy (see Figure 4–9). You've got five options on this popup menu: Any, Date, Time, Number, and Credit Card.

▶ **Any.** The Any option is the default value; when selected, the Viewer lets you type anything into that text box object.

▶ **Date.** If you choose Date, the Immedia Viewer only lets you type a valid date into the text box object. You get to tell Immedia what, exactly, is "valid" on the Format popup menu (see Figure 4–10). Plus, although Immedia always accepts dates delimited with slashes, hyphens, or periods, you can tell it how to display the date after it's entered by selecting from the

Figure 4–9
Data type

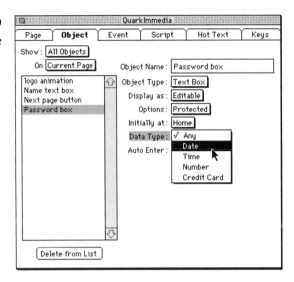

Figure 4–10
Valid dates

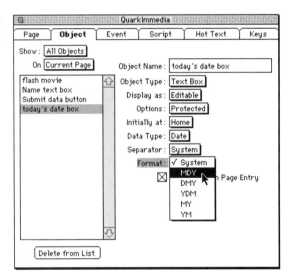

Separator popup menu (see "Auto Enter," below, to see how to make Immedia type the date or time for you).

▶ **Time.** The Time data type is just like the Date data type, except that it forces you to type a time. There are only three options in the Format checkbox: System, 12-hour, and 24-hour. I usually just leave this set to System, unless there's a really good reason to change it. Note that if Immedia expects a time in the 12-hour format, it insists that you type an "AM" or "PM" at the end. If you expect your users to type in a time, you probably want to remind them to type one of these suffixes or else they may receive an error message.

▶ **Number.** If you want your audience to type only numbers in an Editable text box object, you can select Number from the Data Type popup menu (see Figure 4–11). Immedia then asks what kind of numbers you want to allow. The Integer, Decimal, and Money options are on the Format popup menu; Negative OK and Zero OK are separate checkboxes.

Figure 4–11
Allowing
only numbers

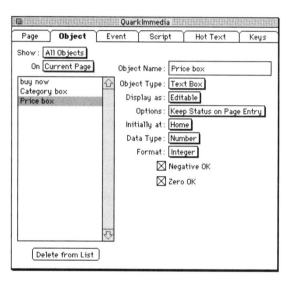

▶ **Credit Card.** Everyone seems to be thinking about electronic commerce these days, and this almost always requires credit cards. If you select Credit Card from the Data Type popup menu, Immedia makes sure that the user types only valid credit card numbers.* Note that you can't type in just any digits; it's got to be a real credit card number.

Auto Enter. Occasionally, you can do your audience a favor, saving them from carpal tunnel syndrome, by typing information into text

---

*Sorry, there's no option for Immedia to automatically enter Quark's corporate VISA number.

box objects for them. There are two ways to automatically enter information in an Editable text box object.

First, you can "hard code" it, filling in the text box object at the project's authoring stage. When you export the project, whatever's in an Editable text box object stays in that box until the user changes it. This is like setting a "default value" for the text box object. If the user changes it, their change only stays for a short time. If they quit the project or turn the page, the text box object resets to whatever you hard coded (you can save their edits from page turns with the Keep Status on Page Entry option discussed earlier).

The second method of auto-entering text box objects is to fill in blank boxes at the time your audience runs the project. For instance, your form may include fields for name, address, e-mail address, and so on. Or perhaps you want the current date or time to appear on your page; you can automatically enter this information, too. Note that for this to work, you must leave the Editable text box object blank.

> ▶ **Personal information.** When the Data Type popup menu is set to Any, Immedia also displays an Auto Enter popup menu that includes items such as Name, Address, Telephone No., and E-Mail Address. When you choose one of these items, the Immedia Viewer reads that particular field from the Viewer's User Preferences dialog box (see Figure 4–12, and "The Quark-Immedia Viewer" in Chapter 14, *Exporting*) and enters it into the text field. Of course, this feature relies on two things. First, the user must have already filled out the User Preferences dialog box properly (I wouldn't bet on it). Second, you cannot embed the Viewer into your project (if you do, the user never has a chance to fill in their pertinent information).

> ▶ **Date.** If you choose Date from the Data Type popup menu, you can insert the current date automatically by selecting the Insert Date on Page Entry option. As the name implies, the current date (according to whatever computer your user is running on) is added as soon as they display that page. Note that the date is displayed using whatever method you've selected on the Separator and Format popup menus.

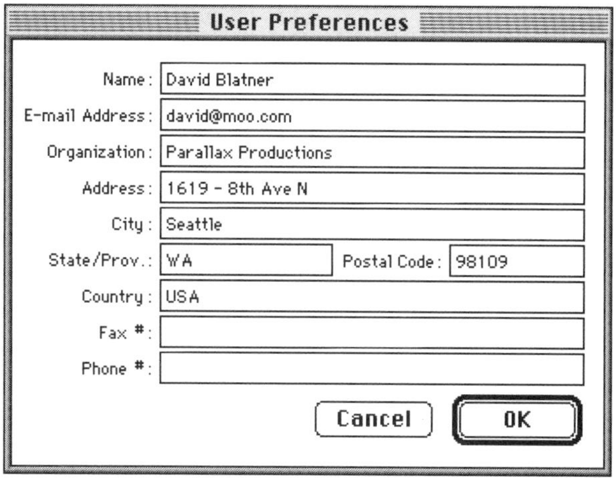

Figure 4–12
User Preferences
dialog box from the
QuarkImmedia Viewer

> ▶ **Time.** To insert the current time into a text box object, choose
> Time from the Data Type popup menu, and select the Insert
> Time on Page Entry option. If you linger on that page for more
> than a minute, the time does not update automatically; it *only*
> updates when you enter the page. To force Immedia to re-
> check the time, you have to display a different page in your
> project and then return.

Scrollable and Editable-and-Scrollable Text Box Objects

Those who are used to designing for print will quickly find that the
instinct to use 10- or 11-point text just won't fly in multimedia projects;
it becomes totally illegible. Instead, you'll need to use larger type. And,
of course, the larger the type, the less will fit into a text box object.
One option is to create Scrollable text box objects (choose Scrollable
or Editable and Scrollable from the Display As popup menu).

All "scrollable" means is that Immedia adds scrollbars to the
right side of the text box object (you only see these when you engage
or export the project; see Figure 4–13). The options for these two
types of text box objects are identical to the previous two types:
Scrollable text box objects are just like Simple text box objects, with
scrollbars. Editable and Scrollable text box objects are just like
Editable text box objects, with scrollbars.

Figure 4-13

Scrollable text boxes

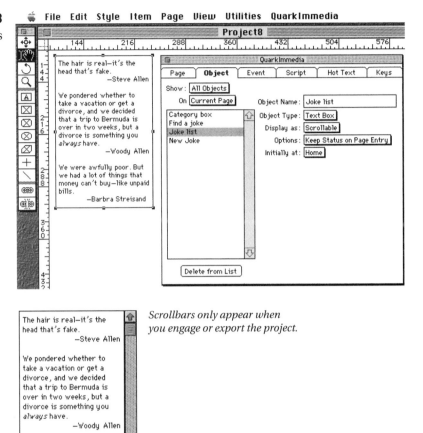

Scrollbars only appear when you engage or export the project.

▼ ▼

Tip: Leave Room for the Scrollbar. When you make a text box object either Scrollable or Editable and Scrollable, Immedia adds a scroll bar (including scroll arrows) to the right of the text box. Even though you can't see the scrollbar when you are designing the page (it won't appear until you engage the project), you have to leave space for it. Scrollbars are about 16 points wide.

▼ ▼

List Text Box Objects

Lists look just like Scrollable text box objects—they even offer the same choices in the Object tab's Options popup menu—but they act differently. I cover all sorts of list things in "Making Lists," later in this chapter; however, here's a quick rundown of the basics.

► Each paragraph in a list sits on a separate line (see Figure 4–14). If the paragraph is wider than the text box, Immedia does not wrap it to the next line.

► Only one item (paragraph) at a time can be selected in a list.

► Some text actions (discussed in the next section) don't work with lists; you've got to use special list actions.

Figure 4–14

Lists

Immedia does not wrap lines that are longer than the text box object.

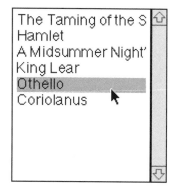

On your page   *In the engaged or exported project*

▼ ▼

Tip: Double-clicking on Lists. Lists are different than Scrollable text box objects in one other way, too: they have a different set of user events. Scrollable text box objects let you assign actions to any of the standard user events. List text box objects, however, only let you assign actions to Click Up, Double-click, and Option-click/Right mouse. The reason: these are the user events that people use when selecting items from the list. Here's one way to take advantage of this feature.

1. Name all the pages in your project (see "Turning the Page" in Chapter 3, *Building Projects*).

2. Type the names of all the pages into a text box and set the box to be a list.

3. On the Event tab of the Immedia palette, select Double-click from the User Event popup menu, then choose Display Page from the Action popup menu (see Figure 4–15).

4. Set the Method popup menu to Text Box Contents and the Text Box popup menu to the name of the list object.

When you engage the project and double-click on one of the page names in the list, Immedia jumps to that page.

Figure 4–15
Assigning an action
to a list object

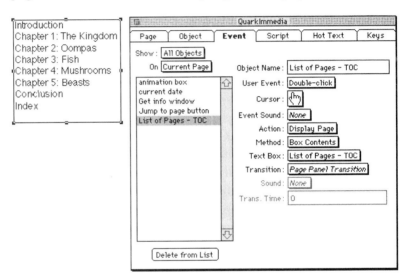

Text Actions

It's time to stop sitting around making text box objects and start doing things with the text *in* the text box objects. For instance, how do you change the text in a text box object? How do you write the text to a text file on disk? There are nine actions that relate directly to text, and nine more that have to do with lists. First, let's cover the actions that appear on the Text popout menu (see Figure 4–16). Then, later in this chapter, I'll explore the various actions in the List popout menu.

Cut, Copy, and Paste Text. The most basic actions in the Text popout menu are Cut Text, Copy Text, and Paste Text. These actions do

Figure 4–16

Text actions

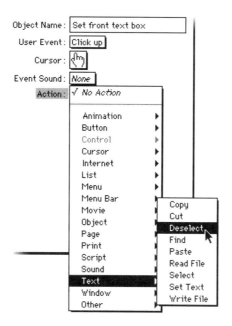

exactly the same thing as selecting Cut, Copy, or Paste from the Edit menu in any program: Cut and Copy grabs whatever text is selected and puts it on the clipboard; Paste inserts the clipboard text into whatever Editable text box object is currently selected. You can copy text from Editable, Scrollable, and Editable and Scrollable text box objects. You can paste text only into Editable and Editable and Scrollable text box objects.

The Immedia Viewer always lets you use the standard keystrokes for Cut, Copy, and Paste (Command-X, Command-C, and Command-V on the Macintosh), even when you don't use these actions. So why bother ever using these actions?

▶ If you want to build a custom menu (see Chapter 11, *Menus*) that contains the Cut, Copy, or Paste items, you'll need to "attach" these actions to those menu items.

▶ If you're trying to move text from one text box object to another, you may want to use these actions to do it, especially if you don't want to copy all the text.

When you trigger one of these actions, it acts on whatever text or text box object is selected. If no text box object is selected, or if the text box object isn't a type that can accept the action, Immedia just ignores it.

Select Text. I hate it when I'm presented with an Editable text box object that I have to click in before typing. Why wasn't it selected for me already? You can put the text cursor in any text box object with the Select Text action. When you choose this action, you must tell Immedia where to place the cursor: what text box object (from the Text Box popup menu), and what text, if any, should be selected (from the Select popup menu).

The Select popup menu gives you four choices: All, Begin, End, and Specify Range (see Figure 4–17).

▶ **All.** This works just as you'd think; it selects all the text in the text box object.

▶ **Begin.** When you choose Begin, Immedia puts the cursor at the beginning of the story in the text box object.

▶ **End.** If you choose End, Immedia places the cursor at the end of the text box object's story; of course, if the Editable text box object is empty, Begin and End do exactly the same thing.

▶ **Specify Range.** In the current version (1.0) of QuarkImmedia, Specify Range only lets you choose a range of characters in the text box object. For instance, you can select the 8th through the 15th characters of a box. I'm sure this has some use—I just don't know what it is. I usually want to specify a range like "the second word" or "the third sentence" or something like that. Well, there's always room to improve.

Note that although you can choose any text box object on the Text Box popup menu, the Select Text action really only works for Editable, Scrollable, and Editable and Scrollable text box objects.

▼ ▼

Tip: The Current Text Box. What good is it to select the beginning or ending point of a Scrollable text box object? You can't edit the text in this kind of box, so it seems meaningless to place the cursor there.

Figure 4–17

Select Text

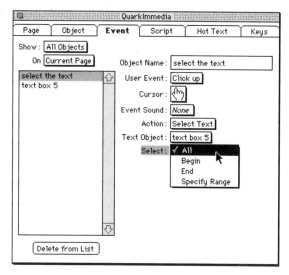

However, it's not as useless as it may seem. If you use Select Text to place the cursor at the beginning or end of a Scrollable text box object (choose Begin or End from the Select popup menu), you effectively set that box as the *current text box*.

Setting the current text box can be very useful for other text box manipulations. The next tip shows you one example of this.

▼ ▼

Tip: Selecting from the Current Box. When you use the Select Text action, it appears as though you must choose a text box object from the Text Box popup menu (I even said you had to, just a moment ago). However, it's not true. If you leave the Text Box popup menu set to None, the Select Text action selects text from whatever text box object is the current text box. For instance, if you've got four text box objects, you can use Select Text to make one of them the current text box (see the previous tip), and then use another Select Text action to select whatever you want from it.

▼ ▼

Deselect Text. When you trigger a Deselect text action, Immedia deselects any text that is selected. If you choose a text box object from the Text Box popup menu, Immedia only deselects text from that particular text box object. However, as in the last tip, if you leave it set to None, Immedia deselects the text from the current text box object, whatever that may be.

Note that the Deselect Text action is also the only way to deselect all the items in a list (see "Tip: Deselecting List Items," later in this chapter).

Set Text. You can place text into any text box object using the Set Text action; what box, what text, and where to put it is completely up to you. You can make all these choices from the three popup menus Immedia provides (see Figure 4–18).

> ▶ **Text Object.** You've got to choose a target text box object from the Text Object popup menu.

> ▶ **Method.** You've got two choices on the Method popup menu: Literal and Text Box Contents. If you choose Literal, you're telling Immedia exactly what text to place in the text box object (type it in the Literal field). If you choose Text Box Contents, you're saying "put whatever's in a different *source* text box object into the target text box object." In this case you have to choose a source text box from the popup menu labeled Text Obj 2.
>
> The Text Box Contents option is basically the same as selecting and copying the text from the source box, then pasting it into the target box; it's just much faster and easier.

> ▶ **Placement.** You can tell Immedia where in the target text box object to place the text by choosing one of the four self-explanatory choices from the Placement popup menu: Add to Beginning, Add to End, Replace All, and Replace Selection.

Reading and Writing Files

As I've said many times before, anything you do in an exported project disappears as soon as you quit the project.* But when it comes to text, you have the option of breaking out of the confines of your

---

*Another way to put this is that the changes you make—forms you fill out, buttons you press, and so on—are volatile . . . they only "live" while the project is running.

project and reading and writing text on your hard drive. The relevant actions are Write Text File and Read Text File.

Write Text File. You can save text from your project to a disk using the Write Text File action. But wait, that's not all . . . you have options to choose from (see Figure 4–19). Note that you can only save text that's in an Editable text box object.

> ▶ **Select.** The first thing you need to decide when using the Write Text File action is what, exactly, you want saved. You can

Figure 4–18
Set Text

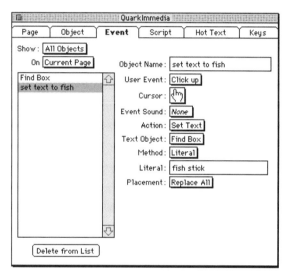

Figure 4–19
Write Text File

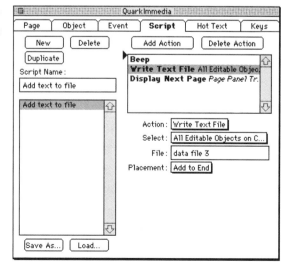

choose either One Editable Object or All Editable Objects on Current Page from the Select popup menu. If you're saving the text from just one text box object, then you have to specify which one in the Text Object popup menu. If you choose All Editable Objects on Current Page, Immedia saves all the text on whatever page is currently visible in the exported project.

If you've got more than one Editable text box object on your page (this includes the pasteboard, by the way), Immedia saves the text from the boxes in a tab-delimited format,* starting with the box on the top layer and ending with the one on the bottom layer. Remember that the layers aren't always what they seem; see "Tip: Putting Boxes in Order," below.

▶ **File.** Once you've figured out what you want to save, you have to tell Immedia what file to save it in. You can just type the name of a file; Immedia looks for that file in the same folder that the project is in. If one already exists, it writes in that file. If there isn't a file with that name, the Immedia Viewer creates one and then writes in it.

If you want Immedia to put the file anywhere other than in that folder, however, you'll have to write out a full file path. For example, instead of writing "MyFile", you might write "MyHardDisk:MyFolder:MyFile". This way, Immedia knows exactly where to put it. Of course, if Immedia can't find volumes and folders with the proper names, it gets mighty confused and puts it in the project's folder anyway. I recommend just letting it save in the project folder to begin with unless you're a system administrator with a firm grasp on your audience's computer system.

▶ **Placement.** The Placement popup menu lets you choose where in the file you want to save this text. You've got two choices: Add to End and Replace All. Replace All is pretty self-explanatory. Add to End, though, may trip you up: it adds the

---

*Tab-delimited means that Immedia saves the text from the first box in the file, then adds a tab, then saves the next text box, then adds another tab, and so on. Immedia always places a carriage return after the last text box's text.

text directly to the end of the file, without adding a carriage return first. However, it always adds a return *after* the text.

▼ ▼

Tip: Writing from CD-ROM or Internet Projects. As I said, Immedia generally tries to write the text file into the same folder that contains the project. But what if the project is being run over the Internet or from a CD-ROM? In the case of a project exported for the Internet, the Immedia Viewer writes the file in the Scratch Directory (the user must have this set up already in the Viewer's Internet Preferences dialog box). If the user hasn't specified a Scratch Directory, the Viewer gives them an error message.

If you're going to run your project from a CD-ROM, you should probably export it in the CD-ROM (two files) format (see Chapter 14, *Exporting*), and then encourage the user to drag the master file over to the hard drive. Otherwise, they'll receive an error message every time they try to write to a disk (you can't write to a CD-ROM, of course). Another option would be for them to choose "Always" in the Apply Security Options section of the Viewer's Security Preferences dialog box; that way, the project would also write to the Scratch Directory.

▼ ▼

Tip: Putting Boxes in Order. When you choose the All Editable Objects on Current Page option in the Write Text File action, Immedia saves the topmost box first. The problem is that there's no easy way to see the how boxes are layered (see Figure 4–20). If you have lots of text boxes on your page, there's a very quick method for setting their order: Select the last box and bring it to the front (press F5), then select the next-to-last box and bring it to the front, then the third-to-last . . . and so on, until you select the box you want to be first (topmost). After you bring that one to the top, you're all set.

▼ ▼

Tip: Inserting Hidden Text. Sometimes it's useful to include text in the file that you don't actually see on screen. Let's say you want to save the status of a button as a "Yes" or a "No" on disk (see Chapter 6, *Buttons*, for more on buttons).

Figure 4–20
Layered boxes

*Which of these is
the topmost box?*

Is this the topmost or
bottommost text box?

1. Create an Editable text box object on your page (it has to be on the page, not on the pasteboard), and turn on Initially Hidden (on the Options popup menu, on the Object tab of the Immedia palette). Make sure this text box is placed in the appropriate layer (see the previous tip).

2. Set up an On/Off button so that when you turn it on, it uses the Set Text action to change the text in your text box to "Yes"; when you turn the button off, it should set the text to "No".

3. Use Write Text File to write either all the Editable text box objects to disk, or just this one.

Because you selected Initially Hidden, the text box object won't appear on the page. However, because it *is* on the page, its text still gets saved to disk with the Write Text File action.

▼ ▼

Read Text File. The Read Text File action lets you read text from a file on your hard drive just as easily as you can write to it. However, you're not limited to what you've already written to disk; you can read any ASCII ("text-only") file from disk. For instance, you could export data from a spreadsheet or a database, save it as a text file on disk, and then pull pieces of that information into your project as necessary.

The Read Text File action does appear a bit intimidating at first, because it offers options in four different popup menus. If we take it step by step, though, it's not too bad (see Figure 4–21).

Figure 4–21
Read Text File

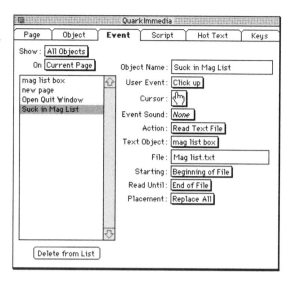

▶ **Text Object.** The first popup menu, labeled Text Object, lets you choose where you want the incoming text to go. This is the target text box object. You can choose any text box object on your page, no matter what type it is. If you want to target a text box object on a different page, select Other.

▶ **File.** In the File field, you have to tell Immedia what file to read, and you have to spell it just right (don't laugh; many a designer has been driven mad because they typed a single letter wrong and couldn't figure out why they were getting so many errors). As with the Write Text File action, if you type just the name of the file, Immedia looks in the same folder that the project is in. But you can also type a file path so that the Viewer tries to find the project in a particular folder on your hard disk (or on a CD-ROM).

▶ **Starting.** Next, from the Starting popup menu, you have to tell Immedia where to start reading in the text file by choosing either Beginning of File or Last Read Position. While the former is rather obvious, the latter is not. The QuarkImmedia Viewer actually keeps track of each file and how much you've already read from it. If you read the first word, then choosing Last Read Position would begin just after that word. Note that the Viewer only keeps track of this position until you leave the project; if you return later, the Last Read Position markers are all reset back to the beginning of the text files.

▶ **Read Until.** How much of the file do you want? A word? A single letter? You can specify how much text Immedia should read by choosing from the Read Until popup menu. The default setting for Read Until is End of File, but you can also choose End of Line ("until the next carriage return"), Tab, Special Character (you can choose any character), or Number of Characters (just type in however many you want).

▶ **Placement.** The last option in the Read Text File action is the Placement popup menu. This tells Immedia where in the target text box you want to place the incoming text. Your options: Add to Beginning, Add to End, Replace All, or Replace Selection. I recently swore in frustration because I wanted to insert the incoming text at the point where my cursor was flashing and there was no "at cursor" option. Then, in embarassment, I realized that the Replace Selection option would do exactly the same thing (you don't have to have anything selected to "replace the selection").

By the way, there's no way that Read Text File can read a text file over the Internet. That's what the Get Text URL action is for (see Chapter 15, *The Internet and the World Wide Web*).

▼ ▼

Tip: Setting Last Read Position. There appears to be a bug in the 1.0 version of QuarkImmedia (this may be fixed by the time you read it . . . or it may not). The problem occurs with the Last Read Position option. If you use the Write Text File action to write some text into a file, and then immediately try to read that text back by using the Read Text File action, the Last Read Position marker gets confused (it thinks the Last Read Position is at the end of the file). One way to work around this is to trigger a Read Text File action that reads zero characters from the beginning of the file—this resets the Last Read Position to the beginning of the file again.

▼ ▼

Searching for Text

Now we come to a couple of actions that I hold very dear. Because I work with so much text, being able to search through a project for a word or a phrase is very important to me. The two key actions that let you do this are Find Text and Add List Items Using Search (the latter is actually a List action, but I'll talk about it here). Neither feature is perfect, but both are powerful enough for most of the work I do.

Find Text. The Find Text feature lets you search for a word or a text string in a particular text box object. The biggest problem with Find Text, in my humble opinion, is that you have to specify the text box object in which to search; you can't search every text box object, or even the current text box object (the one that the cursor is currently in). Nonetheless it's useful, especially for long, scrollable blocks of text. There are several options from which you must choose, two popup menus, a text field, and three checkboxes (see Figure 4–22).

Figure 4–22
Find Text

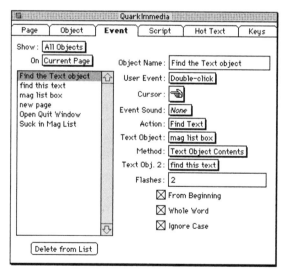

▶ **Text Object.** The first popup menu, Text Object, lets you tell Immedia which text box object to search; you can choose any type of text box object on your page. If you want to search a box that's on a different page, select Other.

▶ **Method.** If you choose Literal from the Method popup menu, you can "hard code" the search string in. I can't imagine why you'd want to do this, but there's probably an awfully good reason (this is the kind of feature that is good to know exists because someday it'll become crucial). The more common selection is Text Object Contents, which lets you choose another text box object from the popup menu labeled Text Obj. 2. This method lets your user type in any word he or she wants.

▶ **Flashes.** When Immedia can't find the requested text in the target text box object, it gives you an error (and an ugly one at that; see Figure 4–23). When it *can* find it, however, it "flashes" it—that is, it highlights the text and then dehighlights it. You can tell Immedia how many times to flash by typing a number in the Flashes field. I recommend setting this to two or three. One often isn't enough, and more can just get annoying to the user. Note that Immedia won't flash at all if the target is a Simple text box object; it flashes only if it's Editable, or Scrollable, or a List.

Figure 4–23
When Immedia can't
find the search string

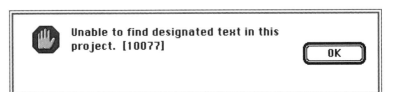

▶ **From Beginning.** When you turn on the From Beginning checkbox (it is on by default), Immedia searches the target text box object from the beginning. When this option is turned off, Immedia searches from wherever the last selection was— that means from wherever you last clicked in the box, selected text using the Select Text action, or found text using Find Text. Of course, you usually need to do both—search from the beginning at first, and then from wherever the last selection was. There are various messy solutions to this problem, from creating multiple buttons to writing complex scripts. If you have some elegant solution, write and let me know.

▶ **Whole Word.** People usually want to search for a whole word, so it's appropriate that the Whole Word checkbox defaults to on. This means that if you search for "dog", Immedia won't find "doggerel"; it will only find "dog". However, sometimes you'll want to let people search for partial words. When Whole Word is turned off and you search for "coat," Immedia finds "coat," "sportcoat," "overcoat," and even "coated."

▶ **Ignore Case.** Finally, you have to decide how important it is to match the uppercase and lowercase characters in your search. When Ignore Case is turned on (it is by default), you're telling Immedia to disregard whether characters are upper- or lowercase in both the text you're searching for, and in the target text. I almost always leave this turned on. Nevertheless, every now and then I find that it matters; for instance, in my hometown of Seattle, there's an important difference between "joe" (what people drink in the morning) and the name "Joe."

▼ ▼

Tip: Selecting What You've Found. At first glance, it appears as though the Find Text action never actually selects the text that it has found. It just flashes and leaves it unselected. However, this isn't actually true—it all depends on the current text box. Let's say you type a search word into an Editable text box object (let's call this the "find box"), and the Find Text action uses this word to search in some other text box (the "target box"). If Immedia finds the word, it'll flash it, but it won't select it because the target box is not the current text box—the find box is, because you just typed in it.

However, when the project is engaged, if you actually click on the target text box before using the Find Text action, Immedia *does* select the word. Clicking on the target box causes it to become the current text box.

Back in "Tip: The Current Text Box," we learned how to use the Select Text action to specify the current text box. I almost always search for text using a little script (see Chapter 13, *Scripting*): first, use Select Text to set the current text box to the target box; next, trigger the Find Text action.

▼ ▼

Add List Items Using Search. There's another way to search for text in your project—the Add List Items Using Search—and though in some ways it appears more powerful, it doesn't include some features in Find Text. The result is that you often have to use the two actions in tandem. Note that all the other list-related actions are discussed later in this chapter, in "Making Lists." However, this action is too good to wait.

The Add List Items Using Search action lets you search for text in a number of places that you can't search with the Find Text action, including page names, page descriptions, multiple text boxes, and even text on your hard drive. Plus, instead of showing you each instance that it found the text one at a time, this action builds a list of every page on which it found what it was looking for.

You need to select from three popup menus: Destination, Search For, and Search what (see Figure 4–24).

▶ **Destination.** First, choose a List text box object from the Destination popup menu. As usual, if the list is on a different page, you can choose Other. The Add List Items Using Search will completely replace any text that is already in the list.

▶ **Search For.** Whereas the Find Text action lets you search for either a literal string or the contents of another text box object, Add List Items Using Search only gives you the latter option.

Figure 4–24
Add List Items
Using Search

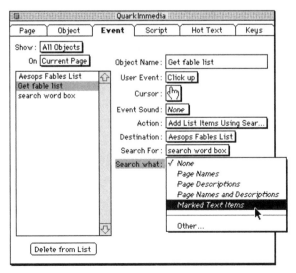

Select the text box object that contains the text you want to search for from the Search For popup menu. This can be any type of text box object, even another list. If it is a list, then whichever list item is selected at the time of the search will be used. If you want to hard-code the search string—the equivalent of using Literal in Find Text—you can put the Search For text box object on the pasteboard so that your user can't change it.

▶ **Search what.** Now it comes time to tell Immedia what you want to search. You have five options in the Search what pop-up menu: Page Names, Page Descriptions, Page Names and Descriptions, Marked Text Items, and Other. The first three search any names and descriptions you've set up on the Page Tab of the Immedia palette (see Figure 4–25). Marked Text Items searches every basic text box and text box object for which you've selected the Searchable Contents option. (That means any basic text box or text box object *other* than Editable text box objects; if it's editable, you can't choose the Searchable Contents option.)

The last option, Other, is a brilliant mystery waiting to unfold. When you choose Other, Immedia asks you to find an index file from your hard drive. I'm going to hold off discussing index files until the next section. Hint: this is how you can search text on your hard drive.

The Add List Items Using Search action is different from Find Text in other ways, too. It always ignores case and always searches for the whole word. Unfortunately, that means that if you search for "computer" it will not find "computers", and *vice versa*. If you search for two or more words using Find Text, it looks for them as a single phrase. Add List Items Using Search, on the other hand, finds every instance where the words appear in the same place (same description, same name, or the same page). For example, if you search for "end up", Find Text would only find each instance of "end up", but Add List Items Using Search would find "end up", "up end", and "up at that end".

Figure 4–25

What you can
search for

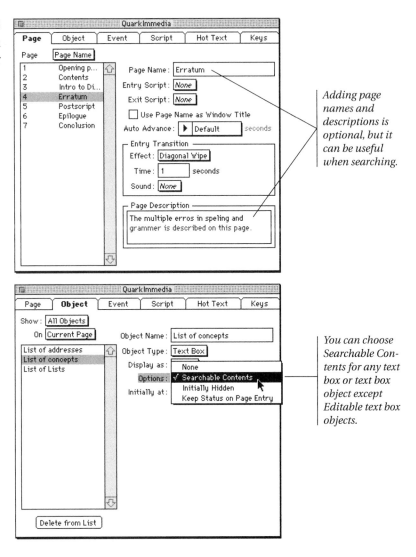

*Adding page
names and
descriptions is
optional, but it
can be useful
when searching.*

*You can choose
Searchable Con-
tents for any text
box or text box
object except
Editable text box
objects.*

▼ ▼

Tip: Searching for Keywords. Let's say you have 100 pages of prize
photographs that you want to search by keywords. There are no
words on the pages, so what do you search for? Remember that Add
List Items Using Search doesn't care if the marked text boxes (text
boxes for which you've chosen the Searchable Contents option) are
on the page or the pasteboard. That makes the pasteboard a perfect
location for keywords or other searchable text that you don't necessarily want to see in your project.

Even if your project is text-heavy, you may still want to include keywords on the pasteboard because the words people are likely to search for may not actually appear on the page. For instance, you could fill a whole page with descriptions of local mushrooms without once mentioning the word "toadstool." If a user searched for "toadstool," they'd be out of luck because the Add List Items Using Search action would never find your mushroom page. Similarly, if your page includes the word "beer" 15 times, a user looking for "beers" wouldn't find it. You can make your project much more user-friendly by anticipating what people will search for and placing these words in a searchable text box on the pasteboard.

Building Indexes

I remember Mr. Duncan, my elementary school librarian, teaching us about the importance of indexes. "An index is the fastest way to a book's contents because it 'knows' where everything is." Searching for "hippopotamus"? Check the index. Searching for *"Boletus mirabilis"*? Check the index. But why bother with an index in a multimedia project if we already have Find Text and Add List Items Using Search? Because sometimes the text we want isn't in the project; sometimes it's on the hard drive or the CD-ROM.

Let's say you have 100 little text files in a folder, each one containing a recipe. You could import each one of these into a text box object and put it on a separate page; but, of course, you'd end up with a 100-page document. What we really want to do is build a single index to all the files, search that index for the one we want, and then only import that one when we want it. That's exactly what Immedia's Make Index feature is all about.

When you select Make Index from the Immedia menu, the program asks you to save an index file somewhere on your hard drive (or on your network; see Figure 4–26). You must save the index file in the same folder as all the text files you want indexed (yes, that means all those text files have to be in the same folder). As soon as

Figure 4-26

Make Index

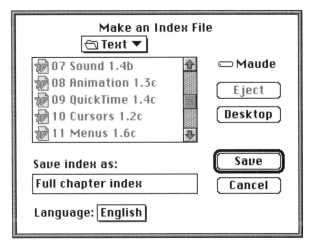

you click Save, Immedia reads each text file to figure out what's in it, then saves that information in the index file.

Language. The Language popup menu in the Make Index dialog box lets you choose some general rules about how the program indexes the files. Basically, it comes down to characters with accents and ligatures. For example, if a file contains the word *après,* should Immedia index it with or without an accent? What about *flügel,* which contains both an fl ligature and a diacritic? How the word is indexed determines how someone can search for it. Will people have to type après or is apres okay? If they type flugel or fluegel, will Immedia recognize the word correctly?

Depending on which language you choose from the Language popup menu, Immedia changes the way it indexes words with ligatures, diacritical marks (such as *é, ö,* or *â*), prefixes (such as *L'* and *d'*), suffixes (such as *'s,* or *'m*), and character equivalents (such as *ue* for *ü*). Selecting General from the Language popup menu is supposed to encompass the widest spectrum of choices, but that turns out not to be true.

To be honest, I generally just use English, and it seems to work just fine (even for other languages).

I may have different feelings about this by the time you read this; check the Update page on my Web site (see *Where to Find Me,* in the back of this book).

Text file formats. While Immedia can always index "text-only" (ASCII) files, Immedia can also index other types. In fact, it'll index any file that QuarkXPress can import using the Get Text feature (under the File menu). If you have the MS-Word filter installed (it gets installed automatically when you install XPress), Immedia indexes your Microsoft Word documents. If you have the WordPerfect filer loaded, it'll index WordPerfect documents, too. You can see which filters and XTensions are loaded by looking in the Environment dialog box (select About QuarkXPress from the Apple menu while holding down the Option key).

Using an Index to Search

Once you've built an index from a folder full of files, you can search it using the Add List Items Using Search action (see "Searching for Text," earlier in this chapter). The key is to choose Other from the action's Search what popup menu, then select the Index file on your hard disk (see Figure 4–27). When you trigger the action, Immedia searches the index for the word or words that are in the Search For text box object, and then displays in the target list the name of each file that contains those words.

Of course, having a list of documents is less than thrilling; it only becomes interesting when you can do something with that list. Here are a few ways in which you can use this list of file names.

Figure 4–27
Selecting an index file

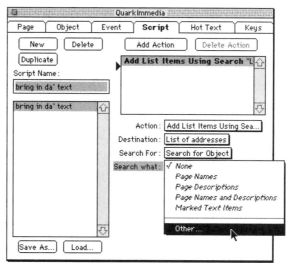

▶ Your project can import any file that is selected in this list with the Get List Selection action (see "Making Lists," later in this chapter). The trick here is to select Indexed Text Document from this action's Get As popup menu.* Note that if you engage the project while in QuarkXPress, text-formatting such as italic, bold, and font actually appears in the text box. However, all text-formatting is lost once you export the project—only the text remains.

▶ If your file names are the same as your page names, you can use the Display Page action to jump to whichever page is selected in your list. For example, let's say you have a file called Soap and a page named Soap. When you click on "Soap" in the list generated by Add List Items Using Search, the Display Page action could jump to the page named "Soap."

▶ You can read a text file over the Internet using Get Text URL, based on the name of a file. For instance, perhaps you have a number of text files that have to be updated each week. If the content of each file doesn't change much (perhaps only dates or part numbers will change), you could index the files, then let people search them as usual. When they select one of the file names from the list, however, you could use the Set Text action to move that file name into a different text box, append a URL header to the beginning of the file name (like "http://www.yourcompany.com/"), and then use the Get Text URL action to import that file over the Internet into a text box.

Exporting with an Index

When it comes time to export your project (this process is covered in more detail in Chapter 14, *Exporting*), any indexes that you've used in the Add List Items Using Search or Get List Selection actions must be present, *as well as* the files you used to build the index. The reason: Immedia actually embeds all that text into your project.

---

*Being able to import a file quickly is the most compelling reason to use indexed files, in my opinion, and I find it ironic that this feature is hardly mentioned at all in Quark's documentation.

▼ ▼

Tip: Encoding your Text. Some people get nervous when they find out that Immedia embeds the indexed text files into the project file. They don't like the idea of someone being able to open the project file with a word processor and copy text out. Fear not: if you turn on Full Compression During Export in the Export dialog box, the embedded text is compressed and encoded; only the project itself—or a cryptologist—can read it now.

▼ ▼

Making Lists

I've already discussed List text box objects, how to make them, and how to fill them during a search. But there are many more things you can do with lists, and that's what we're going to cover next. Immedia has nine different actions that work only on lists; they let you add, remove, and change list items, as well as manipulate the selected list item. We've already seen one list action—Add List Items Using Search. Now, let's take a closer look at the other eight.

▼ ▼

Tip: Keep the List's Status. Don't forget that lists are just text box objects. And, just like other text box objects, you have to turn on the Keep Status on Page Entry option (on the Object tab of the Immedia palette) if you want any changes to be persistent after you jump to a different page. For instance, if you add an item to your list and you don't use this option, when you return to the page, the added item will be gone.

▼ ▼

Set List Selection. As you know, each paragraph in a List text box object is a separate item in the list. When you first engage the project, nothing is selected in the list. You can then select any one list item by clicking on it (you can only have one list item selected at a time). However, you can also make a selection from the list with the Set List Selection action (see Figure 4–28).

Figure 4-28
Set List Selection

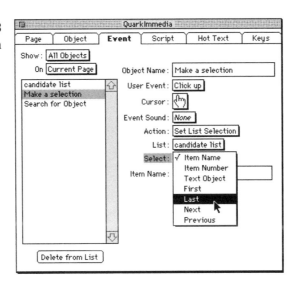

When you choose Set List Selection, you have to tell Immedia which List text box object, and which item in the list, to select. There are seven choices in the Select popup menu.

▶ **Item Name.** If you choose Item Name, the name of the list item you want selected must be typed in exactly the way it appears on the list.

▶ **Item Number.** If you know that you want the third item, but you don't know its name (if, for instance, the list will be generated by some other action), you can choose Item Number. I've never found a use for this, but I'm sure somebody will.

▶ **Text Object.** You can set the list selection based on what's in another text box object. For example, if you have a list of companies, your user could type in a company name and, if it matches any in the list, Immedia would highlight that item. They don't even have to type the entire name; Set List Selection looks for any match it can find, so it recognizes "Xerox Corporation" even if the user only types "Xero". You can even base your selection on whatever is selected in another list (just choose that list in the Text Object popup menu).

▶ **First/Last.** I assume it's obvious that the First and Last options in the Select popup menu select the first or last item in the list.

▶ **Previous/Next.** The Previous and Next options are only slightly less intuitive. If a list item is already selected, these two options select the item before or after it. If no item is selected, nothing happens.

▼ ▼

Tip: Deselecting List Items. As you can see, it's easy enough to select an item from a list. And as soon as you select a different item, the first item is deselected. But how do you deselect all the items? You can do this with the Deselect Text action (see "Text Actions," earlier in this chapter).

▼ ▼

Add List Item. The Add List Item action lets you add an item to a list once the project is engaged or exported. Of course, adding it is temporary; once you quit the project, the list reverts back to its original state. The Add List Item action first asks which list you want to add an item to, then what and where to add it (see Figure 4–29).

Figure 4–29
Add List Item

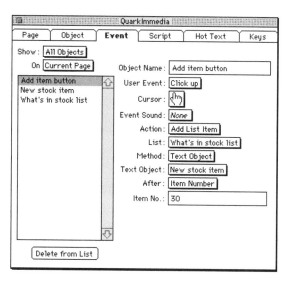

▶ **Method.** If you choose Item Name from the Method popup menu, Immedia expects you to type in the list item, exactly the way you want it to appear. If that's too constraining for you, select Text Object; this lets you choose another text box object. Whatever is in that text box object is added to the list.

▶ **After.** The After popup menu also gives you a choice between Item Name and Item Number. If you choose Item Number, you can specify the item's placement numerically (if you type 4, the new item is placed after the fourth item currently on the list). If you choose Item Name, you have to type in part or all of a list item's name (if you want the list item added after "linoleum," you can tell Immedia to add it after "lino").

▼ ▼

Tip: Adding to the Beginning. To add a new list item at the beginning of the list, select Item Number from the After popup menu (in the Add List Item action) and type 0 (zero). If you want the new list item at the end, type a large number, such as 50.

▼ ▼

Remove List Item. Now you know how to add a list item . . . so let's continue on to removing an item. You can use the Remove List Item action to remove one or more items from any list in your project. Once again, the first step is to select the list from which you want to remove items; the next step is to choose your options.

▶ **Start.** The Start popup menu gives you the same options as the After popup menu in Add List Item: Item Name or Item Number. They work the same way, too: you can choose to remove a list item by its place in the list or by its name.

▶ **No. of Items.** The default value for the No. of Items field is zero, which means "don't remove any items." If you actually want the action to do something, you'd better change this to at least one.

If you only want six items in your list, you could remove the excess by setting the Start popup menu to Item Number 7, and then typing a large number (like 50) into the No. of Items field. That tells Immedia to remove every item from number seven to the end of the list. However, the Remove Excess List Items action is a slightly easier and more elegant solution.

▼ ▼

Tip: Removing All List Items. By the way, you can remove all the items in a list with the Remove List Item action by typing -1 in the No. of Items field.

▼ ▼

Remove Excess List Items. The Remove Excess List Items action has one purpose: to limit the number of items in a list. This action gives you just three options: which list, how many items you want in it, and (if there are too many items) excess items removed from the top or the bottom of the list (see Figure 4–30).

Figure 4–30
Remove Excess
List Items

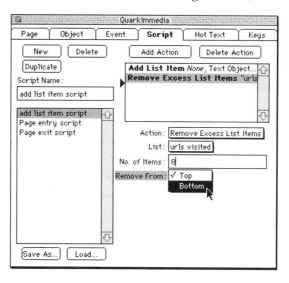

▼ ▼

Tip: Maintaining List Size. An action only happens when you trigger it. So although you may think that using the Remove Excess List Items action once will keep a list trimmed forever, it's just not true. If you want to maintain the length of a list, you might try building a script (see Chapter 13, *Scripting*) that does two things: Add List Item and Remove Excess List Items. Each time you want to add an item to your list, call this script instead. The item is added, and then the list is trimmed to size, ensuring that the list never gets larger than you want it.

▼ ▼

Enable/Disable List Item. You've probably seen menus in programs (like XPress or Microsoft Word) that contain disabled items; they're grayed out and you can't select them. You can do the same thing to items in a list, disabling and then enabling them with the Disable List Item and Enable List Item actions. For instance, you may want to enable or disable different list items depending on what choices your audience has made elsewhere in the project.

In both of these actions, you must first select from the List pop-up menu the list you want to affect. Then you can choose from the Select popup menu which item you want to disable or enable (you can only change one item at a time). The choices on this popup menu are identical to those in the Select List Item action: Item Name, Item Number, Text Object, First, Last, Next, and Previous (see "Select List Item," earlier in this chapter, for more on how each of these options works).

▼ ▼

Tip: Disabling the Whole List. The Disable List Item and Enable List Item only work on a single list item at a time. If you want to disable or enable the entire list, you can use the Disable Object or Enable Object actions (see "Object Actions" in Chapter 3, *Building Objects*). The only real difference is that in the current version of Immedia, although Disable Object stops the user from selecting any list items, it does not gray the list items out.

▼ ▼

Get List Item. The Get List Item copies the text from a list to another text box object (see Figure 4–31). However, you have to know exactly which list item (by number, not name) you want. So if you know you want the first item or the fifth item in the list, this action is perfect for you. If you just want to copy the currently selected item, then check out the Get List Selection action (see below).

You have to make four choices in the Get List Item action.

1. First, choose which list you're targeting from the popup menu labeled "List."

2. Next, choose which list item you want to copy and type it into the Item No. field (again, this has to be a number, not the name of the item).

3. From the Destination popup menu, choose the text box object into which you want to place the copied text. If the text box is on a different page, select Other.

4. Finally, choose from the Placement popup menu where in the destination text box object you want the text to go: Add to Beginning, Add to End, Replace All, or Replace Selection.

To be honest, I don't think I've ever used this action in a project. I just can't for the life of me figure out why I'd want to. E-mail me if you've got any good ideas.

Figure 4–31
Get List Item

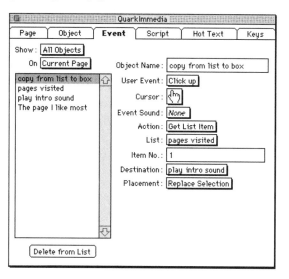

Get List Selection. Get List Selection copies the currently selected list item to another text box object. As much as I find the Get List Item feature useless, I find the Get List Selection action invaluable when working with lists. Most of the options for Get List Selection are exactly the same as that other action—List, Destination, Placement—but two things are new (see Figure 4–32). First, you don't have to specify which item you want to get (because it's always the

Figure 4-32
Get List Selection

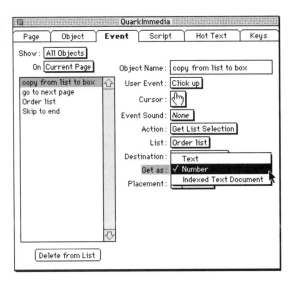

item that is selected). Second, there's a popup menu labeled Get as. The Get as popup menu has three choices: Text, Number, and Indexed Text Document.

▶ **Text.** If you choose Text, the actual text of the selected item is copied to the text box object. If the list item was "Boola-boola," then Immedia would put "Boola-boola" in the text box object.

▶ **Number.** If you choose Number from the Get as popup menu, Immedia writes the position of the selected item in the list. If the fifth item in the list is selected, Immedia will put *5* in the text box object.

▶ **Indexed Text Document.** The Indexed Text Document option is a diamond in the rough. As we saw in "Building Indexes," earlier in this chapter, you can create a list of text files using the Add List Items Using Search action. You can then use the Get List Selection action—with this option—to pull in whichever text file in the list the user selects. Immedia places the text in the text box object that you've chosen on the Destination popup menu. This way, you can avoid importing all those files into text box objects, adding lots of pages to your document. Instead, with this action you can import them as you need them.

By the way, this option only works with lists built using Add List Items Using Search.

▼ ▼

Hot Text

It's curious to note that 30 years ago, when Ted Nelson first conceived a system of nonlinear text-flow called hypertext, it was such a radical notion. Hypertext—the ability to click on a word or a phrase and be transported to a different document or a different part of the same document—is now a standard tool in many computer programs, and is a crucial element of the Internet.

QuarkImmedia takes the concept of hypertext one step farther: in your project you can create not only text that can bring you to some other page or project, but even make text that triggers *any* action in Immedia—playing a movie, opening a window, pausing an animation, printing a page, running a script, and more. Immedia calls this kind of text *hot text*.

Making Hot Text

In the past couple of chapters, you've seen how to make any object (text box, picture box, line, and so on) a hot spot—that is, it'll do something if you click on it. If you want a word or a sentence to be a hot spot, you could just put a box over it, set its Background Color and Runaround to None, and then set up the box to trigger an action. But there's another way to make hot text, and it's better than using the "stupid box trick" for two reasons.

▶ If you edit the text, hot text flows with the paragraph; a box over the text does not.

▶ When you click on hot text, Immedia gives you feedback by flashing the text.

You can turn any text, from a single character to an entire paragraph, into hot text. Plus, you can make hot text in any basic text box *or* text box object (that means your hot text can even be anti-aliased if you want).

1. Select the text (see "Tip: Deselect the Space," below).

2. Open the Hot Text tab of the Immedia palette (Figure 4–33).

3. Give the selected text block a name on the Hot Text tab. You can also assign a color, if you want.*

4. Assign an action to a user event (just as though you were assigning it to an object).

Figure 4–33

Hot Text

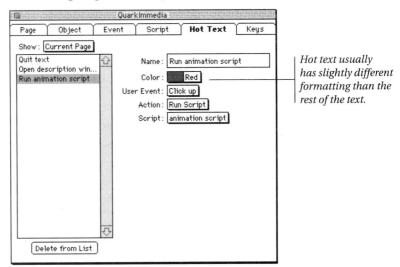

Hot text usually has slightly different formatting than the rest of the text.

That's all there is to it. You'll notice that as soon as you assign an action to the text, XPress changes the text-formatting—the default formatting for hot text is underlined. This is so the hot text stands out from the rest of the text. However, you can always override that formatting just as you would any other text (from the Style menu or the Measurements palette). Overriding the formatting doesn't change the fact that it's hot text.

Editing the hot text. While you can edit the formatting of the hot text, editing the text itself can be problematic. You can do it—for

---

*I don't know why they give you a Color popup menu here; it does exactly the same thing as selecting a color from the Style menu. Well, always nice to have another option, I guess.

instance, if you've got two words selected as hot text, you can delete one of them and the first one remains hot text—but often Immedia loses track of what's supposed to be hot text and what's not.

In general, if you need to do more than simply fix a typo, you should probably remove the hot text tag, edit the text, and then turn it into hot text again. You can remove the hot text tag by selecting the name of the hot text on the Hot Text palette and clicking on the Delete from List button.

Unfortunately, once you've turned text into hot text, there is no way to edit its range. That is, if you've got one word turned into a hot text block called "Open Info Window," you cannot extend that block to two or three words. Again, it's best if you remove the hot text tag, select the whole range, and turn it into hot text again.

▼ ▼

Tip: Deselect the Space. When you double-click on a word in Quark-XPress, the program selects the entire word . . . plus the space after or punctuation on either side of the word. That's fine for editing, but if you're going to turn that text into hot text, you might have grabbed more than you bargained for. You can quickly get rid of that extra space or punctuation after the word by typing Shift-Left Arrow (that deselects the last character). To remove punctuation before the word, you simply have to reselect more carefully.

▼ ▼

Tip: Selecting Hot Text Names. In order to change the action applied to hot text, you must precisely select the word or phrase in the text box; if you have even an extra space selected, the Hot Text tab of the Immedia palette will remain grayed out. This, needless to say, is a pain in the neck. Instead of trying to select the text in the text box, select it quickly and painlessly by clicking once on the name of the hot text on the Hot Text tab.

▼ ▼

Limiting the scope. One more note about the Hot Text tab of the Immedia palette: if you have a *lot* of hot text throughout your document, the Show popup menu quickly becomes your friend. This popup menu offers four choices that let you select what hot text appears in the palette.

▶ **Active Box** shows you all the hot text items in the currently selected box, even if the hot text is overset (if the hot text items are part of text that can't fit in the box, and the box isn't linked to any other boxes).

▶ **Active Story** displays the hot text throughout the current text story. This is the same as Active Box unless you've got more than one box linked together (remember that you cannot link together text box objects, only basic text boxes).

▶ **Current Page** displays all the hot text on the current page (the page currently in the upper-left corner of the window).

▶ **Entire Project** shows you every hot text item in your project. Be careful, though: if you've got more than one hot text item with the same name (but on different pages), as soon as you change to Entire Project, Immedia renames one of them so that there are no duplicates (Immedia really hates having to list duplicate names).

Setting the Default Preferences

Earlier, I said that Immedia automatically changes the text-formatting when you create hot text, and that formatting is usually just an underline. What I didn't mention is that you can set this formatting to be anything you want, and the place to do that is the Quark-Immedia Preferences dialog box (under the Edit menu; see Figure 4–34). As with any other preference, if you change this while a document is open, the change only affects that document. If no document is open, new documents you create will have this formatting.

Formatting. The Hot Text section of the QuarkImmedia Preferences dialog box lets you choose four text styles for your hot text: Bold, Underline, Italic, and Color. This is like a character-level style sheet: whatever text you apply the "hot text style" to gets this formatting automatically. The default setting is a nice, clean, elegant underline.

Figure 4–34
Changing the default
hot text formatting

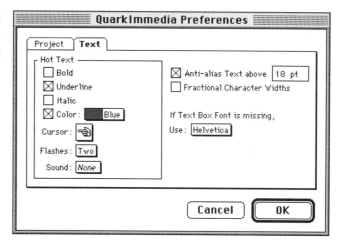

Note that when you change this setting while a document is open, Immedia changes any hot text that you've set up already to this style.

Cursor. The popup menu labeled Cursor lets you tell Immedia which cursor to display when you place the cursor over the hot text. Custom cursors are discussed in Chapter 10, *Cursors*.

Flashes. When you click on some hot text in an engaged or exported project, the text flashes to indicate that you've really accomplished something. You can set the number of times the hot text should flash by selecting One, Two, or Three from the Flashes popup menu. While I usually like this feedback, it'd be nice if they offered a "zero" option, too; sometimes I don't want flashing text.

Sound. When you assign an action to any other object (like a text box or a picture box), you can choose to assign a sound, too (see Chapter 7, *Sounds*). That way, when someone clicks on a box, they can get aural feedback. You can do the same thing with hot text by choosing a sound from the Sound popup menu. However, you get to choose only one sound for every instance of hot text rather than on an item-by-item basis. Immedia plays the sound whenever you click on the hot text.

Note that in version 1.0 of Immedia, there's a bug that disables hot text sound for text box objects.

▼ ▼

Content and ConText

No matter how many flashy graphics and animations you've got, text is often the cornerstone, the *raison d'etre*, for an entire multimedia project. In this chapter we've seen the many different ways that you can use text, basic text boxes, and text box objects both to ground and to enhance your projects, including building lists, making Editable text boxes in forms, creating hot text, and importing and exporting text to your hard disk.

In the next chapter, we'll delve deeper into making your projects interactive by building windows that can appear on command.

Windows

O UT THERE IN THE SO-called business world, when someone says "Windows," they're thinking of "Microsoft Windows." But you and I are different, right? We're part of that weird and wacky group called multimedia authors. So when we say "windows," we're thinking of something that pops up on screen and is in your face. You can create several different types of windows in Immedia, from dialog boxes to alert warnings to windows that give your user more information about something. Building different sorts of windows (especially floating palettes) can be a major pain in some programs, but in Immedia, it's just a popup menu away.

Doing Windows

You can make any text or picture box a window by choosing Window from the Object Type popup menu on the Object tab of the Quark-Immedia palette (see Figure 5–1). Immedia expects (demands) that you place the box on the pasteboard rather than on the page.

Once you've got a window object on the pasteboard, you can start designing what goes in it. Anything you put on top of a window object appears in the window itself, even if it only partially overlaps the window (see Figure 5–2). "Anything" includes animations, movies, buttons, text, and pictures. There are only three constraints.

Figure 5–1

Making a window
in the palette

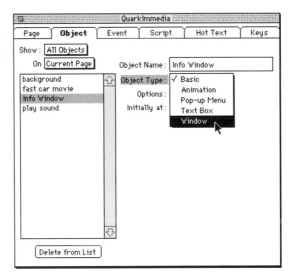

► The window must be rectangular. Even if you make the window a polygon or an oval or whatever, it still always appears as a rectangle in an engaged project.

► The window always ends up with a one-point black border around it in the engaged project.

► Windows stay open even when you move from page to page. If you want to close them, you have to use the Close Window action (see "Window Actions," later in the chapter) or give them close boxes.

▼ ▼

Window Types

Of course, you're not stuck with just one type of window in Immedia. You can specify what *kind* of window it should be in the Display As popup menu (on the Object tab of the QuarkImmedia palette; see Figure 5–3). You have six choices.

► Standard

► Dialog Box

► Movable Dialog Box

Figure 5–2

Making a window on the pasteboard

Before engaging . . .

. . . after engaging. Note what happens to the overlapping objects.

- ▶ Palette

- ▶ Plain

- ▶ Plain Palette

Each window type has several options to choose from; let's look at the window types first, then explore the options.

Standard. The documentation that comes with Immedia insists that Standard windows won't let you click outside of them or move other windows in front of them when your project fills the whole screen. At the time of this writing (version 1.0), this ain't the case. A

Figure 5–3

Display as

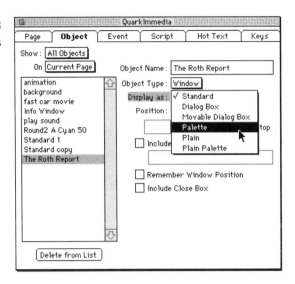

Standard window is simply a window that has a title bar—no more, no less (see Figure 5–4). You can move it around or move other windows in front of it and the project stays active underneath. Standard windows are boring, but they work just fine when you want to send a quick message to your user. I use them rarely, though.

Dialog Box. Dialog boxes are always modal—that means they put you in a mode in which you can't do anything except deal with that dialog box. You can click all day on other parts of the screen, but Immedia only responds to actions within the dialog box window. Then when you close the dialog box, Immedia reverts back to a normal mode in which you can click on other objects.

A window set to display as a dialog box appears with a standard gray dialog box border, and it can't be moved or titled (see Figure 5–5). This is the perfect window style for alert messages.

Movable Dialog Box. Just because a dialog box is modal doesn't mean you can't move it—just change its type to Movable Dialog Box. Immedia treats it the same as a regular dialog box window (you can't click on anything outside of it), but you can move the dialog box anywhere you want on screen by dragging its title bar.

Figure 5–4
Standard windows

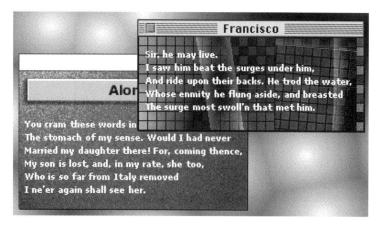

Figure 5–5
Dialog boxes

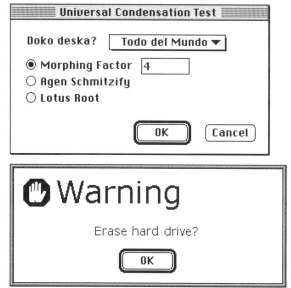

Palette. I'm sure you're all too familiar with palettes; it seems as though they've become *de rigeur* in applications these days.* The key difference between a palette and other window types is cosmetic: the title bar on a palette is . . . well, different (see Figure 5–6). Other than that, palettes sit in front of everything except for dialog boxes. Plus, unlike dialog boxes, you can keep the palette open as long as you like, and the project is still fully functional beneath it.

---

*I can just imagine software developers sitting around saying, "Oh, users won't mind having 18 palettes open at the same time." Please, do the world a favor—keep your palettes to a minimum.

Figure 5–6
Palettes

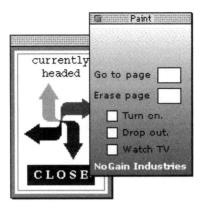

Plain. When it comes to bare-bones, Spartan windows, nothing compares to the Plain window type. Your window appears with nothing but a one-point black rule around it. You can't move it (except with a Drag Window action; see "Window Actions," later in this chapter) and you can't put a title bar on it. Personally, I find Plain windows less useful than other window types; if I just want a box to appear, I typically won't want the black border around it, so I'd use Show Object to make an invisible box appear instead of using the window (see Chapter 3, *Building Projects*).

Plain Palette. The last window type, Plain Palette, looks just like the Plain window, but it has one behavioral difference: it floats in front of windows (the exception is dialog boxes, which appear in front of everything).

Window Options

Don't sit still quite yet; there are up to four more things to pay attention to when making a window. I say "up to" because each window type has a different number of options. Plain windows are the simplest—they have only one option (Position), while Palettes and Standard Windows have four (see Figure 5–7).

Position. Every window type lets you specify where the window will appear when opened. You have two options to choose from on the Position popup menu.

Figure 5-7
Window options

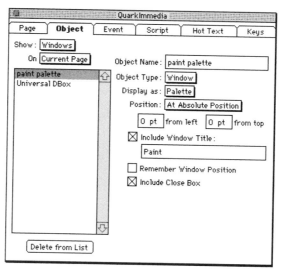

▶ Center on Screen tells Immedia to open the window in the middle of the project. If the project is not centered on the screen, the window may not appear smack-dab in the middle of your monitor.

▶ Absolute lets you tell Immedia exactly where you want the window to appear. The "from left" and "from top" coordinate fields specify the upper-left corner of the window.

▼ ▼

Tip: Catching Coordinates. Here's a fast way to figure out the "from left" and "from top" coordinates for your window, if you're using Absolute positioning.

1. Place the window box (or another similarly sized "proxy" box) where you want it to appear on the page.

2. If your Horizontal and Vertical measurements aren't set to Points in the General Preferences dialog box (under the Edit menu, or press Command-Y), change them now.

3. Write down the values in the x and y fields of the Measurements palette—these are the proper coordinates for the Position fields.

4. Move the window box back to the pasteboard (or delete the proxy) and type these values into the Position area of the QuarkImmedia palette.

▼ ▼

Tip: Windows Outside the Project. There's no reason that a window's position must be within the bounds of the project. As long as the project doesn't fill the entire screen, you can place windows anywhere on the screen you want. Let's say your project is 400 pixels wide; if you set the Horizontal position of a window to 450 pixels, it'll open 50 pixels to the right of the project. Similarly, if you set the Horizontal position of the window to -50 pixels, it'll open to the left of the project (this works with the Vertical position, too, of course).

▼ ▼

Include Window Title. Standard, Movable Dialog Box, and Palette windows have title-bar areas that are usually blank. However, if you turn on the Include Window Title checkbox, you can add whatever title you'd like (see Figure 5–8). Later, when I talk about the Set Window Title action, you'll see how to set this title dynamically while the project is engaged.

Note that the title always appears in the standard system font (Chicago on the Macintosh, Ariel on Windows). If you want it to appear in a different font, you'll have to design and create your own title bar inside the window.

Remember Window Position. You can drag around the screen any window that has a title bar. But if you close the window and then open it again, the window pops back up at its default position (whatever you've set in the Position popup menu). When you turn on the Remember Window Position option on the QuarkImmedia palette, the window "remembers" where your user moves it; next time you open it, it uses this position instead of the default. I always turn this on for palettes, and off for Movable dialog boxes.

Note that even when you do turn on Remember Window Position, the project never remembers the position after you disengage

Figure 5–8
Window titles

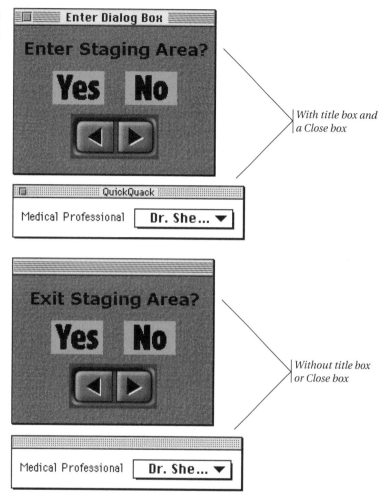

With title box and a Close box

Without title box or Close box

or quit, and there's no good way to automatically reset the window to its original position.

Include Close Box. Palette windows and Standard windows always have title bars, and (accordingly) the title bar can also contain a Close box in its upper-left corner. To include a Close box, turn on the Include Close Box checkbox on the QuarkImmedia palette. Dialog boxes (even if they're movable), Plain windows, and Plain Palettes cannot have Close boxes.*

---

*Have you ever seen a non-moveable dialog box with a Close box in its title bar? No, dialog boxes typically have Close buttons instead.

Window Actions

Windows aren't complicated objects in Immedia, and there's not much you can do with them except to open and close them. Nonetheless, here's a quick rundown on each of the four actions that apply to windows (see Figure 5–9).

Open Window. Any user event can open a window by triggering an Open Window action. When you select Open Window from the Action popup menu (on the Event tab), Immedia asks you which window you want to open (if you want to open a window on a different page from the one you're currently on, select Other). Quark-Immedia also asks you for a transition type, duration, and sound (I discussed these in "Transitions," Chapter 3, *Building Projects*).

Tip: Flush User Events. One of the most common problems developers have is what the user might do in between the time when the Open Window action is triggered and when the window actually opens. If you're running the project over the Internet, it might be a long time. As I discuss later in "Caching User Events" in Chapter 13, *Scripting*, if the user clicks or types during this limbo time, those actions may cause unexpected events once the window opens.

One way to get around this is to build a script that causes a Flush User Events action immediately after the Open Window action (see Chapter 13, *Scripting*). This way, anything the user does will be ignored once the window opens. You can find Flush User Events in the Other popout menu (on the Action popup menu).

Tip: Bring Window to Front. When you click on a window in an engaged project, it comes to the front (except for dialog boxes, which are always in front anyway). You can force a window to the front with the Open Window action. If the window is closed, it opens in front; if the window is already open, it moves to the front.

Figure 5-9

Window actions

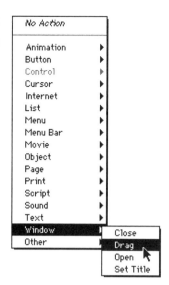

Close Window. The Close Window action closes one or all of the open windows on a page, including palettes and dialog boxes. You can specify whether it closes one or all of the windows by choosing from the Select popup menu. If you're only closing one window, and if the window you want to close doesn't appear on the Window pop-up menu, the window object may be on a different page. In this case, select Other to get the Choose Object dialog box (see "Page Actions" in Chapter 3, *Building Projects*).

Drag Window. As I noted earlier, only certain window types can contain a title bar. And it's the title bar that lets you drag windows around, right? Well, there's one other way to drag a window around the screen: the Drag Window action. This lets you drag *any* kind of window around. However, the way it works is kind of nonintuitive.

You must apply the Drag Window action to an object (a box or a line) that is inside the window—you can't apply it to the window object itself. The action can be triggered by any user event, but the only one that makes sense to use is the Mouse Down event. With this setup, when you press down on that object in the window, you can drag it; when you let go, the window stops dragging.

Set Window Title. Palettes, Movable dialog boxes, and Standard windows all share something in common: they have title bars. And although title bars don't have to have an actual title in them, they often do. If for some strange reason you want to change or add a title to one of these windows at any time while your project is engaged, you can use the Set Title action.

For example, Set Title can save you time and energy (and, for Internet projects, downloading time) if you have to create several dialog boxes that do more or less the same thing but have different titles—just make one of them, and swap the title.

When you select Set Title, Immedia displays the Method popup menu, giving you two choices of where the title should come from.

▶ If you choose Literal from the Method popup menu, you can type in a specific title for the window. (I can't think of a single time I've ever used this in a project. But if you think of a use for this feature, let me know!)

▶ If you choose Text Object Contents, you can pull the title from an editable text box or List (see Chapter 4, *Text*). This text box doesn't have to be on the page itself. You could, for instance, create a list of names on the pasteboard, then build a script that would select one of the list items and use Text Object Contents to apply that list item to the window title. (Whichever item is selected in a list gets used as the title.)

▼ ▼

Opening Windows

Windows are one of the easiest and best ways to create interactivity within your projects. Whether you're building alert messages, floating palettes, or dialog boxes, Immedia lets you customize them to your heart's desire. In the next chapter, I'll discuss another very common interface element: buttons. Between buttons and windows (and putting buttons into windows, and so on), you'll be able to create most of the projects you'll need.

Buttons

W HEN YOU BUILD A QUARKIMMEDIA project, one of your jobs is to be a "human interface designer." Designing an interface shapes how someone will *use* your project; that's a very different thing than making your project look good in print. When you get in a car (any car), you immediately know how to use most of the instruments (the gas pedal, the car radio, and so on) because cars, for the most part, have a standardized interface. On the other hand, every multimedia project created today has its own individual interface. The result: it takes twenty minutes just to find your way around.*

Buttons are one method to build a quasi-standard interface into your projects. Everyone knows how to use a button—you click on it (with a mouse, a pen, or your finger, depending on the system you're using). However, while most buttons are simple rectangles, circles, or arrows, you can can create a button in Immedia that looks like anything you want.

As you know, any object can act like a button: when you click on it, something happens. But a real button has several characteristics

---

*I have no doubt that some designers would say that the process of figuring out how to use the project is part of the overall design. This is akin to using grunge fonts—most designs built with this in mind fail horribly.

that make it special, the most obvious of which is that the button changes visually when you click on it. While you can make something look and act kind of like a button by using boxes, it's usually much easier to just use a real button.

Because you're probably itching to jump in and start adding buttons to your projects, we'll start by discussing how you can use the buttons you already have (some come with QuarkImmedia, plus there are dozens more on the *Real World QuarkImmedia* CD-ROM). Then we'll delve deeper and explore how you can make your own custom buttons.

▼ ▼

Using Buttons

Picture boxes, text boxes, and lines are the three types of objects in QuarkXPress, and everything else is built with them. Until now. Buttons are a new type of object in QuarkXPress.

Buttons live in button libraries, which are more or less like normal XPress libraries, for those of you who are familiar with them. You can open a button library just like you open a document (select Open on the File menu, or double-click on the button library from the desktop). Then you can drag buttons from the library out onto your page.

Button Types

In order to keep life interesting and designers on their toes, there are *two* kinds of buttons: simple buttons and on/off buttons. Each of these can also be built with a *disable* feature. Let's take a look.

Simple Buttons. The most basic of buttons is a Simple button (see Figure 6–1). This is also called a "two-state" button because it just goes in and out, on and off, or up and down. The buttons on your telephone and most of the keys on your keyboard work like this.

Simple Buttons with Disable. You can add a third state to Simple buttons, too. This is the Disable state, which gives you the option of

Figure 6–1
Simple buttons

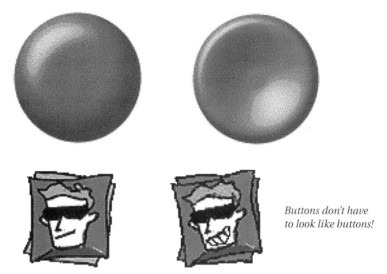

*Buttons don't have
to look like buttons!*

disabling the button (we'll see how later in this chapter, in "Actions to Buttons"). A disabled button doesn't function. People can click on it all day, and nothing happens. For instance, if you don't want a user to click the Next Page button until they've completed a task on the current page, you might disable the Next Page button at first.

If the button does not have a third state (if it's not a Simple with Disable type of button), you can't use the Disable Button action to disable it (you can use the Disable Object action, however; see "Actions to Buttons," later in this chapter). This third state doesn't have to actually look any different, though it's useful if it does. You might make the disabled button grayed out, or perhaps draw an "X" through it.

On/Off Buttons. If a Simple button is like the flush handle on a toilet (just up and down), an On/Off button is like the faucet on your sink—you can turn it on, and it stays on until you turn it off. Another example is the Caps Lock key on your keyboard—press it once and it stays down; press it again and it returns to its original position. On/Off buttons are four-state buttons (see Figure 6–2).

▶ **Off Up.** This is an On/Off button's normal, default state, before you do anything to it.

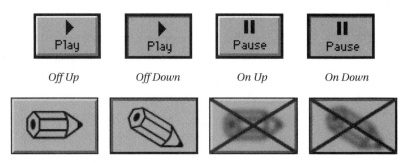

Figure 6–2
On/Off buttons

Off Up   Off Down   On Up   On Down

▶ **Off Down.** When you click an On/Off button, the button first moves to the Off Down state. It stays there as long as you hold down the mouse button.

▶ **On Up.** After you let go of the mouse button, the button moves into an On Up state. In the Caps Lock key example, this is when Caps Lock is turned on.

▶ **On Down.** When you click on the button again, it moves to the On Down state. It stays this way until you lift your finger (or let go of the mouse button, in the case of Immedia buttons). The On Down and Off Down positions of a real-life Caps Lock key look the same, but in QuarkImmedia, they don't have to.

On/Off Buttons with Disable. An On/Off with Disable button has two extra states: On Up Disabled and Off Up Disabled. You can't have a disabled "down" state because disabled buttons don't do anything when clicked. If a button gets disabled while in an "on" position, it changes into an On Up Disabled state. If the button is in a "down" position, it changes into an Off Up Disabled state.

Again, you can only disable On/Off with Disable buttons. If you want to disable an On/Off button, you'll have to change its state to On/Off with Disable in the button library before dragging it onto your page.

Button Libraries

As I said earlier, button libraries are like normal libraries in that you can drag items from the button library palette onto your page. However, the similarities stop there (see Figure 6–3). You cannot

Figure 6-3
Button libraries

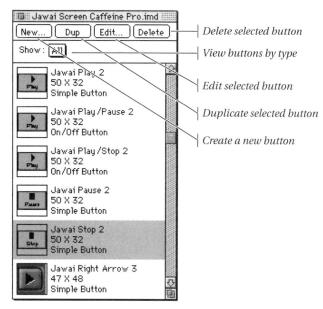

Delete selected button

View buttons by type

Edit selected button

Duplicate selected button

Create a new button

drag a button from your page into a button library. You can give each button a name, but you can't view the buttons by name (you can, however, view them by button type). You can't even drag a button from one library into another library (at least, not in version 1.0). It's incredibly frustrating.

Again, I'll discuss creating and editing buttons in "Making Buttons," later in this chapter.

User Events

Once you've got a button on your page, you can assign an action to each state (two-state buttons can have one or two actions; four-state buttons can have up to four). For example, if you have a simple button, you can assign one action (like running a script) to the Click Down event and another action (like a page turn) to the Click Up event (see Figure 6–4).

I find the act of assigning actions to a button a little confusing because I can't see all the user events at once. Instead, you have to assign actions one event at a time—select an event from the User Event popup menu (Click Up On, Click Down Off, or whatever), then assign an action to it; then select a different event from the popup menu and assign an action to it, and so on. After you assign an action, XPress puts a little checkmark next to that user event (only events that have actions get checkmarks; see Figure 6–5).

Note that you can assign an event sound to a user event (see "User Events" in Chapter 7, *Sound)* even if you don't assign it an action. In this case, XPress won't show you a checkmark (even though the user event *does* do something). This has gotten more than one person in trouble ("Why is it making that sound? I removed the action!").

▼ ▼

Tip: Play/Pause Movies. In the interest of simplifying an interface, it's often nice to minimize the number of buttons on a page. One

Figure 6–4
User Events
popup menu
for buttons

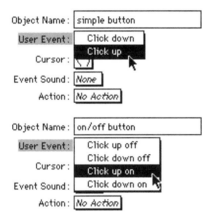

Figure 6–5
User events
and actions

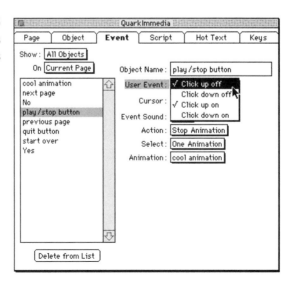

way to do this is to use a single button as a play-and-pause button (this is the way that many CD players work these days). The trick to doing this is the sequence of events attached to an On/Off button. Table 6–1 shows you how.

When you first press down on the mouse button, QuarkImmedia tries to resume the movie. However, if it's not paused (if you haven't started the movie yet), Immedia just ignores the action. When you let go of the mouse button, Immedia tries to play the movie; if it's already playing (if it *did* resume), Immedia ignores this action. Because Immedia conveniently ignores these actions, you don't have to create any fancy scripts.

This trick works for both QuickTime movies and animations (see Chapter 9, *QuickTime Movies*, and Chapter 8, *Animation).*

Table 6–1
Playing and resuming a movie

Button's User Event	Action
Click Up Off	Pause Movie
Click Down Off	Resume Movie
Click Up On	Play Movie
Click Down On	No Action

▼ ▼

Bounding Boxes. As I said, buttons can look round, or triangular or like whatever else your brain can concoct. However, the button always has a rectangular bounding box (see Figure 6–6). Yes, this is annoying, but as Stephen Wright once noted, "You can't have everything. . . . Where would you put it?"

▼ ▼

Tip: Masking Button Areas. If you have a nonrectangular button, you might want to reduce confusion by making sure people don't press it outside of the area that looks like a button. You can do this by drawing polygons over the blank, "non-button" areas (see Figure 6–7). You usually have to change the polygons to movie objects (select Movie on the Object tab of the Immedia palette), though you don't have to specify an actual QuickTime movie in them. When the

Figure 6-6
Button
Bounding boxes

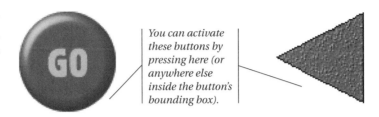

You can activate these buttons by pressing here (or anywhere else inside the button's bounding box).

Figure 6-7
Masking
around buttons

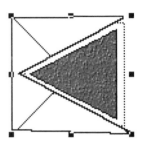

project is engaged, clicking on the polygon won't do anything, but clicking on the uncovered parts of the button will still activate it.

▼ ▼

Button Groups

Sometimes, when you've got several On/Off buttons on your page, you want to make sure that only one of them is turned on at any given time. (Radio buttons in dialog boxes typically work this way; sometimes checkboxes do, too.) You can do this by building a button group.

1. Select the group of buttons (they must all be On/Off or On/Off with Disable buttons).

2. Group them (select Group from the Item menu, or press Command-G).

3. Give the group a name on the Object tab of the QuarkImmedia palette. This is the name of the group, which must be different than any of the button names (see Figure 6–8).

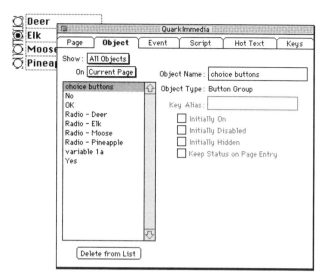

Figure 6-8
Button groups

Immedia now thinks of these buttons as a "button group." When you turn one button on, Immedia automatically turns the others off.

Animated Buttons

We'll take a good hard look at animations in Chapter 8, *Animation*, and at QuickTime movies in Chapter 9, *QuickTime Movies*, but I do want to bring one thing to your attention right here: you can make any animation or movie into a button. The trick is to turn on the Treat as Button option on the Object tab of the Immedia palette. You can then decide whether the animation or movie should act like a Simple button or an On/Off button by choosing one or the other from the popup menu next to the checkbox (see Figure 6–9).

A very interesting thing happens to animations or QuickTime movies when you turn this option on.

▶ If you choose Simple button, the animation or movie runs forward as long as the user holds down the mouse button. When the user lets go of the mouse button, the animation or movie plays in reverse back to the beginning.

▶ If you choose On/Off button, the animation or movie plays from beginning to end when you click the button once. Then when you click the button again, the animation or movie plays in reverse back to the beginning.

Figure 6-9
Animated buttons

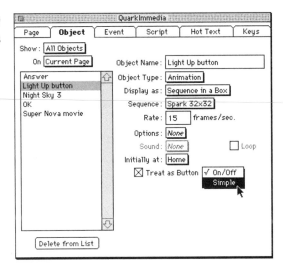

This means that your buttons don't have to look jerky because they only have two or four states. The button can be an entire animation! For instance, there's an animation on the *Real World Quark-Immedia* CD-ROM of a door opening. You can make this a button simply by checking the Treat as Button box option. When you click on the animation, it creaks open. When you click again, it closes.

Animated button actions. As soon as you turn on the Treat as Button option, the whole animation or movie acts like a button. That means you can assign user events and event sounds to it on the Event tab of the Immedia palette. It also means you can run button actions on it (which I discuss in the next section).

▼ ▼

Actions to Buttons

Most people think of buttons as objects that control other events— turning a page, or playing a movie, or whatever. But there are four Immedia actions that control buttons themselves: Button On, Button Off, Button Disable, and Button Enable (see Figure 6–10).

Turning buttons on and off. In most instances, you'll want to let the user control your On/Off buttons, but in some cases, it's useful to

Figure 6–10

Button actions

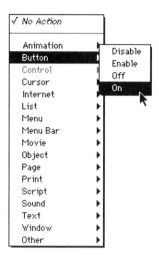

control them from behind the scenes. Let's say you've created an On/Off four-state button that looks like a door—when it's on it looks open, and when it's off it looks closed. Each time you press the door button, it opens or closes, right? You can create another button that shuts the door with the Set Button Off action, or opens the door with the Set Button On action.

These actions simply turn an On/Off button on or off. They do not, however, trigger any actions that you've assigned to the button. For example, if your door button had an event sound that made it creak when you clicked it, you would not hear the creak when your control button opened or closed the door. Button actions and event sounds only happen when someone actually presses the button.

Sometimes you want an On/Off button to start in the "on" position and then give people the option to switch it off. You can do this by checking the Initially On box on the Objects tab of the QuarkImmedia palette (see Figure 6–11).

Disabling buttons. When a button is in a disabled state, you can click on it all you want and nothing will happen. It's like the button is just part of the background. But how does a button become disabled?

▶ You can set a button to be disabled by default by turning on the Initially Disabled checkbox on the Object tab of the QuarkImmedia palette. The button stays disabled until some action enables it.

Figure 6-11
Button options

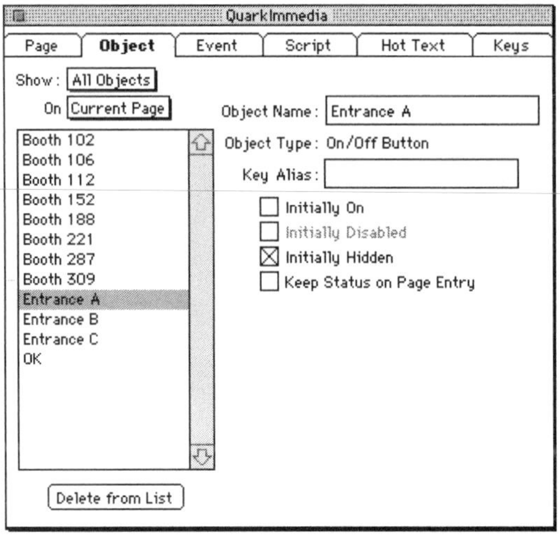

▶ You can enable or disable a button with the Enable Button or Disable Button actions.

Remember that only Simple with Disable buttons or On/Off with Disable buttons can be disabled. You don't have to make the button look any different when it's disabled—though in most circumstances that's useful—but it must be that type of button.

Unfortunately, you cannot disable animated buttons (animations or movies that have the Treat as Button option turned on) or button groups.

▼ ▼

Tip: Disabling Any Kind of Button. You can disable any kind of button—including animations or movies that have the Treat as Button option turned on—with the Disable Object action (see "Object Actions" in Chapter 3, *Building Projects)*. Note that this action does not make a button with a disabled state appear disabled on screen; but it is disabled nonetheless (your user won't be able to click on it).

▼ ▼

Making Buttons

The thing with buttons is that once you use two or three of them, you immediately want to start making your own or customizing the ones you already have. Fortunately, Quark has made it easy to do both of these things—just press New or Edit on the button library palette (you can create a new button library by selecting Button Library from the New submenu (under the File menu; see Figure 6–12). But before you start going hog-wild, let's just take a little walk through the Button Maker.

Figure 6–12
Making a new
button library

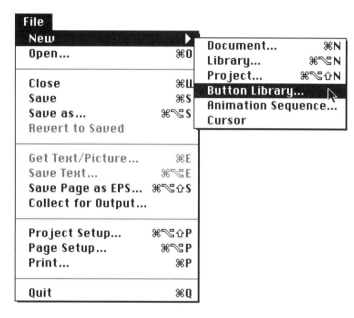

Figure 6–13
Making a new button

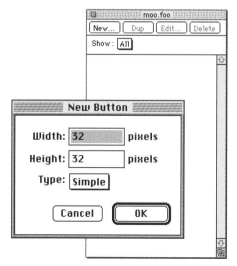

Button Type and Size. When you first create a button (press New on the button library palette), Immedia asks you for two things: frame size and button type (see Figure 6–13). You can create any of the four button types described earlier in this chapter, and at just about any size you want (I've made buttons that fill up an entire 640- by 480-pixel screen, and I've heard talk of buttons bigger than 1,000 by 1,000 pixels). Of course, the size of the button is limited somewhat by how much memory you have allocated to XPress (see "Memory Management" in Chapter 2, *QuarkImmedia Basics)*; if you don't have enough, you might experience crashing or other weirdness.

Don't get too uptight here—if you make a mistake in size or type, you can always change the values in the Button Maker dialog box.

The Button Maker

I don't want to get anyone in trouble, but at least one engineer at Quark has intimated to me that the Button Maker (the dialog box you get when you click New or Edit in a button library; see Figure 6–14) is known internally at Quark as the "paste from Photoshop dialog box." It's not that there aren't cool tools in this dialog box

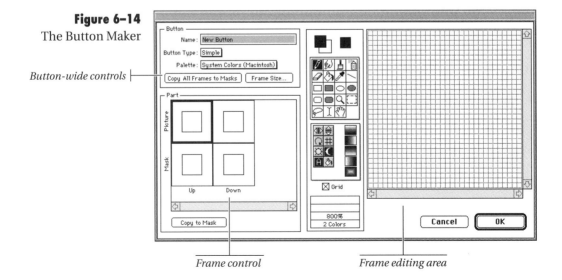

Figure 6–14
The Button Maker

Button-wide controls

Frame control

Frame editing area

(there are), but in general, image editors like Photoshop make creating or editing buttons *much* easier than Immedia does.

Nonetheless, even though I do most of my button building and editing in Photoshop (then cut and paste between the programs), I still use several of the features in this dialog box. In this section, we take a tour around the Button Maker. In the next section, we look at some techniques that involve making buttons with Adobe Photoshop and some other programs.

Button-wide controls. There are three main sections to the dialog box: button-wide controls (just labeled "Button"), frame control (labeled "Part" in the Button Maker), and the frame editing area. In the button-wide controls, you can assign the button's name, change the button size or type, apply a custom palette, or build masks for all the frames (see "Frames," below).

The name you select appears both on the button library palette and as the default name on the Immedia palette's Object and Event tabs. While you can always change it later in the palette, it's always a good idea to use as descriptive a name as possible.

The palette you choose for your button determines which colors you can use in the button. If you paste in pixels (from Photoshop or wherever), the incoming color pixels are mapped to the colors in the button's palette. However, once you drop the button into a project, the project's palette overrides the button's palette. It may look right for a while, but if your button's palette is different from the project's palette, the button's colors will change once you engage. Unless you're using pretty radical color palettes (like 200 shades of blue), or you really need the colors to match, this change won't make too big a difference.

Note that if you change the button's size (by clicking the Frame Size button), Immedia lets you either scale the button up, or—if the new size is smaller—crop it to fit the new size (see Figure 6–15).

Frames. Buttons are made up of two, three, four, or six frames (the term *frame* comes from animations, which I'll discuss in Chapter 8, *Animation)*, depending on the type of button. Each frame is made

Figure 6-15
Changing the
button's size

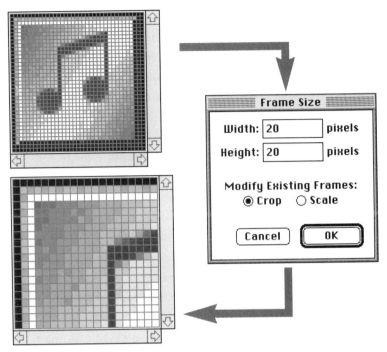

up of two halves: picture and mask. The picture is the entire rectangular button, empty pixels and all. The mask is the part of the button that you don't want people to see.*

The pixels in the picture can be any color in the palette, but the mask can only be black or white (1 bit). This means you cannot create masks with soft anti-aliased edges. If your buttons are anti-aliased in Photoshop before you bring them into the Button Maker, they may end up looking strange on your page (especially if you use the Copy to Mask feature). We'll talk about this more in "Building and Customizing Buttons," later in this chapter.

To make a change to a frame, first click on its picture or mask, then use the editing tools to edit what's already there, or paste something from the Clipboard.

---

*People get very nervous with the word "mask," but it's not a hard concept. If you've ever painted around a window, you already know about masks . . . you just called them "masking tape." You put the masking tape around the areas you didn't want to paint on, then later pulled it off. Masks are the same—anything on the mask acts like masking tape and doesn't let the image show through.

▼ ▼

Tip: Getting White Pixels. You can automatically generate a mask for your button by clicking either Copy to Mask or Copy All Frames to Mask in the Button Maker dialog box. Immedia places a black pixel in the mask to correspond with every non-white pixel in the picture. Even if a pixel is really light gray and looks white on screen, Immedia masks it so that it shows up in the final button.

If you want to include white pixels in your button, make sure you mask them manually using the various editing tools (see "Editing Tools," below).

▼ ▼

Tip: Frame Exchange. Maybe it's just my own problem, but I keep finding myself stuck after having pasted the wrong button into the wrong frame, especially in four- or six-state buttons. There's no good way to switch two frames quickly. Here's one method, however.

1. Select the Picture half of one of the frames (let's call it the "Out" frame).

2. Select all the pixels (double-click on the Marquee tool, or press Command-A), and cut (Command-X).

3. Paste these pixels into the Picture half of any empty frame (the "buffer" frame). If you're working with a two-, three-, or four-state button, and there are no empty frames, change the Button Type popup menu to a type with more frames.

4. Select the pixels in the other frame (let's call it the "In" frame), cut them, and paste them into the now-empty Out frame.

5. Select all the pixels in the buffer frame, cut them, and paste them into the now-empty In frame.

Note that you can change the Button Type popup menu without worrying about losing your frames. If you have an On/Off button (four-state) and accidentally change it to a Simple button, Immedia doesn't throw away the other two frames. When you change back to an On/Off button, those states are still there.

▼ ▼

Editing tools

Of the 33 tools in the Button Maker's frame-editing section (see Figure 6–16), I find myself only rarely using more than seven or eight of them. But, again, I do most of my creation work in Photoshop. Quark has provided most of the drawing tools you'd want, though the interface is sometimes less than optimal. Here's a quick rundown on each of the tools and how you'd want to use them (or not).

Foreground/background color. The overlapping square (foreground color) at the top of the tools lets you control which color you paint with (just click on it and hold down the mouse button; see Figure 6–17). The underlying square (background color) determines the color you get if you erase pixels. If you Option-click on either swatch, it reverts to its default (white or black).

Figure 6–16
Editing in the
Button Maker

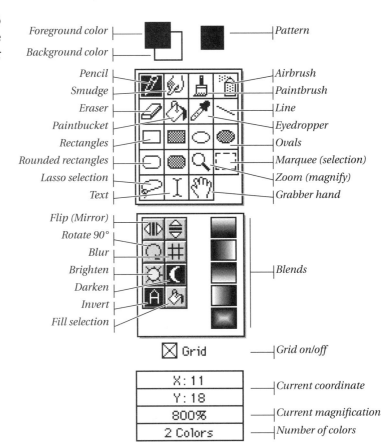

Foreground color
Background color
Pencil
Smudge
Eraser
Paintbucket
Rectangles
Rounded rectangles
Lasso selection
Text
Pattern
Airbrush
Paintbrush
Line
Eyedropper
Ovals
Marquee (selection)
Zoom (magnify)
Grabber hand

Flip (Mirror)
Rotate 90°
Blur
Brighten
Darken
Invert
Fill selection
Blends

Grid on/off

X: 11
Y: 18
800%
2 Colors

Current coordinate
Current magnification
Number of colors

Painting pattern. Back in the good ol' days, when the Macintosh was just a wee liddle lad, Apple included little pattern-painting routines in the operating system. It's so easy for developers to use these routines that for the past ten years almost every paint program has had them. Immedia's Button Maker is no different (see Figure 6–18). Unfortunately, they're almost used for creating really ugly designs that scream, "I'm a novice!" The exceptions are the various

Figure 6–17
Changing colors

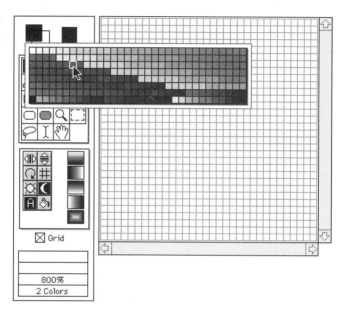

Figure 6–18
Painting patterns

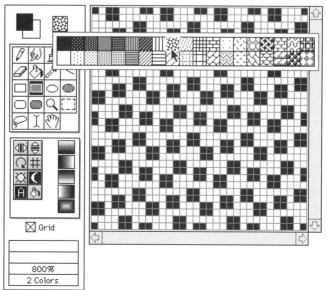

flat-tint patterns, which can come in handy when you need a tint of a color in a limited color palette. If you Option-click on this swatch, it reverts back to a solid color.

Pencil tool. The Pencil tool appears to be the most basic of tools, but it has its tricky side. Typically, if you click on a pixel with the Pencil tool, that pixel changes to the foreground color. The tricky part is that if you click on any pixel that *is* the foreground color, it becomes the background color. This is especially useful when editing a mask, because without even changing colors, black pixels become white, and white pixels become black.

To change the size of the Pencil, click and hold down the mouse button until you get a little popup palette (see Figure 6–19; this works for the other tools, like Eraser, Paintbrush, and Line).

Smudge tool. Smudge is one of the tools I never use. It works just like Photoshop's Smudge tool (click on an area and drag to blend it with the surrounding colors), but I just don't find a need for it. If you think it's invaluable to your work, e-mail me and let me know why.

Paintbrush tool. The Paintbrush is like the Pencil tool, but without the foreground/background trickiness. Also, the Paintbrush tool paints with a rounded brush.

Figure 6–19
Changing tool size

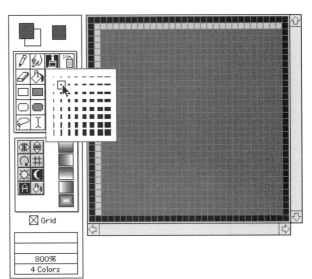

Airbrush tool. The Airbrush tool is like the Paintbrush, but it applies much more diffuse, dithered colors (I assume that Quark decided to use a spray-paint can instead of an airbrush for the icon for trademark reasons). The longer you hold it in one area, the more saturated the color gets.

Eraser tool. I use the Eraser tool all the time, especially for cleaning up large portions of masks. If you click on the tool and hold down, you can change the size of the eraser. If you want drastic action, you can double-click on the Eraser tool to erase the entire frame. Remember that the Eraser tool erases to the background color, not necessarily to white.

Paintbucket tool. When you click on a pixel with the Paintbucket tool, the Button Maker looks around for other pixels of the same color. It then fills them all in with the foreground color. The pixels must be horizontally or vertically adjacent—pixels that only touch at their corners aren't included. Again, this is useful for cleaning up masks or filling flat areas with solid colors.

Eyedropper tool. If you want to paint with a color that is already used in the frame, you can "pick up" a pixel's color as your foreground color with the Eyedropper tool. I rarely take the trouble to select this tool; instead, I hold down the Command key to get it.

Line tool. Need a straight line? Just click and drag with the Line tool. You're also supposed to be able to hold down the Shift key to constrain it horizontally, vertically, or to a 45-degree angle . . . didn't work in the original release (as of this writing). Oh well. 'Nuff said.

Rectangles/ Circles/ Rounded-corners. You can draw a solid or filled rectangle, an oval, or a rounded-corner rectangle* with one of six tools provided for your pleasure. I rarely use anything but the Rectangle tool.

---

*I avoid rounded-corner rectangles like the plague, as my design sense shouts out "desktop publishing" whenever I see one. However, they do seem to be all the rage these days, and they do make pretty good buttons.

Zoom tool. Here's another tool I rarely select, but often use. If you hold down the Control key, you automatically get the Zoom tool, and can zoom in on your button up to 1,600 percent. If you hold down both the Control and Option keys, the zoom tool "reverses," and you can zoom out to 100 percent (no smaller, unfortunately).

Marquee tool and Lasso tool. The Marquee and Lasso tools let you select areas in your button. You can then move, copy, delete, fill, blur, invert, rotate, brighten, or darken that selected area. Note that if you want to select all the pixels, it's probably faster to press Command-A than to use the Marquee tool.

▼ ▼

Tip: Floating Pixels. When you move a selection, Immedia "cuts out" those pixels and leaves a white (or background color) patch where they were. However, if you hold down the Option key, the pixels are copied rather than moved, so there's no bald patch left over. If you want to "float" a selection before flipping or rotating it, Option-click once on the selection before applying those effects.

▼ ▼

Type. While typography has always been one of QuarkXPress's strongest points, it is certainly *not* one of the strong points of the Button Maker. In fact, it's so painful to use that I would rather copy the whole button out of the Button Maker and paste it into Photoshop to handle the type there. However, if you insist on using it, here's what you do.

1. Select a font, size, and style from the Style menu (it's one of the few menus not grayed out while you edit buttons).

2. Click on an area with the Type tool.

3. Start typing. While you're typing—and until you select a different tool or click someplace else—you can change the color, typeface, size, or style of the text.

4. Keep your fingers on Command-Z. You'll often need to undo several times until you get it right.

Grabber hand tool. Here's the third tool that I don't select, but often use. If you have a large button, or have zoomed in so that the entire button does not fit in the editing window, you can display different parts of the button by clicking and dragging with the grabber hand. Instead of selecting this tool, I hold down the Option key at any time to get it.

Flip Horizontal and Flip Vertical buttons. When you click on the Flip Horizontal or Flip Vertical buttons, the selection flips (or if nothing is selected, it flips the entire frame).

Rotate button. Each time you press the Rotate button, the Button Maker rotates the selection (or the entire frame) 90 degrees clockwise. If the frame size isn't big enough to fit the rotated selection, it just clips those pixels off (don't forget Command-Z).

Blur button. Clicking the Blur button blurs the selection (or the entire frame). If you've got a large button, this can take more than just a moment, so be patient. I don't often use Blur, but I have seen some nice effects using Blur to signal a disabled button. If you don't understand this tool's tic-tac-toe icon, you're not alone. Knowing the engineers at Quark, it probably has something to do with math, but it beats me.

Brighten and Darken buttons. The Brighten and Darken buttons are problematic. While they seem like they'd be really useful, in reality I find them less than optimal. The problem is that brightening or darkening pixels within a specific color palette is really complicated. In general, if the image was originally in Photoshop's RGB mode, you'd be better off going back to that original, darkening it there, then reconverting to an indexed-color palette.

Note that darkening a frame darkens everything, including the white pixels (which usually become gray), and that clicking the Brighten button does *not* return you to where you were before darkening.

Invert button. The "A" icon for the Invert button is just about as obscure as the icon for the Blur tool. However, the effect can be just as useful. The Invert button flips the color value for each pixel in the image. But what does that mean? If it's a grayscale image, it's easy: black becomes white, 10-percent gray becomes 90-percent gray, and so on. But with color images, it's much more confusing, and the results are almost never predictable. I like using this when I just want a really wild, far-out effect, especially for the "in" state of a Simple button (see "Customizing Buttons," later in this chapter).

Fill Background button. The button with a paintbucket icon is the Fill Background tool. One click of this button fills a selection (or the entire frame, if nothing's selected) with the foreground color. I'm embarrassed to reveal that until I figured out what this tool was, I spent way too long trying to fill frames using the rectangle tool. No longer! This is much faster.

Blend tools. There are five blend tools in the Button Maker, each generating a different type of blend. One click fills the selection or the entire frame with the blend. The blends always use the foreground and background colors you've selected, picking out other "in-between" colors from the palette as well as it can.

▼ ▼

Tip: Blends and Memory. Beware: building a blend can take a lot of memory. Behind the scenes, Immedia is actually building a high-quality 32-bit blend, then asking the operating system to convert it to the 8-bit color palette. If your blend is very large (hundreds of pixels), this could take up a lot of memory in the background. And if you don't have that memory allocated to QuarkXPress (see "Memory Management" in Chapter 2, *QuarkImmedia Basics)*, you could have troubles. Either it won't blend at all, or you'll get a rougher blend with banding in it.

▼ ▼

Grid checkbox. The Grid checkbox under the editing tools lets you turn the gridlines in the editing frame on and off. I rarely turn this option off, but I suppose it's a matter of preference.

Information. Below all the tools and the Grid checkbox is a feedback area that tells you what pixel coordinates you're currently at (this is helpful for returning to the same pixel later), your zoom percentage, and the number of colors in the button (this counts all the colors in all the frames).

▼ ▼

Building and Customizing Buttons

I've put dozens of buttons on the CD-ROM in the back of this book, Quark has given you many more, and by this time you may have started creating your own. But it seems like no matter how many buttons you have on hand, you need one that's just a little different from them all. In this section, I discuss some techniques for building and customizing buttons.

I have little doubt that after playing with these ideas for a few days you'll say, "Hey, I figured out a much better way to do this." Everyone has their own techniques, and this section is not meant to be fully comprehensive (I could write an entire book on buttons alone). But when you do come up with new, cool methods, I'd love to hear about them (my address is at the end of the book).

What's on the CD-ROM

The buttons on the CD-ROM are saved in several forms, each of which I've included so that you can customize them to your needs (see Chapter 16, *Real World QuarkImmedia CD-ROM)*. Note that all the buttons are copyrighted by their creators, so while you can use them all you want, you cannot give or sell them to other people, even if you customize them.*

▶ **QuarkImmedia button libraries.** The button libraries are organized in folders by button shape (round, square, rectangular, and so on), aliased or anti-aliased (see discussion of

---

*You can, of course, give away or sell projects in which you've used the buttons; you just shouldn't give away or sell the button files themselves.

anti-aliasing in "Editing Buttons," below), size, and color. Yes, that's a lot of folders to wade through, but I hope it'll save you time finding exactly what you need.

▶ **Photoshop files.** Each button in a library was built from an original Adobe Photoshop file, which is saved as an RGB file. You can open these files in almost any image editor (like Adobe Photoshop, Macromedia XRes, or whatever). To create Immedia buttons from them, you'll need to copy and paste the buttons from the image editor into the Button Maker (I'm hoping that Quark or some XTension developer will make this process easier in the near future).

▶ **Illustrator files.** Many of the Photoshop files were built from Adobe Illustrator documents (I step through this process in just a moment). You shouldn't have to change these files, but I've included them anyway.

▶ **Three-dimensional files.** Some of the Illustrator files, in turn, were actually generated by Adobe Dimensions, Adobe's 3-D modeling package. Others were built in other programs. When possible, I've included the original documents for those programs so that you can customize them or see how I did it.

I've also included several sample files that show some interesting possibilities for customizing buttons. They are, however, all in Photoshop format, as many of them use the Layers feature.

Editing Buttons

When it comes time to build your own buttons, you can start from scratch or use some of the tools I've provided on the CD-ROM. Let's take a look at how to start with the files on the disc first, then move into some techniques that use only two ingredients: Photoshop and your imagination.

Opening files in Photoshop. If you want to edit a button by adding a word or a symbol, changing the color, or adding texture, you can open the Photoshop files directly from the disc. When you're finished editing the buttons, make sure you flatten any layers before copying and pasting the button from Photoshop to the Button Maker (you may want to convert the image to indexed color on Photoshop's Mode menu, too).

If you need to change the size of the button, however, you may want to open one of the Illustrator files on the disc (or any other Illustrator-type file*) in Photoshop. When you open the file, Photoshop asks you what size you want it to be, then rasterizes it (changes it from lines into pixels; see Figure 6–20).

A note on the Rasterize Adobe Illustrator Format dialog box: You typically want to keep the resolution of the button set to 72 ppi, and—unless you're working with only grayscale images—open the image in RGB mode. The button still appears as a grayscale image, but you can then colorize it any way you want.

Of course, you can also use the Place or Paste features to rasterize an Illustrator-type file in Photoshop, but they're only applicable when a file is already open. Most of the time I find it easier just to start from scratch by using Open on the file menu.

Figure 6–20
Opening Illustrator
files in Photoshop

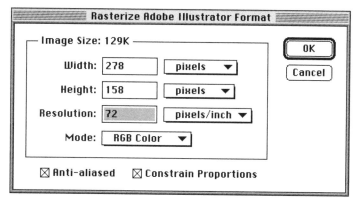

Aliasing versus anti-aliasing. There's one other big decision to make when you open EPS files (other than pixel dimensions, resolution, and color mode): whether to anti-alias the image or not. If your button is going to sit on top of one or more colors in your Immedia project, it's best not to anti-alias the button's edges. Otherwise, you'll get a halo effect.

---

*If you're like me, and use Macromedia FreeHand for many tasks, you can still do this—just export the files in Illustrator 1.1 format first.

The exception is when you can build the background color or texture into the button itself (see Figure 6–21). This way, you're anti-aliasing to the proper background and you won't get a halo. Remember that the edges of rectangular buttons never need anti-aliasing, because they have no diagonals or curves in them.

Figure 6–21
To anti-alias or not

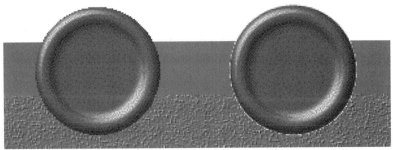

Aliased
Looks great over colors and
textures, but jaggy over white.

Anti-aliased to white
Looks great over white but
jaggy over other colors.

▼ ▼

Tip: Aliasing Anti-aliased Files. If you don't want your button to be anti-aliased because you're concerned about halos, you may still want to consider turning on the Anti-alias checkbox in Photoshop's Rasterize Adobe Illustrator Format dialog box. The reason: if your button has detail on its inside (specular highlights, text, or whatever), you probably *do* want that stuff to be anti-aliased. The problem then is how to un-anti-alias the button's edges. Here's one way you can do it in Photoshop (see Figure 6–22).

1. Open the Illustrator-type file as usual, with the Anti-alias option turned on.

2. Load the button's transparency mask. You can do this in the Load Selection dialog box (choose Load from Photoshop's Select menu), or by pressing Command-Option-T. This selects all the pixels that are not transparent (for more information on masks, see the book I wrote with Bruce Fraser, *Real World Photoshop 3*).

3. Switch to Quick Mask mode (click on the Quick Mask icon on the Tool palette, or press Q).

Figure 6–22
Removing
anti-aliased edges

The original button

*Select the transparency mask
and switch to Quick Mask mode.*

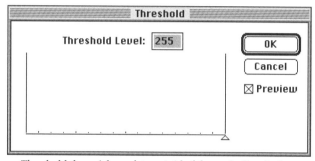

Threshold the quick mask to get rid of the anti-aliased edges.

*Switch out of Quick Mask mode
and invert the selection.*

*Press delete to remove all the
anti-aliased edge pixels.*

4. Use Threshold (under the Image menu, or press Command-T) to push all the pixels to black or white. Here's where you have to make a decision: if the transparent pixels are darkened

in Quick Mask mode, use a Threshold value of 255. If the button's pixels are darkened, use a Threshold value of 1. (Either type of pixel might be darkened, depending on how you have set up Quick Mask Options.)

5. Switch out of Quick Mask mode (press Q again).

6. Invert the Selection (choose Inverse from the Select menu).

7. Choose Clear from the Edit menu (or press Delete). This deletes all the gray pixels from the edges of the button.

The result: the button's edge pixels are aliased, and the internal pixels are anti-aliased. This technique seems long and complicated, but it actually only takes about thirty seconds to complete.

▼ ▼

Adding type and pictures. Once you've opened a grayscale button in Photoshop, you can colorize it in one of many ways—my favorite is the Hue/Saturation feature from the Adjust submenu under Photoshop's Image menu (don't forget to turn on the Colorize option).

From there, creativity is your only limitation. Here's one suggestion, though: When you add text or graphics to your buttons, try using Photoshop's Layers feature as much as possible. That way, you can always change your mind or even create multiple buttons from the same base.

▼ ▼

Tip: Colorizing Many Buttons. When you're working with buttons, you rarely need to colorize just one. If you want to apply the same color to two or more images, you can expedite matters by holding down the Option key when you select Hue/Saturation from the Adjust submenu (or press Command-Option-U). This tells Photoshop to open the dialog box with the same values that you used the last time you were in this dialog box. This technique also works with most of the other items on the Adjust submenu, including both the Levels and Curves features.

▼ ▼

Tip: Colorizing with Layers. You can use layers to colorize your grayscale buttons in Photoshop, too.

1. Create a new layer above the button's layer on the Layers palette, and set the Mode popup menu to Color.

2. Set your foreground color to the color you want the button.

3. Fill the entire layer with the color (press Command-Delete).

4. Make the two layers a *clipping group* by Option-clicking on the gray line between them on the Layers palette (see Figure 6–23). This makes the transparency mask for the button layer into a mask for the color layer, so the transparent areas of the button stay transparent.

Now you can tweak the color using Hue/Saturation, Levels or Curves, or you can fill the layer with an entirely new color.

▼ ▼

Tip: Adding Texture to Buttons. You can use the same clipping-group technique in Photoshop to add texture to your buttons. After adding the new layer, set the Mode popup menu to Overlay. Then fill the new layer with some sort of texture, and Option-click between the layers to create the clipping group.

▼ ▼

Copying and pasting to Immedia. The last step in creating the button (usually after converting it to indexed color mode, which we discussed back in "Pictures" in Chapter 3, *Building Projects)* is, of course, getting the buttons into an Immedia button library. As I said earlier, this is (unfortunately) a case of copying and pasting as many times as it takes. One thing to remember, though: make sure that Export Clipboard is turned on in Photoshop's More Preferences dialog box (press Command-K). When I do prepress work, I almost always keep the Export Clipboard turned off because it can cause

Figure 6–23
Creating a
clipping group

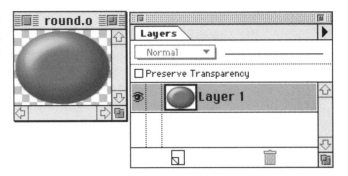

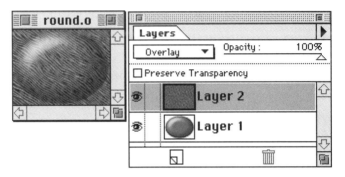

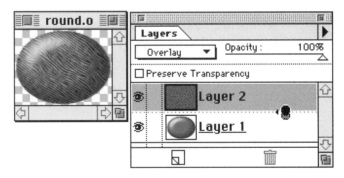

slowdowns and crashes with large files. But it must be turned on in order to get those buttons out of Photoshop and into Quark-Immedia's Button Maker.

Button Tips, Tricks, and Tonics

As I said earlier, it seems like everyone has their own favorite way to make a button these days. Here are just a few ways that I've found particularly easy, useful, and efficient.

Lighting Effects filter. Here's a quick way to make a rectangular button using Photoshop's Lighting Effects filter. To tell you the truth, I still don't entirely understand why it works—but it does, and that's what's important.

1. Make a new document in Photoshop just the size that you want the button.

2. Paste in a texture, an image, or a color.

3. Select All (press Command-A).

4. Turn the selection into a border by choosing Border from the Modify submenu under the Item menu. The width of the border depends on how large your button is; make it about 10 or 15 percent of the button size, so if the button is 100 pixels wide, type "10" or "15" in the Border dialog box.

5. Save this selection (use Save from the Select menu, or press the Selection icon in the Channels palette).

6. Deselect (Command-D).

7. Select Lighting Effects from the Render submenu under the Filter menu.

8. In the Lighting Effects dialog box, choose #4 from the Texture Channel popup menu (see Figure 6–24). Then adjust the various sliders in the dialog box until the preview displays something that looks approximately like what you want. The White is High checkbox makes the light appear as if it's coming from a different direction.

9. Press OK. If you don't like the effect, undo it, and reapply with different settings.

If you want a soft, rounded-edge button instead, omit step 6—don't deselect your bordered selection.

The biggest problem with this technique is that while it's really easy to make buttons look like they're "out," I can't find any good way to make buttons that look like they're pressed in.

Figure 6-24
Lighting Effects in
Adobe Photoshop

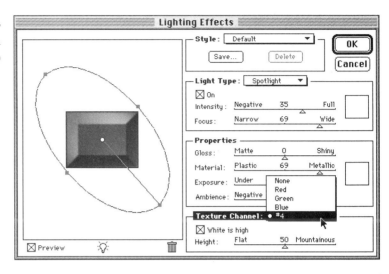

Filters. If you need to make a lot of buttons in Photoshop, your best bet is to buy a third-party plug-in package that does buttons. There are several out there that are good.

▶ The Black Box from Alien Skin Software

▶ PhotoTools from Extensis Corporation

▶ WildRiverSSK from Datastream (this includes an updated, commercial version of DekoBoko—an old shareware product)

There may be more by the time you read this; it seems like everyone wants to get into the Photoshop plug-in market. Only Extensis, however, has built their bevel technology (which can make buttons) into a QuarkXTension (called QX-Tools). That means you can build buttons right in XPress without having to bother with Photoshop at all (I've put demo copies of WildRiverSSK, PhotoTools, and QX-Tools on the CD-ROM at the back of the book; see Chapter 16, *The Real World QuarkImmedia CD-ROM).*

Other programs. You can use a host of other programs to build buttons, as well. For instance, Specular's 3D Web Workshop makes building and editing buttons a breeze. Sure, the program is designed for people who are authoring for the World Wide Web, but who cares? It builds 72-dpi buttons, animations, and graphics quickly and easily.

Other programs you should consider (this is clearly not a complete list) include Adobe Dimensions, Adobe TextureMaker, Strata Studio Pro, and Ray Dream Designer.

▼ ▼

Simple Interfaces

You can build all sorts of interfaces for your projects in Quark-Immedia, but if your audience can't figure out how to navigate through them, all your hard work will be for naught. One solution is to use buttons; unless your buttons are really obscure, almost everyone will know how to use them. Even better, buttons have a built-in ability to give you feedback when you press them.

In the next chapter, we'll explore a less interactive (yet extremely important) element of multimedia projects: sound.

Sound

WE HUMANS TAKE IN THE VAST majority of sensory information around us through our eyes, but we often forget how much we take in through our ears. A door closing behind us, a telephone ringing in the other room, the click of a radio turning on—without these aural cues, we'd lose out on a world of information. And just as sound plays a significant role in our lives, it can play just as important a role in our multimedia presentations.

When you think of sound in multimedia, you probably think of fast-paced video-game music playing in the background; but you can use sound in a number of subtle and important ways to enhance your presentation without creating a Nintendo nightmare or a Sega splash.

Digital sound is not a complicated subject, but a little ignorance can go a long way toward making your life miserable. So in this chapter, we'll first take a look at what sound on a computer is all about, and then see how you can use it in your Immedia projects. By the end, you'll be ready to roll the sound files.

▼ ▼

Digitized Sound

If you don't understand the basics of digitized sound, you're in for an Extra-Strength Tylenol evening next time a deadline comes around. Fortunately, these basics don't take long to master.

In the real world, we hear sound because something vibrates. Those vibrations make the air vibrate, which vibrates in our ears. Really deep sounds make long, slow vibrations, and high squeaky sounds make short, quick vibrations. For instance, my washing machine starts off churning slowly, making long, slow vibrations that sound like low-pitched grumbles. Later, when it's in spin mode, it vibrates really fast (which sounds like a high-pitched whine).

Similarly, the sound system in your living room works by vibrating a piece of paper in the speaker. (It's hard to imagine all that great sound coming from paper rattling, but it's true!)

Getting it in a computer. There are things called analog-to-digital converters, which—like our ears—convert sound vibrations into electrical signals, and then—unlike our ears—convert those signals into zeros and ones. The numbers can be easily stored on a computer hard drive or a compact disc. Later (when you play the sound), another converter reads the zeros and ones and converts them back into sounds we can hear.

Just Like Bitmaps

When you scan a photograph, the scanner takes thousands of tiny samples of the image: one is black, one is white, one is light gray, one is dark gray, and so on. This is called "digitizing" the image. After each sample is saved to disk, you've got a bitmapped image that you can print out or see on your screen.

Digitizing sound is basically the same as digitizing an image. The "scanner" (the analog-to-digital converter) takes tiny slices of the sound, one after the other. It then looks at each slice, figures out the vibration rate and loudness at each moment, and saves that information to disk as a set of zeros and ones. Later, various programs let you manipulate that information or play it back.

The key to working with digitized sound efficiently is to understand the information that is saved to disk.

Resolution. You know that when you print a 300-ppi (pixel per inch) scan, it looks better and less coarse than a 50-ppi scan does, right? That's because the scanner actually took more samples per inch— so it picked up more details. With sound, what's important is how many samples per second you've captured. People talk about samples per second as *hertz* (Hz), and thousands of samples per second as *kilohertz* (kHz).

High-quality CD music is recorded at 44,100 samples per second (44.1 kHz). This ensures that every nuance of vibration is captured.* That's a lot of data! In fact, each minute of CD-quality sound takes up about 10.5 MB of disk space.

Lower sampling rates are almost always sufficient in multimedia work—for two reasons.

▶ Most computers have dinky speakers that can't reproduce rich, high-resolution sounds anyway.

▶ Even if they've got good speakers, the computers sometimes can't process that amount of data quickly enough to make it play smoothly. For instance, playing sound over the Internet or from a computer's CD-ROM drive can be pretty slow— you'd better use lower resolutions.

Other typical sampling rates are 22.05 kHz, 11.025 kHz, or even 5.5 kHz. The lower the resolution, the fewer high notes are captured, and the more twangy the sound becomes. Unless you've got great speakers, you probably won't notice any difference between 44.1 and 22.05 kHz. And while 11.025 kHz may sound fine on a small

---

* For those who care: the highest sounds we can hear vibrate at about 20 kHz (20,000 cycles per second). In a perfect world, you could just sample at 20 kHz and still capture everything. However, as it turns out, you can't. The laws of physics require you to sample at twice that rate—44.1 kHz—in order to capture those really high notes.

computer speaker, if you hook up good, amplified speakers to the computer, it'll sound pretty rough. 5.5 kHz is like a bad telephone connection, but sometimes it's all you can use (I discuss why in just a moment).

▼ ▼

Tip: Sample High, Resample Low. When possible, try to record your sound at 44.1 kHz. Later, you can use third-party software—like Macromedia's SoundEdit 16, Wave's WaveConvert, or SndConverterPro—or Immedia's compression (see "Compression" in Chapter 14, *Exporting*) to downsample to a more reasonable rate. The reason: you'll have more flexibility and control over the sound, and you can resample for different uses. For example, if you're making a CD-ROM, but are also planning on exporting your project for the Internet, you can compress the same sound at two different resolutions. On the other hand, if you know you're going to do only one thing with the sound, it's often fine just to sample at the rate at which you'll be using it.

▼ ▼

Bit depth. Just as important as the sampling rate is the amount of information stored about each sample (called *bit depth*). Each pixel in a digitized black-and-white line-art image is described with only one bit of information: black (0) or white (1). In a 2-bit image, each pixel is described with two zeros or ones, and the result is four levels of gray: black (00), dark gray (01), light gray (10), and white (11). Eight-bit images can contain up to 256 levels of gray.

If you only saved one bit of information for each sample of digitized sound, you'd just be saving static—each sample would simply be "sound on" or "sound off." Most sound is recorded at 16 bits per sample—that means each sample can be one of 65,536 different steps in the sound waveform. In most multimedia applications, however, you don't need that kind of fidelity, and eight bits per sample (256 different sounds) is acceptable.

Note that when you downsample from 16-bit sound to 8-bit sound, you often introduce a significant amount of distortion or noise in the background. While you may not notice this in hard-driving rock music, a soft classical piece may be damaged by the conversion. Many sound-editing programs provide tools that handle downsampling bit depth better than Immedia does.

Channels. When you listen to stereo sound on two speakers, each speaker is being fed different information—you're literally playing two different sound channels at the same time, each through a different speaker. In most music, however, the two channels overlap to create a richer ambiance than if you heard just one.

The opposite of stereo sound is monaural sound—only one sound comes out of the speaker (or speakers). If you're playing a multimedia project on a computer with only one speaker, stereo sound won't help you any. But if you're playing the sound through a larger, amplified sound system, you can create great effects by using stereo sound.

As we'll see in a moment, however, the difference between stereo and monaural sound is significant when it comes to file size.

▼ ▼

Tip: Low Res for Clicks and Beeps. It's all very well and good to want the very best, but when it comes to clicks, beeps, and other short special-effect sounds, there's just no reason to use high resolution. A click is a click, whether you've recorded it in stereo at 16-bit 44 kHz, or at 8-bit 22 kHz. Not that I'd tell you what to do; I just want to encourage you to think about each of your sounds and decide what's best for them *and* for your project.

▼ ▼

File size. The more data you've sampled, the larger the file size on your disk. And because sound has to be played back in a specific amount of time, the rate at which you can move data from your hard drive or CD to your computer's memory is vital.

Let's say that a one-second sound file has 180 K of data. That means you've got to transfer 180 K per second in order to play that sound properly, right? A CD-ROM drive can transfer at this speed, so you shouldn't have a problem. However, if you're playing the project on the Internet with a 28.8 Kbps modem, you've got troubles: you can only transfer two or three K per second. That means it's going to take over a minute to play that single one-second sound.

This is why if you're running the project on a slow computer, a slow disk drive, or a slow network, the difference between a 16-bit 44.1 kHz stereo sound and an 8-bit 11 kHz monaural sound can be the difference between the life and death of your project. On the other hand, if you know that your project will be played on a fast computer with good speakers, you can really pack a wallop with the higher-quality sounds.

The important thing to remember is that when you increase resolution, bit depth, or channels, you *double* the size of the file. A 44.1 kHz sound file is twice as big as one at 22.05 kHz. A 16-bit sound file is twice as big as an 8-bit sound file. A stereo sound is twice as big as a monaural sound (see Table 7–1).

Compression. If you've got a large sound file, how do you make it smaller? The zeros and ones that make up a sound file can be compressed down to even more compact forms in two ways.

▶ **Resampling.** This actually strips out data. For example, you can downsample a 44.1 kHz sound to a 22.05 kHz sound by throwing away every other sample. You can get the same reduction in file size by downsampling 16-bit sound to 8-bit sound. Sure, you'll lose a little fidelity; but in many sounds, you'd hardly know the difference.

▶ **Compression.** There are mathematical algorithms that can compact data into smaller chunks, and then later decompress the data so that it's whole again. My favorite example is socks: you can stare into your sock drawer and say you have "one black sock and one black sock, and one red sock and one red sock"; or you can say, "I've got one pair of black socks and one pair of red socks." In the latter case, you've compressed four pieces of information into two pieces.

The problem with compressing sound is that it has to be decompressed before you play it. This takes a computer a lit-

	Resolution	Bit depth	Channels	File size (MB/minute)	Data rate (KB/second)
Table 7–1 Sound file size and required data rate	5.5 kHz	8	mono	0.33	5.5
		16 *	mono	0.66	11.0
	11.025 kHz	8	mono	0.66	11.0
		16	mono	1.32	22.1
	22.05 kHz	8	mono	1.32	22.1
		16	mono	2.64	44.1
		16	stereo	5.29	88.2
	44.1 kHz	8	mono	2.64	44.1
			stereo	5.29	88.2
		16	mono	5.29	88.2
			stereo	10.50	176.4

tle while, so if you run your project on a slow computer, the sound may skip, or not play exactly when you want it to.

▶ **Combination.** You can also use software to both compact and resample sound data at the same time. This often results in files that sound better than if they were simply resampled, but they must still be decompressed.

I'll discuss how you can resample and compress sounds in QuarkImmedia in Chapter 14, *Exporting.*

File Formats

Just as you can save the same scanned photograph as a PICT, TIFF, or EPS file, you can save a digitized sound to disk in one of several formats. QuarkImmedia imports and plays five types of sound files.

▶ **SND.** Most sounds on the Macintosh are saved in the SND format; it's the format used for System sounds (the kind of sounds you can put in your System file). This is the format that I most often use with Immedia. One benefit: you can double-click on the sound file from the desktop to make the System

---

*There's no reason to use 16-bit sound when the resolution is so low; I just included it for the sake of completeness.

play the sound (if you do this, remember that you can stop the sound from playing by pressing Command-period).

▶ **AIFF.** Apple developed AIFF (Audio Interchange File Format) for sounds longer than a beep, a click, or a whirr. For instance, when you save a track from an audio CD to disk using FWB's CD-ROM Toolkit, it automatically saves the sound in the AIFF format. You can then import it directly into an Immedia project. You can also open AIFF files from within Apple's freeware SimplePlayer utility to convert them to QuickTime format.

▶ **AU.** If you download sounds from the Internet, the file names will often have a ".au" suffix. These sound files are technically called µLaw ("mu-law"), but people also call them "ay-yoo" files. These sound files show up all the time on Unix-based computers—like those used for many Internet servers—but you *don't* have to use this format if you're creating Internet projects. µLaw files have a 2:1 compression, so they're smaller than AIFF files, but they suffer from some sound degradation because of it.

▶ **WAV.** The wav ("wave") format is standard on Windows-based computers (Microsoft designed it). I'd still rather use SND.

▶ **QuickTime.** You can also save sounds on the audio track of a QuickTime movie. In fact, you can save a QuickTime movie that doesn't even have any images—just sounds! Because Immedia is so flexible when it comes to importing and playing sounds, there's not much reason to save them in Quick-Time format unless you're using General MIDI soundtracks (see the tip below).

▼ ▼

Tip: General MIDI QuickTime Files. Bitmapped images make pictures one pixel at a time, and it takes thousands of pixels to make an image of anything, even a basic geometric shape. However, object-oriented graphics—like those written in PostScript—simply describe shapes on a page. For instance, you can just tell PostScript to draw a circle with a certain radius, and it does that.

The sound files I've been talking about are like bitmapped images because they contain thousands (or millions) of bits of data to describe sounds—even simple sounds. Even 8-bit 11 kHz monaural sound, which sounds reasonably decent on most computer speakers, takes up more than 600 K per minute of sound.

Wouldn't it be great to have a computer language for sound, so that you could say, "Just give me a middle C played for two seconds on a trumpet"? As it turns out, there is: MIDI (Musical Instrument Digital Interface). Whole books have been written on MIDI, but suffice it to say that you can create a MIDI file a hundredth or a thousandth the size of the equivalent SND or AIFF file. There is, of course, no free lunch in this business . . . .

▶ You can create MIDI files from most music-sequencing programs on Macintosh or Windows (like Performer or Finale), but in order for it to work properly, you'll have to save it using General MIDI standards. This limits the types of instruments that you can use.

▶ General MIDI files must be played on any Macintosh that has QuickTime loaded, but in order to get the right sounds, the computer also has to have the QuickTime Musical Instruments file loaded (this is standard in System 7.5).

▶ You have to convert the General MIDI file into a QuickTime movie format. You can do this by opening it in Apple's (free) Movie Player utility, and saving it out again. QuarkImmedia can then play this file as a movie (using Play Movie rather than Play Sound; see Chapter 9, *QuickTime Movies*).

The great benefit, of course, is that these MIDI files are relatively tiny, even after being saved as QuickTime movies. The file size depends on how many instruments and how many MIDI commands there are—I have a 6 K file that plays a song more than two minutes long! The sound is rarely as rich or as good in QuickTime, but for many applications (Internet, mostly), these files can be incredibly useful.

I'll discuss playing sounds over the Internet in more depth in Chapter 15, *The Internet and the World Wide Web.*

▼ ▼

Happenin' Sounds

There's much more to digitized sound than I can cover in this one little chapter, but with what you know so far, you'll be able to at least make some intelligent choices about the kinds of sound you're going to use in projects. Next we need to explore how sound is used in Immedia, and what you can do with it.

There are five times when a sound can be played in a project.

▶ When the user does something with the mouse, such as Click Down or Double-click (event sounds)

▶ When a page turns (transition sounds)

▶ When a sound action is triggered by a user event or in a script

▶ While an animation is playing

▶ While a QuickTime movie is playing

I'll discuss the first three here, but I'll cover the last two in Chapter 8, *Animation,* and Chapter 9, *QuickTime Movies.*

Event Sounds

Clicking on a box, pressing a button, or selecting something from a list can trigger an action. As you know, each of these actions is called a "user event," and any user event can trigger an action. But as you may not know, each user event can trigger a sound *as well as* an action. The trick is to select a sound from the Event Sound popup menu on the Event tab of the QuarkImmedia palette (see Figure 7–1). If you haven't already used the sound in your project, select Other from the popup menu (see Figure 7–2).

You can have an event sound, even if the event doesn't start an action. For instance, you could select a button, and set the event sound for Click Down to a beep, and still leave the Click Down action set to No Action. When you click down on the button, Immedia plays that sound. Because you can have a user event sound *and* an action, you're triggering two actions for the price of one.

Figure 7–1
User event sounds

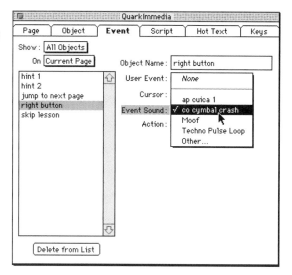

Figure 7–2
Opening a new sound

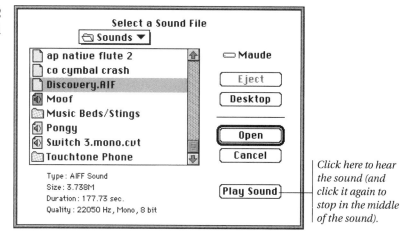

Click here to hear the sound (and click it again to stop in the middle of the sound).

Note that there's no way to make user event sounds fade in or out. They just play.

Transition Sounds

To every page-turn there is a sound, turn, turn, turn.* Or at least, there *can* be: every page transition can have an accompanying sound (see "Transitions" in Chapter 3, *Building Projects*). And because page transitions are handled both on the Page tab and with Page actions, you can also assign sounds in each of these, too.

---

*Ecclesiastes 13:1

Entry Transition. You can assign an entry sound to each page in the Entry Transition section of the Page tab (on the QuarkImmedia palette; see Figure 7–3). The sound starts playing as soon as the entry transition begins. This means that if you've got a two-second digital dissolve between pages, and the sound is only one second long, the sound will finish before the page is fully displayed!

Page actions. Most of the time, users jump from page to page using one of the Page actions (Display Page, Next Page, Previous Page, and so on). Most of the Page actions let you specify a transition effect and

Figure 7–3
Entry transition
sounds

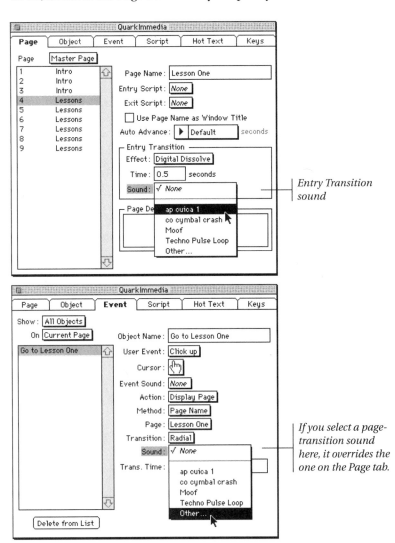

Entry Transition sound

If you select a page-transition sound here, it overrides the one on the Page tab.

a sound, and these effects override any transition effect or sound you've set up on the Page tab of the QuarkImmedia palette.

In general, it's easier to specify page transitions and sounds as Entry Transitions, and to override them with a Page action only when you're trying to create some special effect. Let's say you're creating a kiosk, and six different pages contain links to your table-of-contents page. You can specify the same entry transition and sound for all six Display Page actions, or you can specify them once on the Page tab.

Sound Actions

The third time a sound can be triggered is when you use a Sound action like Play Sound. This is the most blatant method, of course, but there are some subtleties that we should explore before cutting you loose to play with sounds.

Sound versus Background Sound. Take one look at the Sound action popout menu (see Figure 7–4), and you'll immediately notice something: it contains references to "sound" and "background sound."

Figure 7–4
Sound actions

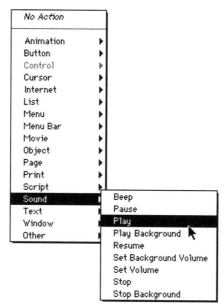

The difference is actually pretty minor, but it can really make or break your project.

▶ Immedia repeats the background sound until you tell it to stop. Normal sounds play only once, unless you specifically tell Immedia to loop them.

▶ There can be only one background sound playing at any one time. However, you can play as many normal sounds over each other as you want, and you can play normal sounds over the background sound.

Beep

Let's start our exploration of Sound actions with Immedia's simplest action: Beep. Do I really need to say that all this action does is to play whichever system beep the user's computer is set to? I find this action most valuable when I'm trying to debug my scripts,* and when I'm popping up alert windows.

Play Sound

You can play any sound file that Immedia understands (see "File Formats," earlier in this chapter) by selecting Play Sound from the Action popup menu. Then select the sound from the Sound popup menu (see Figure 7–5). If you haven't already imported a sound, nothing appears in the Sound popup menu; choose Other to import a new sound.

You can also fade sounds in gradually, rather than have them begin at full volume immediately. To fade a sound in, specify a number of seconds in the Fade In field.

▼ ▼

Tip: Fast Fades.   People often type in whole numbers out of habit, or perhaps an irrational fear of decimals. Fear not! Fractions of a second are helpful, especially when you're working with short sounds.

---

*I find it useful to place a Beep action in a complicated script that uses conditionals, so that I can quickly tell when Immedia has reached a certain place in the script. Or sometimes I place a Beep at the end of the script, so that I know when the script has finished running.

For instance, if you want to take the sharp edge off the beginning of a sound, you might try a fade-in of .25 second.

Figure 7–5
Play Sound

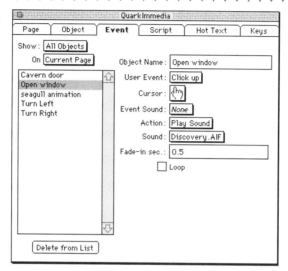

Stop Sound

As fast as you can start a sound, you can stop it, too. When you select the Stop Sound action, Immedia displays the Sound popup menu, asking you whether you want to stop one particular sound or all the currently playing sounds. And just as you can fade a sound in, you can fade it out, too. It's often jarring to have a sound stop suddenly; a fade-out of even half a second can make a difference in quality.

Pause Sound and Resume Sound

You can also pause any playing sound—or all the currently playing sounds—by choosing the Pause Sound action. A paused sound is held in stasis indefinitely, until you start it again with a Resume Sound action. Pause Sound lets you fade the sound out, and Resume Sound lets you fade it back in again.

Tip: Play/Pause Buttons. Immedia ignores the Play Sound action when a sound is already paused, and ignores the Resume Sound action when a sound is already playing. This makes it easy to use a four-state button that both plays and pauses a sound. Once you've got an On/Off button on your page, you can assign the proper actions to the proper user events—like this.

1. Set Click Down Off to Resume Sound. In the beginning, when the sound has not yet played, this event will be ignored.

2. Set Click Up On to Play Sound. In the beginning, Immedia will trigger this action; however, once the sound has begun to play, Immedia will ignore it.

3. Set Click Up Off to Pause Sound.

Yes, it seems nonintuitive and a hassle, but the opportunity to put fewer buttons on your page is well worth the extra trouble.

▼ ▼

Play Background Sound

As I said earlier, a background sound repeats continuously until the project ends, until you replace it with a different background sound (there can be only one playing at a time), or until you stop it. To make life easy for us, Immedia includes three actions specifically for background sounds. The first two, Play Background Sound and Stop Background Sound, are self-explanatory and work the same as Play Sound and Stop Sound. They even let you specify fade-in and fade-out times.

I discuss the last action, Set Background Sound Volume, in the next section.

▼ ▼

Tip: Removing Sounds. If you're like me, you build projects in a somewhat nonlinear fashion, bringing sounds in when you need them, or using other sounds as proxies until you get the sound you're looking for. The problem is that Immedia won't "forget" a sound just because you're not using it. Therefore, your Sound pop-up menus may be filled with sounds you no longer care about. The solution is easy to overlook: click the Remove button in the Quark

Immedia Usage dialog box (on the QuarkImmedia menu; see "QuarkImmedia Usage" in Chapter 14, *Exporting*).

▼ ▼

Pump Up the Volume

Immedia cannot change a computer's default sound volume settings by itself.* On the Macintosh, you make these settings in the Control Panels folder of the System Folder. When you use Play Sound or Play Background Sound, Immedia plays the sound at the full-volume setting.

You can, however, use the Set Sound Volume and Set Background Sound Volume actions to make a sound's volume softer than its maximum setting. When you use either of these actions, Immedia asks you for a volume setting between zero and 255. Zero is "off;" you won't hear any sound at all. The loudest volume Immedia can play is a setting of 255; but this is never louder than the volume that the computer is set to (see Figure 7–6).

Figure 7–6
Set Background
Volume

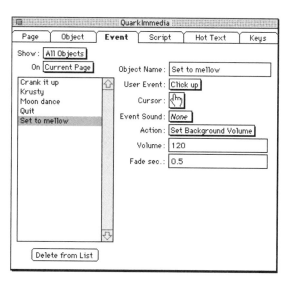

---

*There are ways to do this using AppleScript on the Macintosh, however. See "AppleScript Project" on the Real World QuarkImmedia CD-ROM at the back of this book.

Fade In. Both actions let you specify a Fade In time. This is different than Fade In in the Play Sound action. Here, Fade In determines the time it takes Immedia to transition from one volume to another. If you're at full volume and you want to switch to a very low volume, you probably want to adjust over a half second or so; otherwise, the transition may be too harsh.

All or some. The Set Sound Volume action lets you specify which sound in your project to adjust, or whether to adjust all of them (select All from the Sound popup menu). However, because you can only have one background sound playing at a time, the Set Background Sound Volume action changes the default background sound volume—for any background sound that you play.

▼ ▼

Tip: Global Volume Changes. The only way to create a single volume control—one that sets the volume for all the sounds in your document—is to trigger a script that uses both the Set Background Sound Volume action and the Set Sound Volume action. Of course, the Sound popup menu in the Set Sound Volume action has to be set to All (see Figure 7–7).

Figure 7–7
Global volume
changes

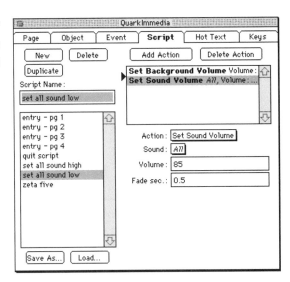

▼ ▼

Incorporating Sound

Sound is one of the key factors in making multimedia live up to its name. A project with no sound may get the job done, but more often than not, the addition of sound will make using your piece a lot more fun and interesting. In many cases, sound can make your project more functional, too, since you can do things with sound that would be difficult to convey visually.

Immedia gives you all the tools you need for including and controlling sound in your projects. It does not, however, provide much in the way of creating, recording, or editing sounds. When I hear people grumble about this, I like to remind them: Immedia is a *screen*-layout tool, and other programs are always going to be better at those other chores.

In the next chapter, as we take on animation, we'll go even further into multimedia effects.

Animation 8

MAKING BUTTONS YOU CAN PUSH and sounds you can play is all very well and good, but let's face it: the world loves animation. When a client hires you to build a multimedia project, the first thing they inevitably suggest is to fly their logo around the screen. Then they want the credits to roll up the screen, "You know, like in the movies." Don't worry; you can do all this and a whole lot more in QuarkImmedia.

In this chapter we'll take a look at the various types of animations you can create in your QuarkImmedia projects, from playing a sequence in a box to moving something along a path. I won't, however, talk about playing QuickTime movies until the next chapter, because Immedia makes a distinction between animation objects and movies.

Animation Objects

There are two kinds of animations in Immedia: *items* (like picture boxes, text boxes, or lines) that move around the screen, and *animation sequences* that are composed of two or more frames. A frame is like a cell in traditional animation; each frame is slightly different from the next, so that when they're played in sequence the picture appears to be moving. Sequences must be built using the Animation Editor.

For instance, the easiest way to make a word fly across the screen is to just put it in a text box and animate the whole box along a path. However, if you want a little animation of a ladybug doing a May Day jig, you'll probably want to use an animation sequence.

Making an Animation

In order to make either type of animation, you must first make a text box or picture box (or a line) into an *animation object* by selecting Animation from the Object Type popup menu on the Object tab of the QuarkImmedia palette (see Figure 8–1).

Once you make an animation object, you can tell Immedia what kind of animation you want it to be on the Display As popup menu (see Figure 8–2). You have three choices here: Item on a Path, Sequence in a Box, and Sequence on a Path. Note that while text boxes, picture boxes, or lines can be "items on a path," only picture boxes can contain sequences.

Item on a Path

In order to make a text box, a picture box, or a line move along a path, you've got to create a path first. A *path* is the edge of a box, line,

Figure 8–1
Animation objects

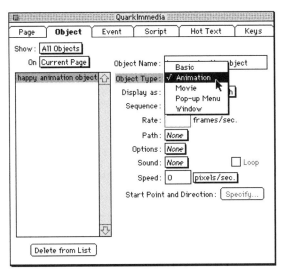

or polygon. For example, a diagonal line can be a path; a triangle-shaped polygon can be a path; an oval picture box can be a path. *Any* object can be a path, with one requirement: you have to give it a name on the Object tab of the QuarkImmedia palette. It doesn't matter what object type it is; it just needs a name.

When you choose Item on a Path from the Display As popup menu, Immedia gives you several more options (see Figure 8–3).

Figure 8–2

Display As

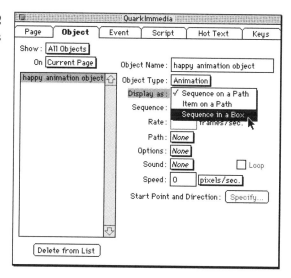

Figure 8–3

Item on a Path

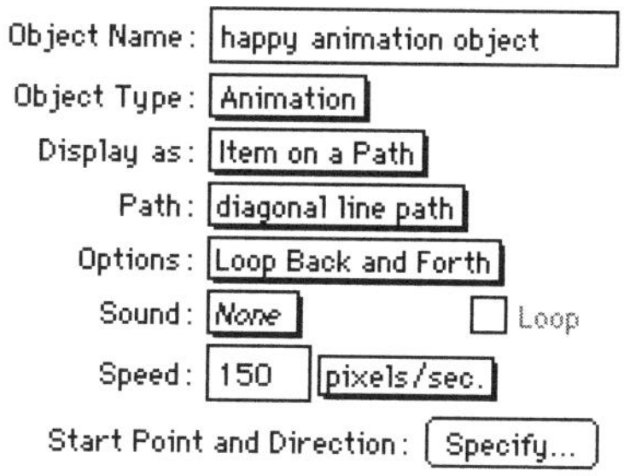

Path. The first thing Immedia needs to know is what path you want the animation to follow. Again, any named object on the same page as the animation can be a path.

Note that it's always the upper-left corner of the item that moves along the path. If the item (like an oval) doesn't have an upper-left corner, Immedia uses the upper-left corner of the object's bounding box (see Figure 8–4).

Figure 8–4
Where items
sit on the path

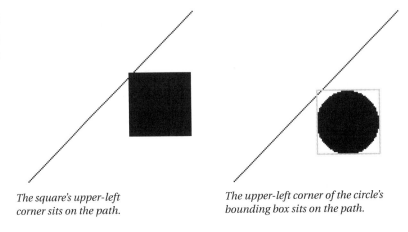

*The square's upper-left
corner sits on the path.*

*The upper-left corner of the circle's
bounding box sits on the path.*

Speed. The Speed field is the second option you need to change. The default value of zero means the item won't move at all. You can specify the speed of the item in three ways.

▶ You can use pixels per second. Try starting with a value around 100 or 150; then adjust the value, making it faster or slower, as necessary.

▶ You can use inches or centimeters per second (if you think better in those terms; note that Immedia assumes that there are 72 pixels per inch and about 28.4 pixels per centimeter). If you want a box to move exactly one inch per second, you can set this to "1 inch/sec."

▶ You can use seconds per path traversal. For instance, if you want a box to move across the length of a line in exactly 10 seconds, you can set this value to "10 sec/path traversal." This is very useful when you need to synchronize several animations with each other, or an animation with a sound.

Options. The Options popup menu for an Item on a Path provides five choices from which to pick. In most cases, you can choose more than one (for example, you can choose Initially Hidden *and* Loop, but you can't choose Loop *and* Loop Back and Forth).

▶ **Loop** makes the animation start over from the beginning, once it has finished traversing the path.

- ▶ **Loop Back and Forth** makes the animation play in reverse after it reaches the end of the path; then it starts from the beginning again.

- ▶ **Initially Hidden** makes the animation object invisible until it begins playing (then it suddenly appears—not subtle at all).

- ▶ **Hidden at End** makes the animation object disappear as soon as the animation stops playing.

- ▶ **Keep Status on Page Exit** makes sure, when you leave the page, that Immedia remembers whether the animation is playing or paused. Later, if you return to that page, the animation picks up where it left off.

Sound. If you choose a sound from the Sound popup menu, that sound begins playing when the animation begins. This is much more convenient than having to build scripts that start or stop an animation *and* a sound. If it's a short sound (shorter than the animation itself), you can repeat it automatically by turning on the Loop option; with this turned on, the sound keeps repeating until the animation is finished or has stopped. For more information, see Chapter 7, *Sound.*

Start Point and Direction. The final option you get to set is Start Point and Direction. If you click the Specify button, Immedia displays the Animation Start Point dialog box (see Figure 8–5) with a preview of the path you've chosen from the Path popup menu. Here you can control where on the path the animation should begin, and in what direction it should move. To change the placement, just click somewhere else on the path; to switch the direction of travel, click the Change Direction button.

Don't worry if the direction arrow doesn't point exactly where you want it to go; it should just point in the general direction.

Note that when you engage the project, the object you set to Item on a Path does *not* appear where you've put it on the page. Instead, it appears at the point you've specified in this dialog box (unless, of course, you've turned on the Initially Hidden option).

Figure 8–5
Start Point
and Direction

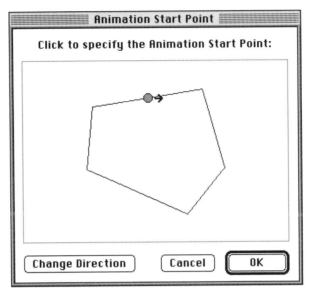

Sequence in a Box

As I said earlier, sequences of frames can be saved in QuarkImmedia's Animation Maker as animation files. Once you have a sequence saved to disk (or once you want to use one of the animation sequences on the *Real World QuarkImmedia* CD-ROM), you can incorporate it into your project in one of two ways: in a picture box, or in a picture box that travels along a path.

Here's how to put the animation into a plain old picture box.

1. Create a picture box, and set its Object Type to Animation on the QuarkImmedia palette.

2. Next, choose Sequence in a Box from the Display As popup menu (see Figure 8–6).

3. Choose the animation sequence from the Sequence popup menu. If you haven't already imported it (if you're reading this, you probably haven't), select Other from the popup menu.

▼ ▼

Tip: Importing Animations Quickly. There's a much faster way to import an animation into a picture box: choose Get Picture from the File menu. I included the step-by-step method above because it's

Figure 8–6

Sequence in a Box

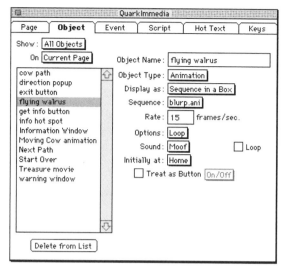

important to understand what the Object Type, Display As, and Sequence popup menus do. But honestly, I almost always just use Get Picture.

▼ ▼

The sequence looks like a picture in the picture box—it won't actually animate until you engage the project and use the Play Animation action (see "Animation Actions," below). After importing the animation, you can choose from several other options in the form of popup menus and checkboxes.

Frames per second. Immedia simply plays animation sequences, one frame after another; but you can tell it how fast to move from one frame to the next. Animation sequences are always saved with a default frame speed, usually between 10 and 30 frames per second. Immedia places this value in the Frames per Second field, but you can always override it. If you set this field to zero, Immedia won't play the animation at all.

Options. The choices on the Options popup menu (Loop, Loop Back and Forth, and so on) are the same as those on the Options popup menu for Item on a Path.

Sound. Sound works in exactly the same way as it does for Item on a Path (see above); any sound you select begins playing when the animation begins, and repeats itself if you turn on the Loop option.

Initially at. As I said earlier, an object set to Item on a Path always appears at the beginning of the path (unless you have the Initially Hidden option turned on). Sequences follow the same rules as other types of objects—they sit at their home position unless you choose an option from the Initially at popup menu (see "Initially at" in Chapter 2, *Immedia Basics*).

Treat as Button. One of the coolest features of animation sequences is that they can act as buttons. I'll discuss in depth how to do this in "Animations as Buttons," later in the chapter.

▼ ▼

Tip: One-Frame Animations. I discuss the importance of transmission speed (how fast a project transmits across the Internet) in Chapter 15, *The Internet and the World Wide Web*, but suffice it to say that smaller files mean faster transmission speeds, which means happier users. Quark's multimedia team taught me an awesome method for streamlining some projects.

If you've got a project that contains the same image on multiple pages, you can replace that graphic with a one-frame animation. Animations are downloaded from the Internet only once each time the project is run, no matter how many pages the animation is on. The QuarkImmedia Viewer then caches the animation on the local hard drive. So if you build an animation consisting of a single frame (the picture you want to use), you can put it on as many pages as you want and it'll only get downloaded once.

For optimum performance, if the single-frame animation is on top of a busy background, put a white box underneath it. The reason: even though you can't see anything under the animation, Immedia includes it anyway when it rasterizes the page for export. A white box compresses really well, whereas a busy background does not (see Chapter 14, *Exporting*).

▼ ▼

Sequence on a Path

Let's say your boss has decided that the flying logo is a *must* in this project. If the logo is just going to move around, you could make it an Item on a Path. But your boss wants it to spin around, too.

1. Create a spinning-logo sequence (that's a whole discussion in itself; see "Animation Editor," later in this chapter).

2. Make a picture box and set its type to Animation on the Object tab of the QuarkImmedia palette (see Figure 8–7).

3. Set the Display As popup menu to Sequence on a Path, and select the animation you've created. Even if you import the animation using Get Picture (see "Tip: Importing Animations Quickly," above), you still need to set this popup menu to Sequence on a Path.

Immedia presents you with a combination of all the options from Item on a Path and Sequence in a Box. (Of course, the Initially At popup menu is missing because Sequence on a Path objects always appear on a path—just like Item on a Path objects.)

▼ ▼

Tip: Don't Change the Picture Box. As if sequence animations weren't cool enough, some people try to skew or rotate animation objects.

Figure 8–7
Sequence on a Path

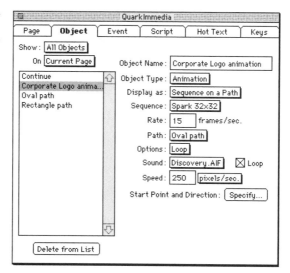

This works for Item on a Path, but you cannot rotate, skew, scale, or flip a Sequence on a Path or a Sequence in a Box. Immedia just won't engage or export the project if you do. If you need effects like these, you should build them directly into the animation sequence itself.

However, while you're not supposed to be able to run animation sequences inside nonrectangular polygons (Quark says you can't), you actually can. That means you can crop the animation any way you want.

Animation Actions

Now that you've got your various animations set up in your project, it's time to start playing them! Animations don't play by themselves—you need an animation action. There are six actions that pertain to animations: Play Animation, Play Animation in Object, Play Animation on Path, Pause Animation, Resume Animation, and Stop Animation.

Play Animation. You can start any animation with a Play Animation action. The animation follows the default settings you've specified on the Object tab (where to play, to play along a path, or whatever) unless you've previously used one of the Play Animation in Object or Play Animation on Path actions (see below). This is the action you'll use to start animations most of the time.

Play Animation in Object. You can play more than one animation sequence in the same box, but you can play only one of them at a time. For instance, let's say you've got four animations of spinning balls: a basketball, a soccer ball, a baseball, and a football. Depending on which button the user presses, you want one of those animations to play in the upper-left corner of the screen.

You can put a single picture box in the proper place and set it up as a Sequence in a Box object (you don't have to put a sequence in it yet if you don't want to). Then (for this example) you can set up four buttons, each one triggering a Play Animation in Object action, each playing a different sequence in that same box. The Play Animation in Object action is relatively simple (see Figure 8–8).

1. First you must specify the picture box in which you want the sequence to play (on the Object popup menu).

2. Next you can choose which animation sequence you want to play (from the Sequence popup menu).

3. Finally, you can determine how fast you want it to play by typing a number in the Frame Rate field. If you want the animation to repeat after playing, turn on the Loop option, too.

Note that once you use a Play Animation in Object action, that object (the picture box that plays the sequence) gets set to the new animation. For example, let's say you've got an animation of a spinning football inside a picture box. Later, you use the Play Animation in Object action to play the spinning-basketball animation in that box. Now if you trigger a Play Animation action, it will run the basketball sequence rather than the original football sequence. If you display a different page and then return, the object resets to the football animation (unless you've turned on the Keep Status on Page Entry option on the Object tab of the QuarkImmedia palette).

Play Animation on Path. The Play Animation on Path action is sort of the "super-animation-action"—it lets you play any animation

Figure 8–8
Play Animation
in Object

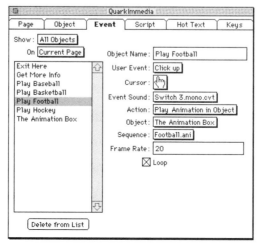

sequence inside any animation-type picture box, along any path on your page. You can use it to play different animations in the same box along the same path (only one animation at a time, of course) or to override the settings in a Sequence on a Path animation.

At first, the Play Animation on Path action appears to be a hopelessly complex jumble of popup menus (see Figure 8–9). But on closer inspection, we find it's really as simple as anything else in Immedia. The key is to take one option at a time.

▶ **Object.** The Object popup menu lets you specify which box you want the sequence to play in. The box must be set up as some type of animation object already (though it doesn't matter which kind).

▶ **Sequence.** You can pick which animated sequence you want to play from the Sequence popup menu. If you haven't already used the sequence in your project, you can select it from your hard drive by choosing Other from this popup menu.

▶ **Frame Rate.** The Play Animation on Path action always overrides the default frame-rate setting you've assigned to the box and the sequence.

▶ **Path.** What can I say about the Path popup menu? Select the path you want the animation to play on.

▶ **Pixels/sec.** This action also overrides the animation object's Pixels per second setting, so you'll have to specify it yourself.

Figure 8–9
Play Animation
on Path

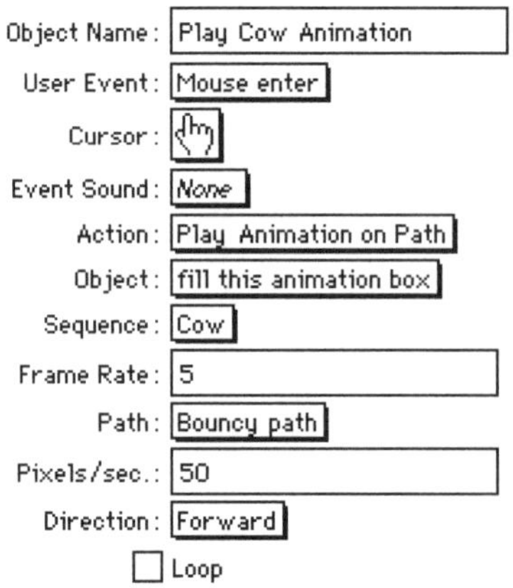

Object Name : [Play Cow Animation]
User Event : [Mouse enter]
Cursor : [🖐]
Event Sound : [None]
Action : [Play Animation on Path]
Object : [fill this animation box]
Sequence : [Cow]
Frame Rate : [5]
Path : [Bouncy path]
Pixels/sec. : [50]
Direction : [Forward]
☐ Loop

No, you can't set this to Inches per second or any of the other traversal settings. Maybe in the next version.

▶ **Direction.** It seems like the Play Animation on Path action should provide you with a Start Point and Direction button so that you can (more or less) precisely specify where you want the sequence to begin. Unfortunately, you're not that lucky. Instead, you get a Direction popup menu with two options: Forward and Reverse.

Pause Animation. Once you've got an animation playing (either a Sequence on a Path or an Item on a Path), you can pause it in midstream with the Pause Animation action. Immedia lets you pause any one animation on the page; if the animation isn't already playing, Immedia just ignores this action.

Resume Animation. After pausing an animation, you can start it again using the Resume Animation action. Note that Immedia ignores this action when the animation is already playing or if it's stopped. If you resume a paused animation, it restarts from the same point at which it was paused. If you use Play Animation instead, Immedia starts the animation again from the beginning.

See "Tip: Play/Pause Movies" in Chapter 6, *Buttons*, for a tip on how to make a single On/Off button handle a big part of playing, pausing, and resuming animations.

Stop Animation. The last animation-based action is Stop Animation, which does just what it says: it stops any or all animations—you can choose One Animation or All Animations from the Select popup menu. If you then restart an animation, it will start from the beginning point.

▼ ▼

Animations as Buttons

As I said earlier, you can make any Sequence in a Box act like a button (see Chapter 6, *Buttons*). At first I found this very nonintuitive, and couldn't figure out why they put this feature in. Then it occurred to me: you can make buttons that actually animate! Instead of a button that has four states (Off Up, Off Down, On Up, and On Down), you can make a button that smoothly slides in when you turn it on, and then out when you click again; or a button that looks like a door that swings open when you click on it and closed when you click again, meanwhile acting as a button to trigger other actions.

The trick is turning on the Treat as Button option on the Object tab of the QuarkImmedia palette (see Figure 8–10). You can then tell

Figure 8–10
Animations as buttons

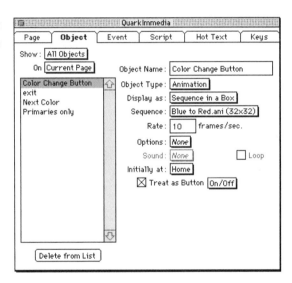

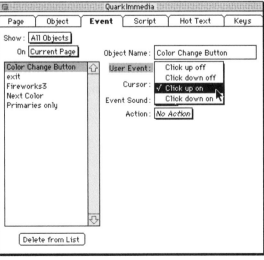

Immedia whether you want it to act like a Simple button or an On/Off button.

▶ An animation set up as a Simple button plays forward as long as you hold the mouse button down over it. Then when you release the mouse button, the animation plays in reverse back to the beginning.

▶ An animation set up as an On/Off button plays forward when you first click it, and continues to play until the end of the animation. Then when you click it again, the animation reverses back to the beginning.

Animation User Events. The User Events popup menu on the Events tab of the QuarkImmedia palette changes when you turn on the Treat as Button option. Normally (when this option is turned off), you can assign actions to the basic user events for that animation object—Click Down, Click Up, Double-click, Mouse Enter, and so on. However, when the Treat as Button box is checked, the User Event popup menu lists the standard button events—Click Down Off, Click Up On, Click Down On, Click Up Off. You can then specify different actions for each of these user events, just as though the animation object were a button.

▼ ▼

Animation Editor

While it may be true, as Maude says in *Harold and Maude*, that "consistency is not really a human trait," the folks at Quark try their best to keep some sort of consistent interface throughout QuarkImmedia. With that in mind, they developed the Animation Editor to look almost exactly like the Button Editor. Fortunately, this means two things.

▶ You don't have to learn a whole new set of tools.

▶ I don't have to write about those tools and features all over again. Instead, you can just go look at Chapter 6, *Buttons*.

In this section I'll discuss the differences between the Button Editor and the Animation Editor (see Figure 8–11), along with some important issues that are specific to animations. One of the first things you'll notice about the Animation Editor is that it's a non-modal dialog box. That means you can leave it open while you move between QuarkXPress and other programs; you can even switch between the Animation Editor and your QuarkXPress document.

Animation

The Animation area in the upper-left corner of the Animation Editor contains features that apply to the whole animation (like the Button area in the Button Editor). However, there are a few features

Figure 8–11
Animation Editor
vs. Button Editor

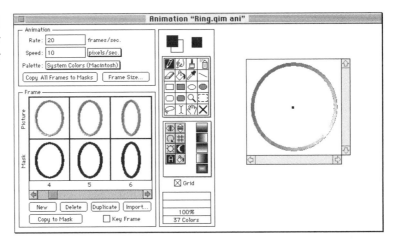

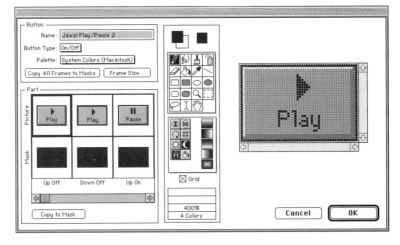

very different from those in the Button Editor, due to the inherent differences between animations and buttons.

Naming and saving. You have to name buttons in the Button Editor itself, because buttons are just saved within libraries. Animations, on the other hand, are saved on disk, so you name them in the Save As dialog box, like any other file.*

Rate. As I noted earlier, an animation is a sequence of frames, and you have to tell Immedia how fast you want it to go from frame to frame. Immedia uses the value you type in the Rate field of the Animation Editor as the default frame rate for the animation, but you can always override that value once you've imported the animation into your project (see "Sequence in a Box," earlier in this chapter).

Frame rate can be a tricky thing. Fast computers can process animations faster, so they can tolerate faster frame rates. Slower computers may not be able to handle a fast frame rate, so they'll drop frames when necessary (making a very jerky animation). So even though you can set the frame rate up to 30 frames per second, you often may not want to. Besides, a rate of 20 or 25 typically won't appear jerky; and some animations appear smooth even at rates under 15 frames per second.

By the way, when I talk about slow computers, I'm *not* talking about running the animation over a slow Internet connection. When you run an animation over the Internet, the Viewer downloads every frame of the animation before starting to play it, so the speed of the connection has no effect on the frame-by-frame playing speed.

Speed. If your animation is destined to be played along a path, you should enter a value in the Speed field of the Animation Editor. However, once again, this is only the default value, and you can

---

*You'd think that after creating a new animation, you'd select Save As from the File menu. Unfortunately, as of this writing, you have to select Save instead of Save As. It's an annoying inconsistency on Quark's part, but as Emerson once noted, "With consistency, a great soul has simply nothing to do."

always override it later on the QuarkImmedia palette (see "Sequence on a Path," earlier in this chapter). Out of habit, I almost always enter a value of 100 pixels per second—for two reasons.

▶ If you leave the Speed value set to zero, and later decide to put the animation on a path, it's easy to forget to override the zero with a different value. The result will be an animation that doesn't move along the path at all.

▶ I'm just one of those guys who can't leave well enough alone; I like fiddling with the knobs.

Palette and Frame Size. The Palette popup menu and the Frame Size feature work exactly the same in both editors, but because people often forget, I should reiterate that no matter which color palette you use in the animation, it is always overridden by the project's palette (see "Palettes" in Chapter 3, *Building Projects*).

Frame

The Frame area of the Animation Editor displays each of the frames in sequence, along with its mask. Remember that every frame must have a mask in order to display properly. The Animation Editor has five features in this area that don't appear in the Button Editor.

▶ **New.** All animations start with only a single frame. You can create a new frame by clicking the New button. This adds a frame to the right of whatever frame is currently selected.

▶ **Delete.** You can delete any frame (including its mask) by selecting it and clicking the Delete button.

▶ **Duplicate.** When you click the Duplicate button, Immedia places a copy of the selected frame right after the original. This is helpful when you draw animations directly in the Animation Editor because you can draw one frame, then duplicate it, then edit this copy, then duplicate it and edit that copy, and so on. If nothing else, it saves a lot of copying and pasting.

▶ **Import.** You can import a PICS file into the Animation Editor by clicking the Import button (I'll say more on that subject in just a moment).

▶ **Key Frame.** Remember when I said that slower computers can't always keep up with the animation's frame rate? The result is that Immedia starts dropping out frames, and you get a jerky animation. That's where the Key Frame checkbox comes in. Selecting the frame and checking this box tells Immedia that a frame is important and shouldn't be dropped.

Turning on the Key Frame option won't guarantee that the frame won't get dropped, but Immedia has at least been informed of your desires and will do its best. Of course, the temptation is to turn on Key Frame for every frame; they're all important, right? Trust me: it's a rare case when every frame of an animation is important; and if every frame were, you wouldn't be running the animation at such a high frame rate.

▼ ▼

Tip: Missing Animations. I can't tell you how many times I've built animations, imported them into a project, played them, and then growled in frustration because the animation has disappeared. The problem is almost always the same: I forgot to build a mask for every frame of the animation. Masks can be a pain, but they're a necessary evil. Remember the Copy All Frames to Masks button? Although you sometimes need to do some cleanup in the masks (if you *want* some of the pixels to be white instead of clear, for example), it's a great place to start.

▼ ▼

Importing PICS

Few people draw their animations directly in the Animation Editor. Just as the Button Editor is called the "paste from Photoshop" tool, the Animation Editor could be called the "import from somewhere else" feature. It's not that the tools in the editor window are necessarily bad, it's just that it's often much easier to do this sort of work in a program that's really designed for it.

QuarkImmedia can only import animations that are exported from other programs in the PICS format. If your program cannot save in this format, you'll be reduced to copying and pasting the animation, frame by frame. Fortunately, most animation applications can save in this format—there are two things to note, however.

▶ Importing an animation doesn't delete any frames already present in it. If you create a new animation and immediately import a PICS file, you then have to go back and delete the first empty frame of the animation (the one that was there before you imported the file).

▶ If the PICS file contains frames that are larger than the value you've specified in the Frame Size dialog box, Immedia scales the animation down to fit. This sometimes looks good, but to be honest, it often looks ugly. The best thing is to save the PICS file at the size you want the animation to be in Immedia. On the other hand, if the frames are smaller in the PICS file, they simply get dropped into the upper-left corner of the animation—and no damage is done.

No, there's no way to import a PICS file directly into your project; you have to save it as an Immedia animation file first. (There are actually good technical reasons for this, but it's not worth getting into them here.)

▼ ▼

Tip: You Can Import Anything. The Import button lets you import more than just PICS files. In fact, you can import any kind of picture that XPress usually can import: TIFF, PICT, EPS, JPEG*, PCX*, BMP, or PhotoCD*. As with PICS animations, if these images are too big, they'll get scaled to fit the animation's dimensions.

---

*These file formats require that an XTension be present; the XTensions all ship with XPress, so you won't have a problem unless you've moved them.

Note that while Immedia imports PICS animations following the currently selected frame, these other types of graphics are imported *into* the currently selected frame.

▼ ▼

Editing Tools

If you *do* want to draw your animation in the Animation Editor, or perhaps use it to edit an imported animation, you can use the tools in the center of the editor (see Figure 8–12). Every tool in this area works the same way as I described back in Chapter 6, *Buttons*. There is, however, one additional tool: the Hot Spot tool.

Hot Spot. Every frame of an animation has one pixel called the "hot spot." QuarkImmedia uses the hot-spot pixel for two things.

▶ In an animation set up as a Sequence on a Path, Immedia aligns the hot spot with the path.

▶ In an animation set up as a Sequence in a Box, where the hot spot goes is a little more complicated. Generally, Immedia ignores the hot spot, and the top left corner of the animation appears in the top-left corner of the picture box. However, if

Figure 8–12
Animation
Editor tools

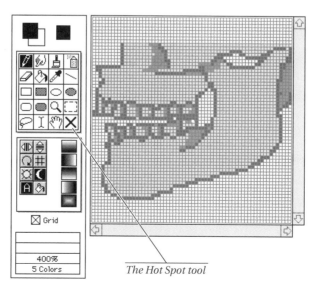

The Hot Spot tool

you later edit the animation and move its hot spot . . . well, weird things happen. I don't recommend it.

When you click on a pixel with the Hot Spot tool—that's the one with the "X" icon—QuarkImmedia makes that pixel every frame's hot spot.

If (for some obscure reason) you want to set the hot spot on a frame-by-frame basis, you can Shift-click with the Hot Spot tool; that sets the hot spot for a single frame only.*

▼ ▼

Tip: Animations and Memory. When you build animations in the Animation Editor, you may run into memory problems if you haven't allocated enough RAM to QuarkXPress (see "Memory Management" in Chapter 2, *QuarkImmedia Basics*). The key is that Immedia has to hold each and every frame of the animation in memory at all times. If you're working with small animations, this isn't such a big deal, but if your animations are large in size or number of frames, you need to pay attention.

Each frame in an animation is a bitmapped image, and each pixel in the frame takes up eight bits of information. So a single frame of a 100-by-100 animation takes up 80,000 bits, which is about 10 K. If this animation has 60 frames, Immedia has to hold on to about 600 K every time you edit it (60×10 K). And 30 frames of a 200-by-200 animation take up a megabyte of RAM!

With numbers like these, you have to make sure you've allocated extra memory to QuarkXPress, or else you could suffer all sorts of memory-related errors (crashing, quitting, and so on).

▼ ▼

Tip: Transparent Animations. You can make your animation "semi-transparent" by filling the mask with a tint of black (because you can't use grays in the mask, you have to simulate them with a tint).

---

*The only time I've needed to set the hot spot on a frame-by-frame basis is when I wanted to make a Sequence on a Path wobble along the path instead of move smoothly along it. By "randomly" changing the hot spot in each frame, I got the impression I was looking for.

One easy way to do this is to use the MacPaint-like patterns in the Animation Editor (see "Editing Tools" in Chapter 6, *Buttons;* also see Figure 8–13).

Figure 8-13
Transparent masks

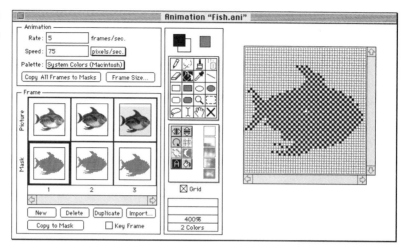

▼ ▼

Tip: Transition Effects. Once you start playing with transparent animations (see the last tip), you're just a short step away from building your own custom transitions. For instance, you can change the opacity of each frame in an animation using different mask patterns, so that the animation appears to fade in or fade out.

▼ ▼

Sliding Objects

There's one other kind of animation in QuarkImmedia that we should discuss before moving on to QuickTime movies: the sliding object. This is like an Item on a Path, but it works with *any* kind of object—not just those objects that you've defined as animations— and you don't need a path. Sliding objects work really well for titles or pictures that you want to fly across the screen, or for objects that you want to move just a little distance.

Note that the Slide Object action works with any object (text box, picture box, line, button, or whatever), as long as you've given it a name on the Object tab of the QuarkImmedia palette.

Slide Object

Slide Object is an action, so it has to be triggered by something—a user event or a script. When you select this action from the Object popout menu on the Action popup menu, Immedia gives you a lot of options, and it can be a little overwhelming at first (see Figure 8–14). Just take the options one at a time, and as Douglas Adams once wrote: "Don't Panic!"

Object. The first option is easy: the Object popup menu lets you choose which object you want to slide. This doesn't have to be an object on the current page, by the way. If you choose Other from the popup menu, you can choose to slide an object on a different page.

Figure 8–14
Slide Object

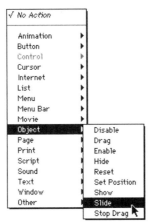

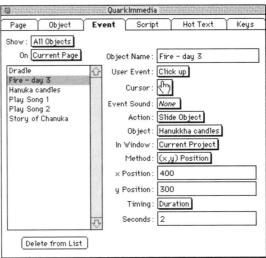

(Don't forget to turn on Keep Status on Page Entry for the box you're sliding, or else you won't see a difference when you get to that page.) I can't think of many (okay . . . *any*) reasons to slide an object on a different page, however.

In Window. You can slide the object across the screen in the project itself by leaving the In Window popup menu set to the default setting of Current Project. However, if you want to slide an object inside a window, you can do that too: just select the window name from the popup menu (or choose Other, if the Window is on a different page).

I've had mixed luck with using Slide Object inside windows; often the coordinates get mixed up, or the objects don't slide from where I'd expect them to. You can do it; you just might have to spend a little time playing around until it works.

Method. The Method popup menu defines where you slide the object. This is really the heart of Slide Object, and where you can set up the cool stuff. You've got five options on this popup menu (see Figure 8–15).

▶ **(x,y) Position.** When you select (x,y) Position, you can tell Immedia exactly where on the page (or the window) you want the object to end up. Just type in the x and y coordinates; this coordinate defines the object's origin (the upper-left corner).

One of the best ways to figure out a coordinate is to change the Vertical and Horizontal measurements to Points in the General Preferences dialog box (Command-Y). Then place the object where you want it to go, and read the x and y coordinates from the Measurements palette. Type those numbers into the x and y position fields of the QuarkImmedia palette, and move the object back to where you want it.

▶ **(x,y) Offset.** If you want to move the object some distance relative to where it already is, you can use the (x,y) Offset option. This lets you specify a distance to the left or right (the x value) and up or down (the y value). Negative numbers mean left and up; positive numbers mean right and down (this is easy

Figure 8–15
Slide Object methods

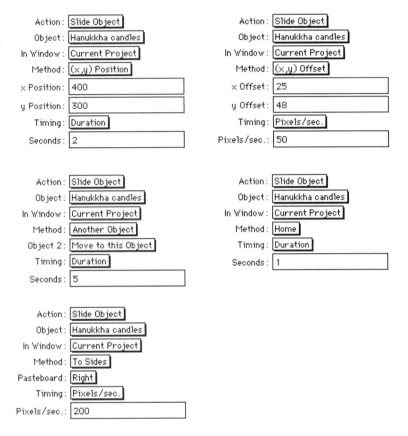

to remember, because it's exactly how QuarkXPress's rulers typically work).

▶ **Another Object.** I don't much like working with coordinates, so I find myself using the Another Object option a lot. This lets you slide an object from where it is initially to where another object is. Like all the slides, Immedia focuses on the upper-left corner of the object—in this case, sliding the upper-left corner of one object to the upper-left corner of the other.

Note that the "target" object doesn't have to be visible—it just has to be named (so you can choose it from the popup menu). If I'm not in a coordinate kind of mood, I'll just put a little empty picture box on the page where I want my object to slide, give it a name, set the background to None so it won't interfere with anything behind it, and finally set up my Slide Object action so that the object slides to that box.

▶ **Home.** If you've ever wondered what the Initially At feature on the Object tab of the QuarkImmedia palette is for, this is it! Let's say you place a red box somewhere on your page. You give the box a name and set the Initially At popup menu to Left. When you engage the project, the red box is nowhere to be seen because Immedia has put it just outside the project boundaries, off to the left.

Now you can use the Slide Object action to slide the red box back to Home (select Home from the Method popup menu). The object flies in from the left and stops exactly where you originally put it on your page. When you slide back to Home, the object always flies in from the left, right, top, or bottom, depending on how you set Initially At.

You can also use Home if you've moved the object around using Slide Object or Drag Object, and later want to return it to its original position. No matter where you move the object, Immedia remembers that Home is where you actually placed it on the page before engaging or exporting the project.

▶ **To Sides.** When you select To Sides from the Method popup menu, Immedia slides the object from wherever it currently is to the Left, Right, Top, or Bottom (you choose). For instance, let's say you want a title to scroll up the project, from "down below" to "up above." First you could set the text box's Initially At popup menu to Bottom. Then use the Slide Object action, and choose To Sides from the Method popup menu. Finally, select Top from the Pasteboard popup menu.

The result is that the object starts out off the page at the bottom, slides up the screen, and ends up off the page at the top. Note that To Sides always moves the object horizontally or vertically out of the project window.

Timing. The last two options offered to you when you choose Slide Object let you specify how fast you want the object to slide—either by pixels per second, or over a duration. These are identical to the settings you'll find when using Item on a Path or Sequence on a Path: you can choose either Duration or Pixels/sec from the Timing popup menu—depending on your mood, the arrangement of the stars, or other whimsy.

Again, if you're trying to synchronize the object to a soundtrack, Duration might be the best bet. On the other hand, some people find Pixels/sec more intuitive and more precise (it's not more precise, but for folks who like numbers, it *feels* that way).

▼ ▼

Animating Immedia

I don't know why, but people love animations. Maybe Freud was right, and animations are an unconscious wish to return to Bugs Bunny. Or maybe Jung had it right when he surmised that animation is an archetypal synthesis of anima and animus. Whatever the case—whether you're moving an item around the page, or playing a sequence of frames—animations are cool, and they can really make or break the success of your projects.

But animations aren't the only thing that can move in your QuarkImmedia projects. You can use QuickTime movies, too. And that's exactly where we're going in the next chapter.

QuickTime Movies

IN THE LAST CHAPTER, I TALKED about animations—how to make them, how to use them, and so on. In this chapter, I'll explore the world of QuickTime movies. Both animations and movies can make something appear to move on the screen by displaying one frame after another. Both are imported into QuarkImmedia from files saved on disk. The difference between the two lies almost entirely in who is running the show.

QuarkImmedia plays animations by itself. You tell Immedia how fast to play the animation—in frames per second—and where the animation's mask is (what parts of the frame to display and what parts to hide). When it comes to QuickTime movies, though, Immedia lets the system software play them. The QuickTime movie is like a little encapsulated bubble; when you say "Play," Immedia hands it off to the system and says, "Play this for me."

This means Immedia cannot control how fast the movie plays, what the key frames are, or where the movie's hot spot is (it's always in the upper-left corner). On the other hand, there are all sorts of things you can do with QuickTime movies in Immedia that you can't do with animations.

QuickTime versus Animations

If you want a little box rotating around its axis or a little cartoon-like person doing a dance inside an alert icon, you should probably be thinking, "I can do this with an animation." But when it comes to a music video or a fancy 3-D logo changing colors and spinning around a picture of the earth, it's time to start thinking about Quick-Time. And there are other reasons you might choose QuickTime instead of animation.

▶ In general, QuickTime movies may appear less jerky on screen than animations (Immedia may have a hard time running an animation at the same time that it processes other actions; but it can just pass a QuickTime movie to the system to run).

▶ You can synch up sound and pictures together in QuickTime (the sound is actually a track in the QuickTime movie). A QuickTime movie can even contain just audio, or contain MIDI audio information (see "Tip: General MIDI QuickTime Files," in Chapter 7, *Sound*).

▶ You can put a QuickTime movie inside a polygon if you don't want it to be rectangular (you don't have to worry about building masks).

▶ Many different programs use QuickTime movies; only Immedia uses its own particular form of animation file.

▶ QuickTime is often better than animation for longer pieces (anything over a second or two) because it has built-in video compression.

Where Movies Come From

You cannot build QuickTime movies inside Immedia. They must come from some other program. Fortunately, there are lots of other programs that create QuickTime movies, including Adobe Premier and Adobe AfterEffects. There are also smaller utilities that specialize in editing and tweaking QuickTime movies, such as Movie Cleaner (see Chapter 16, *The Real World QuarkImmedia CD-ROM*) and DesktopMovie.

I hate to pass the buck like this, but building and editing Quick-Time movies are really outside the scope of this book. You can find much more information on QuickTime movies in a book such as *Desktop Video Studio* by Andrew Soderberg and Tom Hudson.

▼ ▼

Importing QuickTime Movies

You've got a QuickTime movie all set and ready to roll (there are several you can use on the *Real World QuarkImmedia* CD-ROM at the back of this book). So how do you get it into your Immedia project?

1. Create a picture box (any picture box will do).

2. Open the Object tab of the QuarkImmedia palette, and give the picture box a name.

3. Set the Object Type popup menu on the QuarkImmedia palette to Movie (see Figure 9–1).

4. Select a movie from the Movie popup menu. If the movie's name doesn't already appear on the popup menu (unless you've used it in this project before, it won't), choose Other and then select the movie from your hard disk.

Figure 9–1
Creating a
movie object

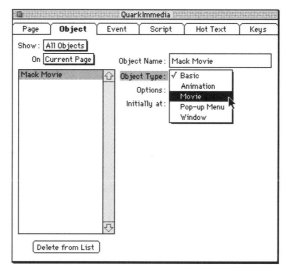

5. Choose some options for playing the movie (we'll talk about options in a moment).

That's all there is to it. When you choose a movie, Immedia displays its first frame in the picture box (just like an ordinary picture).

▼ ▼

Tip: Importing QuickTime Movies Quickly. In the last chapter I mentioned that you could import an animation into a picture box using Get Picture. As it turns out, you can do the same thing with QuickTime movies, too. Again, while it's important to understand the various popup menus on the Object tab, I generally just use Get Picture.

▼ ▼

Tip: Blank Frames. Every now and again, a QuickTime movie begins with a plain white frame. And every now and again, someone gets confused by this and thinks that the movie hasn't imported correctly. If you're not sure, always remember to try to play the movie first. It may be there after all!

▼ ▼

The QuickTime Rules

As I said earlier, you can put a QuickTime movie in a picture box of any shape or size, including polygons and ovals. However, it's important to be aware of what Immedia will and won't do with that movie.

▶ You can stretch the movie by changing the horizontal and vertical scaling percentages on the Measurements palette (or by holding down the Command key while you drag one of the box's corner handles).

▶ You can move the movie within the picture box with the Content tool, or crop the movie by making the picture box smaller than the movie frame.

▶ If the movie doesn't fill the entire box, you can specify the background color of the box.

▶ You can put a frame around the box. I usually leave the Frames setting in General Preferences (under the Edit menu) at Inside because . . . well, just because I like it that way. However, when I want to add a border to a movie, I change the setting to Outside so that I don't lop off the sides of the movie.

▶ You *cannot* rotate, skew, or flip (mirror) the movie.

▶ Remember that on the Windows platform, your movies are controlled by QuickTime for Windows. One of the limitations of QuickTime for Windows is that it only allows one sound to play at a time. If your movie has sound, you won't hear any other sounds that you've set up (see Chapter 7, *Sound*).

▶ Another limitation of QuickTime for Windows is that movies always play on the topmost layer, above any other objects you have on your page (at least they do in the initial version of Immedia). Plus, movie boxes are always rectangular in Windows, so your masking may be messed up. In general, if you're working with QuickTime movies, it's important to test the project thoroughly on a PC—it may look very different there.

▼ ▼

Tip: Pixel Doubling. You can often get away with playing a small QuickTime movie at twice its size. Sure, it looks more pixelated (you can see the pixels), but it hardly matters in some movies. For instance, those fast-motion videos with a lot of quick edits that are all the rage these days can often be pixel-doubled without a noticeable loss of quality.

▼ ▼

The Options Popup Menu

When it comes to movies, you've got a slew of options to choose from on the Object tab of the QuarkImmedia palette. The first three—Initially Hidden, Initially Disabled, and Keep Status on Page Exit—appear on the Options popup menu, just like they do for most other object types. You can, of course, select more than one option from the popup menu by choosing them one at a time.

Initially Hidden. You may find that you don't want the QuickTime movie to be visible when you first enter the page it's on. In this case, select the Initially Hidden option. Note that you can play a movie even when it's hidden (you might think of this as a "bug" or as a feature, depending on what you're trying to do).

Initially Disabled. Some people get confused about the meaning of Initially Disabled. It doesn't disable the movie itself; it disables the movie object. Let's say you selected the movie's picture box and assigned a Display Next Page action to the Click Up event. The movie is now both a movie and a "hot spot" that you can click on. If you turn on Initially Disabled on the Options popup menu, however, the movie runs normally, but clicking on the movie has no effect. You can then use the Enable Object action to "turn it back on."

Keep Status on Page Exit. When you select the Keep Status on Page Exit option, Immedia remembers the status of the movie when you switch to a different page.

▶ Whether or not the movie was playing

▶ Which frame was displayed last

▶ Whether the movie was paused or stopped

When you return to the page that contains the movie, Immedia picks up right where you left off. (Don't worry, it won't keep playing the movie while you're off on some other page.)

Movie Options

The keen of eye will notice immediately that I skipped right past the Initially At popup menu. Remember that we talked about this back in Chapter 2, *QuarkImmedia Basics,* and again in "Slide Object" in Chapter 8, *Animation.* So we won't bother covering that old ground again.* There are, however, five other movie-related settings on the

---

*Perhaps I should mention that in the version of Immedia that just shipped, setting the Initially At popup menu to a movie object causes very odd things to happen to the movie. Quark tells me that the bug will be fixed soon, perhaps by the time you read this.

Object tab of the QuarkImmedia palette that we should pay some attention to when working with QuickTime movies.

Loop. A QuickTime movie is just a sequence of frames, right? If you turn on the Loop option, Immedia starts playing the first frame right after the last one, so the movie keeps looping around. If you also turn on the Back and Forth option, however, once the movie reaches its end, QuarkImmedia turns around and plays the movie backward to the beginning.

Show QuickTime Controls. QuickTime has a standard control bar that pilots QuickTime movies. It's very functional, but unless your project is designed to look like a computer interface, the controller sticks out worse than a pit bull at a cat show (see Figure 9–2). That's why QuarkImmedia lets you build your own controls (see "Movie Actions," later in this chapter). But if you have a strong stomach and feel like using the default controls, you can get them by turning on the Show QuickTime Controls option.

Note that the control-bar displays just under the movie's picture box is as wide as the picture box—not as wide as the movie itself.

Preload Movie. The QuarkImmedia Viewer usually loads a small portion of the QuickTime movie into RAM when you first display the

Figure 9–2
QuickTime Controls

The QuickTime controls rarely blend in well.

page that the movie is on; the more of the movie in RAM, the more smoothly it should play.

The Preload Movie option tells the Immedia Viewer to load as much as possible of the QuickTime movie into RAM. How much it loads depends on how much RAM you have allocated to the Viewer (in the Viewer's Get Info dialog box; see "Memory Management" in Chapter 2, *QuarkImmedia Basics*) and how much RAM you've got in your machine (or perhaps more importantly, how much RAM your user has).

To be honest, I've never seen it make any difference whether I have this option turned on or off. Perhaps I'm not working with large enough movies. But it might be worth trying if you're experiencing jerky playback on a large movie file.

Treat as Button. Ordinarily, the picture box that contains the movie acts like any other object in your project when it comes to assigning actions to it. That is, you can assign an action to any normal user event: Click Down, Mouse Enter, and so on. When you turn on the Treat as Button option, however, the movie acts in a totally different way. I talked about this in detail in Chapter 6, *Buttons*, and in "Animation Buttons" in Chapter 8, *Animation*, so I won't repeat myself here.

Control Strip. The last option on the Object tab of the QuarkImmedia palette is the Control Strip (see Figure 9–3). This looks and acts exactly the same way as the QuickTime controls mentioned above, but it only lets you control the movie from the QuarkImmedia palette. The Control Strip lets you do three things.

▶ You can preview the movie without engaging the project (very helpful if you have several movies that are similar).

▶ You can set the movie's volume (if the movie has sound) by clicking the volume control button on the left side of the strip. If you're trying to get consistent sound levels from several different movies, this is one way to do it.

Figure 9-3
Movie options

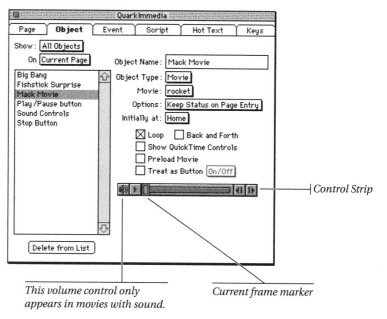

Control Strip

This volume control only appears in movies with sound.

Current frame marker

▶ If you don't want the movie to play from the beginning, or if you don't want the first frame of the movie to be the one you see in the project, you can choose a different beginning frame in the Control Strip (either drag the current frame marker, or just pause the movie at that point).

▼ ▼

Movie Actions

If you're not going to use the plain old QuickTime controls to run your movie, how are you going to get it to play? Immedia provides nine different actions that control QuickTime movies (see Figure 9–4). There's plenty more I wish Immedia could do, but these actions are sufficient for the majority of work you'll use QuickTime for. And the most important thing is that you can use any object or user event to trigger these actions (you can design your own interface: buttons, scripts, and so on).

Figure 9–4
Movie actions

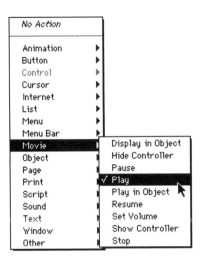

For each of the following actions, you have to specify which movie you want to affect (and for some actions, whether you want to affect all the movies on a page).

Play Movie. Unless the QuickTime movie is already playing, the Play Movie action starts the movie from the beginning (or from whatever frame you selected in the Control Strip). If the movie is already playing, Immedia just ignores this action. Note that if your movie is paused, Play Movie does *not* begin playing it from where it was paused; it starts again from the beginning.

Pause/ Resume/ Stop Movie. If you want to pause the movie at any time, you can invoke the Pause Movie action. Then, to begin again, use Resume Movie. And finally, if you want to stop the movie so that it cannot be resumed, you can use the Stop Movie action. I rarely use Stop Movie—I use Pause Movie instead because I get the same result, plus this gives me the option of starting up again.

The one advantage Stop Movie has over Pause Movie is that the former lets you stop all currently playing movies, while the latter only lets you pause a single movie.

Play Movie in Object. Let's say you've got a training CD with a list of ten training movies your user can play. Instead of having 10 different picture boxes set up as movie objects with the appropriate movie in each one, you can make just one picture box, and then use the Play Movie in Object action to swap in different movies when requested. The Play Movie in Object action is very similar to the Play Animation in Object action—you specify a movie, and which movie object to play the movie in (this can be any picture box for which you've chosen Movie from the Object Type popup menu on the Object tab of the QuarkImmedia palette; see Figure 9–5).

One important difference between this and the Play Animation in Object action, however, is that the new movie is resized to the same dimensions as the original movie (or to the dimensions of the empty movie object, if you haven't specified a movie for it yet). If all your movies are the same size, this isn't a problem; but be careful if they're not!

Note that this action actually swaps the movie in the box, so that if you later use a Play Movie action, it plays the newer movie—not the box's original movie.

Display Movie in Object. In the training-CD example above, when the user clicks on one of the subjects, that movie plays immediately in the picture box (because you used the Play Movie in Object action). If you want to place the movie in the picture box (so you can see it), but you don't want to start playing it yet, you can use the Display Movie in Object action instead. Then you can use the Play

Figure 9–5
Play Movie
in Object

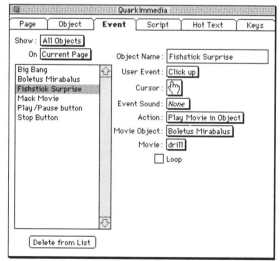

Movie action later to start it. Again, the movies must have the same dimensions, or Immedia will resize the new one.

Show Movie Controller and Hide Movie Controller. Remember that lovely QuickTime controller that I spoke of so fondly earlier? Just in case you're making a habit of using the control bar under your QuickTime movies, you can turn it on and off with the Show Movie Controller and Hide Movie Controller actions. It's as easy as telling Immedia which movie box you want to affect.

Set Movie Volume. Some movies have audio tracks as well as video tracks (others *only* have audio tracks; see "Tip: General MIDI Quick-Time files" in Chapter 7, *Sound*), and Immedia dutifully plays the audio portion of the movie alongside the video portion. This is probably the best way to synchronize sound and video, by the way— much better than trying to start a movie and then start a sound, and hoping they synch up properly.

You can set the volume of a QuickTime movie on the Object tab of the QuarkImmedia palette (see "Control Strip," above). But if you want to change the volume later, you can use the Set Movie Volume action (see Figure 9–6). As with sound, a value of 255 is the loudest the computer can play, and 0 (zero) is no sound at all.

The Method popup menu lets you set the volume of a particular movie, or set the volume of whatever movie is currently in a movie object.

▼ ▼

Tip: Movies versus Sounds. Sometimes you can design, implement, test, and finalize an entire project and something can still go wrong. That's what happened to one company I know of. They had a project working beautifully, but after they wrote it to a CD-ROM (the way the final piece was going to be distributed), they noticed that when sounds and movies with audio tracks were playing at the same time, one or both would be more jerky than when either was played alone. After much searching, they found out why: movies and sounds are stored in different places on the disc; the CD-ROM drive just couldn't skip back and forth between the two areas on the disc quickly enough.

This is the kind of problem that makes people who have been working in prepress for years (like me) want to give up on multimedia completely. But don't run quite yet; there is almost always a workaround. In this case, they were able to strip out the movie's sound into a separate file and play it along with the movie, using a Play Sound action.

▼ ▼

Tip: Full-Color QuickTime Movies. Back in Chapter 3, *Building Projects*, I told you that everything in your project gets converted to your project's 8-bit color palette when you engage or export the project. The one exception, I noted, was QuickTime movies. Remember, once you play the QuickTime movie, the operating system—not Immedia—displays the image, so it can display all the colors in the movie (even out-of-palette colors). There are two caveats to this.

▶ The project must be played on a screen that is displaying more than eight bits of color. That means you've got to set the If Wrong Screen Settings popup menu to Continue (in the Export Settings dialog box; see "Screen Settings" in Chapter 14, *Exporting*).

Figure 9–6
Set Movie Volume

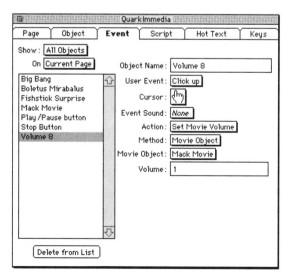

▶ The movie must be playing. Before and after the movie plays, Immedia just displays the movie using the project's custom color palette.

With these caveats in mind, you can use one of the following two tricks to make a movie appear in full color while it's not playing.

▶ You can make a script (see Chapter 13, *Scripting*) with two actions: Play Movie and Pause Movie. Set up this script to run when you enter the page. Because the movie pauses immediately after it begins playing, its color is retained.

▶ You can display the movie's QuickTime controls by turning on Show QuickTime Controls on the Object tab of the Quark-Immedia palette. For some reason, the movie is displayed in color when the controls are visible. One trick I've seen used is to put the picture box at the bottom of the page; that way, the QuickTime controls are displayed outside of the project.

▼ ▼

Tip: One-Frame Movies. With the last tip fresh in mind, don't forget that a QuickTime movie can be any length, even a single frame. If you've got a picture in your project that really must be displayed in full color, you can convert it into a single-frame QuickTime movie (using Apple's MoviePlayer or ConvertToMovie utility, for instance), then use the last tip to make sure it appears on screen correctly.

▼ ▼

Movie Magic

QuickTime movies are one of the easiest and most powerful methods of getting animation, video, and moving objects into your projects. They can often be more reliable and smooth than animations, especially for longer sequences. But even better, there are many programs out there that create and edit QuickTime movies, and many stock-footage sources you can quickly draw from.

As the film projectionist's motto goes, "If you can't be in the movies, you can at least *play* the movies!

Cursors 10

I F GOD IS TRULY IN THE DETAILS, then the lowly cursor is as holy as can be. Many multimedia authors neglect the cursor—that tiny icon whose job it is to follow your mouse movements and point at things on the screen. While there's nothing necessarily wrong with leaving the cursor set to the default arrow, you can score big points with your users (and your art director) if you take the time to design a custom cursor for your project.

Immedia lets you specify a different cursor just about any time you want. In fact, once you get into the habit, it becomes easy to use a different cursor for each page or each event. But you know what they say about too much of a good thing . . . .

Changing Cursors

It turns out that cursors are really just little animations that Immedia plays wherever the cursor should be. If the animation has only one frame, it looks static—it doesn't change at all. If the animation has more than one frame, then it becomes an animated cursor. Animated or static, it's created the same way, saved to disk the same way, and imported into your projects the same way.

In this first section, I'll discuss how to use cursors in your projects. QuarkImmedia ships with several you can use, and there are even more on the *Real World QuarkImmedia* CD-ROM at the back of this book. Later, I'll talk about how you can make your own.

Cursor Preferences

There are four default cursor settings in Immedia: Default, Busy, User Event, and Hot Text. Immedia starts you off on the right foot by setting reasonable default cursors, but you can change any of these in the QuarkImmedia Preferences dialog box (see Figure 10–1). In addition, you can always change a cursor for a specific action or object . . . but we'll get to that soon enough.

Figure 10–1

Default cursors

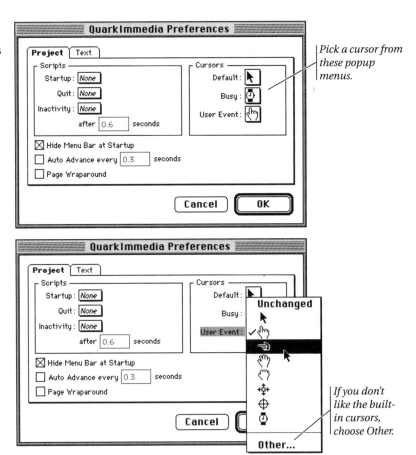

Pick a cursor from these popup menus.

If you don't like the built-in cursors, choose Other.

Default. Immedia uses the default cursor when the user isn't pointing at anything that will trigger an action—this is the project's "normal" state. It's usually just an arrow cursor.

User Event. As soon as the cursor moves over something that triggers an action, Immedia switches to the User Event cursor. The change of cursor doesn't tell you which user event will trigger the action, just that some type of event—mouse click, double-click, or so on—will do something.

Busy. Some actions take time to perform. For instance, if you're running a project over the Internet and you start to load a movie or display a new page, it may take a little while. If it's going to take more than a couple of seconds, Immedia kicks in the Busy cursor. As soon as Immedia is no longer "busy," it switches back to whatever cursor it was using before.

Hot Text. I said above that any time the cursor moves over something that triggers an action, Immedia switches to the User Event cursor. The one exception to this is when the cursor moves over some hot text (text that has been set up to trigger an action; see Chapter 4, *Text*). In this case, the program uses the Hot Text cursor. Just to confuse you, the folks at Quark put this setting in a different place: on the Text tab of the QuarkImmedia Preferences dialog box (see Figure 10–2).

User Event Cursors

Just because you set up the default cursors one way in the Quark-Immedia Preferences dialog box doesn't mean you have to stick with them! You can accompany any user event with a cursor by changing the Cursor popup menu on the Event tab.

For example, let's say you want a special warning cursor to appear only when the user moves over one particular area of the screen. Here's one way to do it.

Figure 10-2

Hot Text cursor

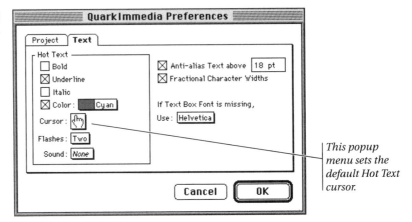

This popup menu sets the default Hot Text cursor.

1. Select the object over which you want the cursor to change (if there isn't an object there already, make one, and give it a name on the Object tab of the QuarkImmedia palette).

2. Select Mouse Enter from the User Event popup menu on the Event tab of the palette.

3. Select a cursor from the Cursor popup menu (see Figure 10-3). If you don't want one of the built-in cursors, choose Other, and select one from your hard drive. Note that you don't have to assign any action to this user event; just choosing a cursor is enough.

Now when you move the cursor over that area, Immedia switches to your custom cursor. When you move it beyond the bounds of the object, Immedia reverts to the default cursor.

Similarly, if you want a special cursor to appear only when the user is holding down the mouse button, you can choose Click Down from the User Event popup menu and pick a cursor from the Cursor popup menu.

▼ ▼

Tip: Watch Out for Cursors. As I said, you don't have to assign an action to a user event in order to change that event's cursor. However, if you do this, you need to be careful. As you know, if you assign an action to a user event, Immedia puts a little checkmark next to it on the User Event popup menu. But the popup menu does not

Figure 10–3
User Event cursors

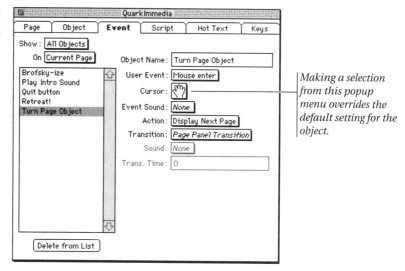

Making a selection from this popup menu overrides the default setting for the object.

indicate that you've changed a user event's cursor! The only way to tell is by selecting each user event, one at a time, and checking the Cursor popup menu.

▼ ▼

Tip: Ignore Some Events. There are some user events you can just ignore when it comes to assigning cursors. For instance, assigning a cursor to the Cursor Up user event won't help you much—you only see the cursor for about a tenth of a second (if that) when you let go of the mouse button. Same thing with Double-click and Mouse Exit—why bother if you'll never really see any change?

▼ ▼

Cursor Actions

You can use the QuarkImmedia Preferences dialog box or the User Event popup menu to change your cursors; or you can use a cursor action. There are three such actions: Use Cursor, Hide Cursor, and Show Cursor. Any action or script can trigger one of these actions.

Use Cursor. The Use Cursor action changes the current default cursor (the one Immedia uses when the mouse isn't over any object that can trigger an action). For example, let's say you want a particular cursor to appear on one particular page of your project. You could write a script with one command in it—Use Cursor (see Figure 10–4)—and then use that script as an entry script for that page (see Chapter 13, *Scripting*, for more information on entry scripts).

As soon as you jump to that page, your script changes the cursor. Then you'll need another script that changes the cursor back to the original cursor icon (you could set this up as the Exit Script so that it's triggered automatically when you jump to a different page).

Hiding and showing cursors. You can also hide the cursor and then show it again. Hiding the cursor (with the Hide Cursor action) makes it disappear from the project. It's a little deceiving, because a hidden cursor is still active—if you start rolling the mouse around spastically while clicking, you can still accidentally trigger actions.

However, hiding the cursor is often helpful when you're playing a QuickTime movie or slowly displaying a hidden object. I just wish you could hide *and* disable it.

Note that if your project is set up to play in a window (with or without a title), the cursor is only hidden inside the boundaries of the project. As soon as you move the cursor outside the project, it appears again. Of course, you can make it visible again at any time by invoking the Show Cursor action.

Figure 10–4
Use Cursor

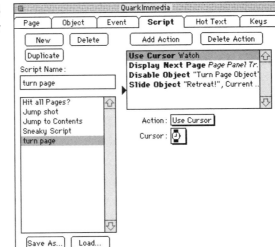

▼ ▼

Building Cursors

Now that you know how to use (and abuse) cursors, it's time to learn how to make them yourself. Remember when I said that cursors were just little animations? Well, strangely enough, the Cursor Editor looks and acts almost exactly like the Animation Editor (which, in turn, bears a striking resemblance to the Button Editor). I won't go into the details of how this dialog box works because I've said it all before in Chapter 6, *Buttons,* and Chapter 8, *Animation;* however, let me give a little explanation of the differences.

Rolling Your Own

Cursors are always 16 pixels wide and 16 pixels tall. There's no argument there, at least not in this first version of the product. When you create a new cursor (select Cursor from the New submenu under the File menu) or want to edit one already saved to disk (choose Open from the File menu, or double-click on it from the desktop), Quark-Immedia opens the Cursor Editor (see Figure 10–5).

The only differences between the Cursor Editor and the Animation Editor are the absence of the Speed field and the Frame Size button; clearly, neither are necessary because cursors don't move along a path, and they must remain a fixed size.

Figure 10–5
Cursor editor

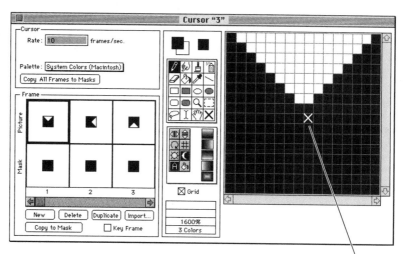

The hot spot

If you want a static cursor, make sure there is only a single frame in the Frame section of the Cursor Editor. If you want an animated cursor, add all the additional frames you want.

While your cursors can include any color in the color palette, remember that the QuarkImmedia Viewer for Windows can't display color cursors. If your project will be viewed on a PC, you probably want to stick with black-and-white cursors.

Hot Spot. There are two other subtle differences between a cursor and an animation, and they both have to do with the hot spot—the pixel that contains the "X". First of all, the hot spot has a different meaning when it's in a cursor: it shows where the cursor is "live." For instance, that particular pixel must be over a button before you can click on that button; if every pixel *except* the hot spot is over the button, you could click all day and not activate it. To change the hot spot, click on one pixel with the Hot Spot tool.

The second difference is that the hot spot must be the same in every frame of a cursor; you can't change it from frame to frame (I can't think of why you'd want to).

▼ ▼

Tip: Reversible Cursors. You remember how I was harping in the *Buttons* and *Animation* chapters on how you always have to make sure your mask is correct for each frame? If you don't create a mask for each frame, the button or animation won't appear properly on the page. Well, you almost always want to use a proper mask with cursors, too.

But you know, something really interesting happens if you don't create masks for cursors. The cursors *do* work. And what's more, the cursors react to whatever is underneath them. If you have a black cursor with a mask, it stays black when you move it over a dark-blue area. But if there is no mask, the cursor actually inverts to a lighter color when it moves over a dark area, so you can still see it!

To tell you the truth, I don't know if this is a bug in the program or not (Quark's documentation doesn't mention it), but it sure can be helpful if you need to see the cursor even when it's over a color similar to its own (like black over black).

▼ ▼

Importing Animations

The tools in the Cursor Editor are pretty rudimentary, though they are usually adequate for building cursors. Nonetheless, it's often easier to build animated cursors elsewhere, even though you still have to get them into the Cursor Editor in order to save them to disk in the proper format.

There are two ways that you can import animated cursors into the Cursor Editor.

▶ You can copy and paste them into Immedia, frame by frame, from another program (such as Photoshop). If there aren't many frames, this is a reasonable choice.

▶ You can save them from some other program in PICS format, then use the Import button to bring them into the Cursor Editor. Immedia always leaves the first frame blank when you import PICS files, so you'll probably want to delete that frame before saving the cursor. Note that the Import button also lets you import any other kind of picture XPress can handle (TIFF, EPS, and so on).

▼ ▼

A Last Cursory Glance

I don't want to suggest that a cursor is going to make or break your project; there are many other issues that are clearly more important to your project's success than a little icon that moves around the screen. But I do want to emphasize that even a little attention paid to the most mundane aspects of your piece can lift it from being "just another multimedia project" to a more professional and satisfactory level.

Menus

11

The pulldown menu has been incorporated into programs and operating systems probably more than any of the other computer interface innovations developed at Xerox PARC and SRI over the past 30 years. It's easy to see why: a menu is a simple but elegant way to offer options to computer users. Too often people forget that these programs are meant to be used by humans, and they clutter their pages up with 20 buttons instead of just using two or three menus.

QuarkImmedia makes creating menus easy—both the kind that drop down from the top of the screen, and also the "popup" type that you can put anywhere. However, unlike many other features in Immedia, you cannot customize how a menu looks. When viewed on a Mac, you get Mac-looking menus; on the PC, you get Windows-looking menus. No, you can't colorize the menus; no, you can't use a different font. If you want a specialized menu, take a look at the Aesop's Fables project on the *Real World QuarkImmedia* CD-ROM.

▼ ▼

Making a Menu

Before you can do *anything* with menus—including viewing or placing them—you must first create one using the MenuMaker (on the QuarkImmedia menu; see Figure 11–1). The MenuMaker is a quick and easy way to construct menus. Menus you create here can later appear on the menu bar, or as popup menus, or not appear at all—it's up to you.

Note that the left side of the MenuMaker dialog box lists the menus; the right side lists the menu items.

1. To create a new menu, press the New button on the left side of the MenuMaker dialog box.

Figure 11–1

The MenuMaker

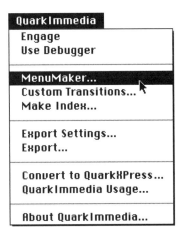

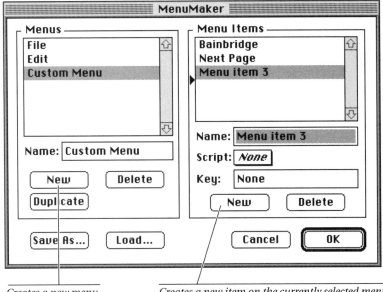

Creates a new menu   *Creates a new item on the currently selected menu*

2. Type in the name of the menu. (If the menu is going to sit on the menu bar, whatever you type is how it'll appear; if it's going to be a popup menu, it doesn't matter what you name it, 'cause it won't appear on screen.)

3. Click the New button on the right side of the dialog box to add an item to the menu; then give the item a name. You don't have to create the items in any particular order, because you can always change them around later. However, if you've already got a few menu items on the list, you can specify where you want the next one to be by moving the black triangle-pointer and clicking New.

4. If you want something to happen when the user selects a menu item, you have to assign a script to that item. First build the script (see Chapter 13, *Scripting*), then assign it to the menu item here by selecting it from the Script popup menu.

5. You can also use the Key field to assign keyboard shortcuts to menu items. The keystroke combination can be anything on the keyboard, along with the Command key (unfortunately, you cannot use the Option, Shift, or Control keys).

Moving and Deleting

The list of menus on the left side of the MenuMaker dialog box is fixed—you cannot change the order of the menus. But that's okay, because there's really no need to. The order of this list has nothing to do with the order of the menus on the menu bar, or with anything else. So stop worrying about it.

On the other hand, the order of these items on the list on the right side *is* important—it's the order in which the items appear on the menu. Fortunately, you can change the order easily by dragging items from one place to another on the list.

If you want to delete a whole menu or a single menu item, select it, and click one of the Delete buttons (be careful which one you press; you may be deleting more or less than you want). If you want to delete more than one item at a time, Shift-click on each of them (or Command-click to select noncontiguous items).

▼ ▼

Tip: Gray Bars and Spaces. If you want to put a blank line between two menu items, create a new item and enter a single wordspace in the Name field. Later, when you show the menu, use the Disable Item action so that the user can't select it.

Instead of using a blank space, you might want to separate two items with a gray bar. You can't make a gray bar that looks like a real separator bar (see Figure 11–2). However, you can fake it easily enough: just type a line of underscores in the name field (a menu item's name can have up to 31 characters). Later, use a Disable Item action to gray this item out.

Figure 11–2
Gray bars and
spaces in menus

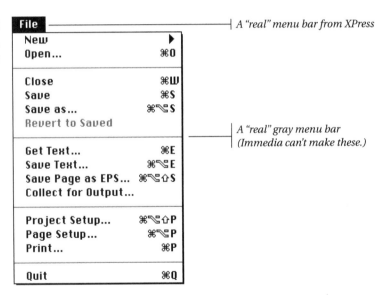

A "real" menu bar from XPress

A "real" gray menu bar
(Immedia can't make these.)

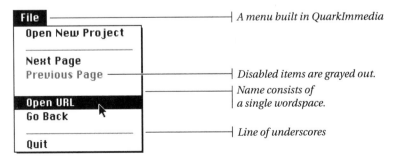

A menu built in QuarkImmedia

Disabled items are grayed out.

Name consists of
a single wordspace.

Line of underscores

▼ ▼

Popup Menus

Once you've created a menu with the MenuMaker, you can incorporate it into your project either as a popup menu or as a menu on the menu bar. Let's first take a quick look at how to make popup menus; then we'll explore the wild world of the menu bar.

Popup menus (some Windows folks call these "popdown" menus) are an "object type." That means you can turn any rectangular picture box or text box into a popup menu by selecting it and choosing Pop-up Menu from the Object Type popup on the Object tab of the QuarkImmedia palette (see Figure 11–3). Immedia automatically sets the height of the object to 19 points; the width remains the same.

Popup objects have various optional attributes. However, no matter what you do, the box never actually looks like a popup menu until you engage or export the project (see "Tip: Where's the Popup?"). That's because Immedia leaves the "drawing" of the popup menu to the operating system (Macintosh or Windows), and it only asks for it when the project is running.

Figure 11–3
Making a
popup menu

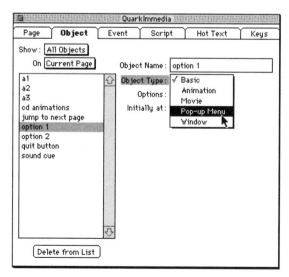

Title Box

You don't *need* a label on your popup menu, but unless it's painfully clear what the menu is for, a label sure is useful. You can label your popup menu however you like, just by putting a text box next to it (or above it or under it or whatever). But if you don't need high-falutin design, Immedia makes labeling popup menus easy.

1. Create a text box anywhere on your page (or, preferably, on the pasteboard) and type in the label you want.

2. Set the text to 12-point Chicago. Actually, you can use any font or size you want, but when you engage the project, Immedia will use 12-point Chicago (on a computer running Windows, you'll probably get 12-point Ariel). No, you can't do any other special text formatting; Immedia just ignores it.

3. Make the text box approximately 12 pixels wider than the text itself.

4. Give that text box a name on the Object tab of the Quark-Immedia palette, and select Text Box from the Object type popup menu (see Figure 11–4).

5. Select the popup menu object again, and on the Object tab of the palette, choose the name of the text box from the Title Box popup menu.

If you later decide to remove the label, set the Title Box popup menu back to None.

You need to set the width of the label's text box (in step 3) because this width determines where the popup title is in relation to the popup menu. If the text box is too narrow, Immedia truncates the label (see Figure 11–5). If the text box is too wide, Immedia places the label strangely.

Options

Popup menu objects have options, just like any other kind of object (all objects are created equal, and so on). You've seen the three choices on the Options popup menu in other chapters: Initially Hidden,

Figure 11–4
Labeling a
popup menu

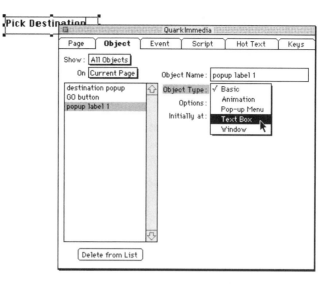

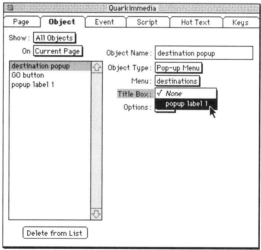

Initially Disabled, and Keep Status on Page Entry. You can, of course, choose one or more of them, or leave the popup set to None.

Initially Hidden. Popup menus are so ugly (compared to all but the most spartan of designs) that you may want to show them only when necessary. Accordingly, you can choose Initially Hidden from the Options popup menu and later show the menu with the Show Object action.

Figure 11–5
Labels and
text box width

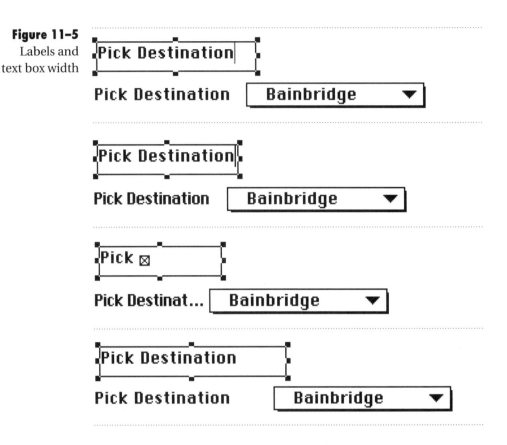

Initially Disabled. If you don't want someone to mess around with a popup menu, you can disable it. Immedia grays it out and makes it unusable. Later, you can enable it with the Enable Menu action. For example, you might have three popup menus on a page, with the last two disabled. Depending on what the user selects from the first menu, one of the other two could become enabled.

Keep Status on Page Entry. Let's say you select an item from a popup menu, then move to another page. When you return to the page with the popup menu, it will have reset itself back to the first item on the list. You can force the popup menu to remember what you last selected by turning on the Keep Status on Page Entry option. When this option is on, the only way to reset the popup menu is with the Set Pop-up Selection Action (see "Other Menu Actions," later in this chapter).

▼ ▼

Tip: Where's the Popup? I find it annoying that I can't see popup menus on my screen until I engage the project. What's the difference between a popup menu and a little empty picture box or text box? Nothing. Here's my advice: use a text box to create a popup menu. Then color it, or type the name of the popup in it (see Figure 11–6). This has no effect on the look of the popup menu, because Immedia totally replaces the text box with the actual popup menu when the project is engaged or exported.

Figure 11–6
Identifying
popup menus

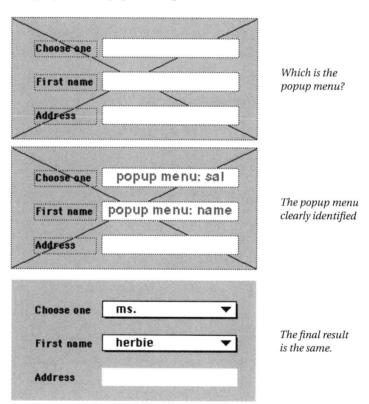

Which is the popup menu?

The popup menu clearly identified

The final result is the same.

▼ ▼

The Menu Bar

When you engage an Immedia project, the menu bar at the top of the screen remains visible unless you tell Immedia to hide it. If the project fills the entire screen and you aren't using any menus in your project, you should probably hide the menu bar—it just looks odd sitting there with nothing in it.* If the project is running in a window (see "Making a New Project" in Chapter 3, *Building Projects*), there's little reason to hide the menu bar. In fact, people usually expect a menu bar—at least one that has a Quit command in it (yes, *you* know you can always just press Command-Q to quit, but your user may not know that).

You can hide the menu bar in two ways. The first method is to turn on the Hide Menu Bar at Startup option in the Immedia Preferences dialog box (choose QuarkImmedia Preferences from the Edit menu; see Figure 11–7). When this option is on, the program makes the menu bar invisible as soon as you engage the project. You can later make it visible with the Show Menu Bar action (see below).

Note that like most preferences, if you turn this option on while no document is open, it stays on for all subsequent projects you make. If a document *is* open when you turn this option on, you only affect that one document.

Figure 11–7
Hide Menu
Bar at Startup

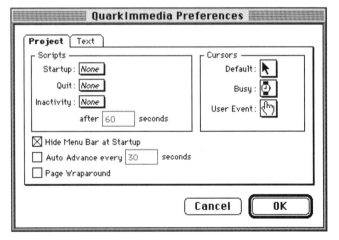

Show Menu Bar and Hide Menu Bar. The second method for hiding the menu bar is to trigger a Hide Menu Bar action. There are no options for this action; Immedia just turns off the whole menu bar.

---

*Actually, the menu bar isn't entirely blank. System-level items that appear in every program—like the Apple menu in the left corner and the application menu in the right corner—are still visible. The same thing goes when the project is viewed in Windows—except that the system items are different.

If you want to make the menu bar visible again, you can trigger a Show Menu Bar action. Here you've got one option: the Include Viewer Menus checkbox (see Figure 11–8). When you check this box, Immedia displays three menus on the menu bar: File, Edit, and View. Any menu you add to the menu bar (we'll see how to do that in a moment) follows to the right of these.

▼ ▼

Tip: Leave Space at the Top. When you show the menu bar in a project that fills the screen (like a 640-by-480-pixel project on a 640-by-480-pixel screen), the Macintosh menu bar cuts off the top 20 pixels of the page. In Microsoft Windows, the menu bar won't cut off the top of the screen; instead, the whole screen moves down, so you lose about 20 pixels from the bottom. You might want to set your margin guides at 20 pixels from the top and from the bottom to remind you not to put important page elements there.

▼ ▼

Add Menu and Remove Menu. Just because you've got the menu bar visible doesn't mean any of the menus you've made will show up. In fact, a custom menu won't appear in the menu bar until you use an Add Menu action to put it there. The Add Menu action lets you choose which menu you want displayed; you can add one at a time.

If your menu bar is dynamic (that is, if it changes depending on what page you're on, or what the user is doing), you may want to remove menus, too. You can do this easily enough with the Remove Menu action.

▼ ▼

Tip: Building a Menu Bar. You typically add or remove menus in a script. You don't *have* to do it that way; it just usually turns out that way because you generally want to use more than just one Add Menu or Remove Menu action at a time. For example, when you start up a project, you may want several menus to appear on the menu bar all at once.

You can create this effect with a few short steps.

Figure 11-8

Include Viewer Menus

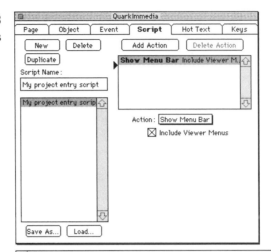

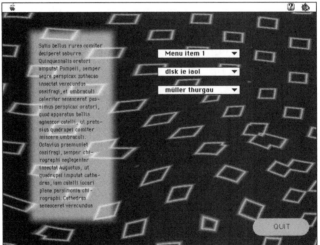

Include Viewer Menus turned off . . .

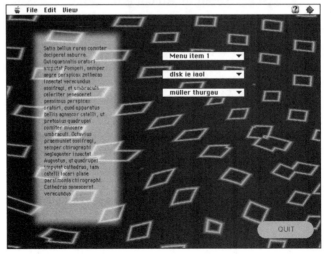

. . . turned on

1. Create a short script (see Chapter 13, *Scripting*) that adds the menus to the menu bar with a series of Add Menu actions. Make sure you add the menus in the order you want them to appear (add the first menu first, and so on). The last action in the script should be Show Menu. Name your script something like "Build Menu Bar."

2. Turn on the Hide Menu Bar at Startup option in the Immedia Preferences dialog box.

3. While you're still in the Immedia Preferences dialog box, choose your Build Menu Bar script from the Startup Script popup menu.

When you engage the project, your script adds the menus while the menu bar is still hidden. At the end of the script, the menu bar appears with all the menus in place.

▼ ▼

Tip: Including Viewer Menus. If you want the Viewer's menus to appear when you start up the project, you can use a variation on the technique in the last tip.

1. Turn on the Hide Menu Bar at Startup option in the Quark-Immedia Preferences dialog box.

2. Build a script that contains only one action: Show Menu Bar. Make sure the Include Viewer Menus option is turned on.

3. Make this script your Startup script in QuarkImmedia Preferences.

▼ ▼

Tip: Quitting from Projects. What happens when your user presses Command-Q? The project quits, right? Not necessarily.

▶ If the Viewer's menus are visible in your project (that is, if you used a Show Menu Bar action with the Include Viewer Menus option turned on) when the user presses Command-Q, both the project *and* the Viewer quit.

▶ If the Viewer's menus are not visible, only the project quits and the Viewer stays open (presumably waiting for the user to open a new project).

▶ If the Viewer's menus are not visible and you've assigned the Command-Q keystroke to a script (on the Keys tab of the QuarkImmedia palette), then Immedia runs that script and does not quit the project at all.

Note that the first two items assume that the Viewer is not embedded in the project; in that case, the project and the Viewer quit together when the user presses Command-Q.

Of course, the user can always quit by pressing F15 . . . .

▼ ▼

Menu Enable and Menu Disable. Instead of hiding and showing menus on the menu bar, you might find it more elegant to disable (gray out and deactivate) and enable menus with the Menu Disable and Menu Enable actions (see Figure 11–9). The only option you get with these actions is which menu you can disable or enable.

Figure 11-9
Disabled menus

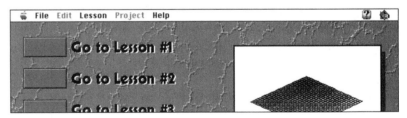

Check Menu Item and Uncheck Menu Item. You know how sometimes menu items have a checkmark next to them? They're like on/off switches—when you select the item from the menu, the checkmark toggles off. Not to be outdone, Immedia lets you put checkmarks next to menu items with the Check Menu Item and Uncheck Menu Item actions. When you use either of these actions,* you have to

---

*You might be tempted to look for these actions on the Menu popout menu (under the Action menu). But you won't find them there. They're on the Menu Bar popout because you can only check and uncheck items that are on menu bars . . . not on popup menus. Odd logic, but there you are.

specify a menu and an item, either by name or by their place on the menu (see Figure 11–10).

Figure 11–10
Checking menu items

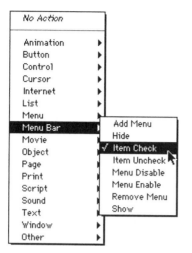

Check Menu Item adds a checkmark next to a menu item.

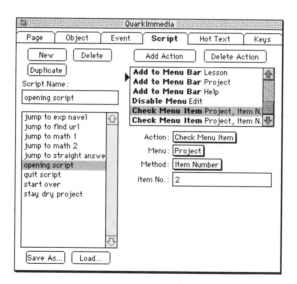

▼ ▼

Tip: Checking and Unchecking Menu Items. Of course, if you want a menu item to be *unchecked* when you select it, you've got to tell Immedia that, too. You might want to make a script that either checks or unchecks the menu item, depending on its current status. Unfortunately, Immedia's If action currently can't tell the status of a menu item. Annoying, but true.

The only good way I've seen to do this is to create a proxy button on the pasteboard that you can turn on or off (you *can* check to see if buttons are on or off). Let's say you want a menu item called "Run" to be checked the first time you select it, and then unchecked the next time you select it. First, put a small On/Off button on the pasteboard and call it "RunButton." Then build this little snippet at the beginning of Run's script.

```
If Button "RunButton" is On
Uncheck Menu Item "Run"
Turn On Button "Run"
Else
Check Menu Item "Run"
Turn Off Button "Run"
End If
```

Yes, this is kind of a pain. But sometimes you need to make three right turns when you're not allowed to make a single left turn.

▼ ▼

Other Menu Actions

We've looked at all the actions on the Menu Bar popout menu, but Immedia also provides you with six actions on the Menu popout menu. The difference? The Menu popout gives you control over the content of both menu-bar menus *and* popup menus. You can add, remove, or disable menu items. You can also change the current popup menu selection or find out which popup menu item is currently selected.

Add Menu Item. Quarkmmedia's menus, as I've said before, are dynamic—you can change them whenever you want. The Add Menu Item action lets you add a menu item. The multitude of options for adding menu items seems overwhelming at first, but at second glance the options are really straightforward (see Figure 11–11). The process can be broken down into five steps: choosing

Figure 11–11
Add Item

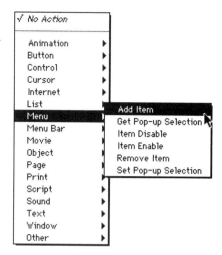

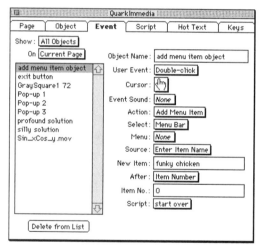

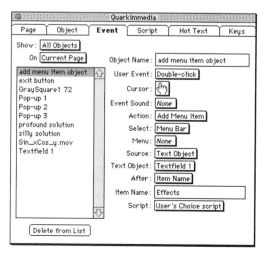

what kind of menu you want to change, choosing *which* menu you want to change, specifying the name of the new menu item, specifying where on the menu it should go, and then choosing which script should be triggered when the menu item is selected.

1. First you must choose either Menu Bar or Popup Menu Object from the Select popup menu—you can't add an item to both types at the same time.

2. The next popup menu you must contend with is called either "Object" or "Menu," depending on what you selected in the previous step. If you're dealing with a menu on the menu bar, choose the name of the menu. If it's a popup menu, choose the name of the popup menu object—that is, the name of the object on your page. Note that neither the menu, menu bar, nor popup menu has to be visible when you do this.

3. The Source popup menu lets you choose how the item will be named. The default setting Enter Item Name lets you choose a name for the menu item right there on the QuarkImmedia palette (type it in the New Item text field that follows the popup menu).

   The second option, Text Box, lets you use the content of a text box as the menu item name. For instance, after the user types an Internet URL into a text box, you could place that URL on a popup menu. When Text Box is selected, Immedia expects you to choose the name of an editable text-box object from the Text Object popup menu. As usual, you can choose a text box object from another page by selecting Other from the Text Object popup menu.

4. Now you've got to tell Immedia where to place this new item on the menu. You must choose either Item Name or Item Number from the After popup menu. Personally, I most often add menu items to the beginning or end of a menu (see the next tip to find out how to do this). But if you know that you want your menu item to be third on the list, you can choose Item Number, then type "2" in the Item No. text field.

5. Finally, you can attach a script to this menu item by choosing one from the Script popup menu. This script plays when the user chooses this menu item. Note that you don't have to attach a script to a menu item, although the menu item just won't do anything unless you do. Sorry, you can't add keyboard shortcuts to menu items dynamically. You have to add them ahead of time in the MenuMaker dialog box.

Remove Menu Item. There are many fewer steps when you remove items from a menu (see Figure 11–12). You still must first decide whether you want to remove the item from a menu on the menu bar or from a popup menu. Then you must choose which menu or popup menu object you want to remove it from.

Finally, you have to choose which item you want to remove. In this case, you must specify either the particular name or number of the menu item. I recently wanted to choose an item based on what was selected from another popup menu (or based on what was written in an editable text box), and found to my dismay that there was no way to do this. I suppose the engineers need to have something to work on in future versions.

Figure 11–12
Remove Item

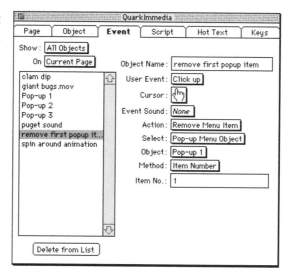

▼ ▼

Tip: The Beginning or the End of Menus. If you want to place a new menu item at the beginning of a menu, set the After popup menu to Item Number, and type "0" (zero) in the Item No. text field. If you want to add the new item to the end of a menu, type in a number that's larger than the number of items already on the menu. For example, if you tell Immedia to put the new item after item number 200, even if you only have 10 items on the menu, Immedia places it as item number 11.

The same thing holds true for removing menu items—if you tell Immedia to remove item number 200, it removes the last item.

▼ ▼

Disable Menu Item and Enable Menu Item. Just as you can gray out an entire menu on the menu bar (see "Menu Enable and Menu Disable," earlier in this chapter), you can disable (gray out) a single item on a menu using Disable Menu Item (see Figure 11–13). You can enable it later using Enable Menu Item. The options for these two actions are exactly the same as those for Remove Menu Item: you must choose either a menu or a popup menu object, then specify a

Figure 11–13
Disabling a
menu item

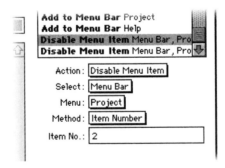

menu or popup menu, and finally choose which item you want (either by name or by number).

Get Pop-up Menu Selection. As soon as you choose an item from a popup menu, Immedia runs the script attached to that popup menu (if there is one). But that doesn't mean that you know *which* item is currently selected on that popup menu. You can find this out with the Get Pop-up Selection action (see Figure 11–14).

Get Pop-up Menu Selection requires that you choose from four popup menus: Object, Get As, Destination, and Placement.

▶ **Object.** This is the name of the popup menu object you're inquiring about—not the name of the menu, but the object on the page itself. It doesn't have to be on the same page you're currently on; if it isn't, choose Other from the popup menu.

▶ **Get As.** You can ask for either the Item Name or the Item Number (Item Name is the default). Item Number just gives you the item's placement on the popup menu; I'm not sure why you'd want this (if you can think of a good use for it, let me know). Item Name is exactly what you see on the popup menu.

▶ **Destination.** This action provides you with a name (or number) which must be inserted somewhere. That somewhere can be any text box that has been named and set up as a text box

Figure 11–14
Get Pop-up
Menu Selection

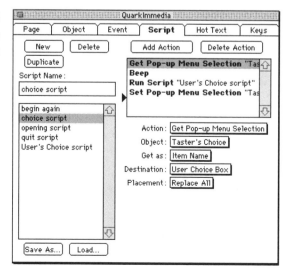

object on the Object tab of the QuarkImmedia palette (any kind of text box object will do—simple, editable, scrolling, or even a list). If you leave Destination set to None, the action won't have any result at all.

▶ **Placement.** Where in the text box do you want to put the result? You've got four choices: Beginning, End, Replace All, and Replace Selection. The only thing that may not be self-explanatory here is that Immedia does not add a return at the end of whatever you add. If you add some text at the end of the text block, then add some more text, there's no line break (or even a space) between the two text blocks. The only exception to this is when the text box is a list object; then each chunk of text sits on its own line.

Set Pop-up Menu Selection. The final menu action is Set Pop-up Menu Selection. This simply lets you choose which menu item is visible on the popup menu. For example, you could use this action to reset the popup menu to show the first item, or to switch to a different menu item if a particular button is pressed. The Set Popup Menu Selection action lets you choose a popup menu, and an item from that popup menu (you have to specify it by name or number).

Note that using this action does not run the script attached to the menu item you select. Scripts attached to menu items are run only when a user selects the menu item.

▼ ▼

What's on the Menu?

While it's true that menus are utilitarian and somewhat less than cool when it comes to fancy multimedia projects, what *is* cool is how easily you can create and manipulate menus in QuarkImmedia. Menus work because we all know how to use them, and while flashy multicolored buttons and animations are fun to see and play with, a basic menu-driven interface is often simply easier to use.

In the next chapter we'll take a trip into the world of printing, where you can get your work out of the computer and onto paper.

Printing 12

I F YOU'VE EVER SEEN WHERE I WORK, you know that the idea of the "paperless office" is a joke. Sure, everyone is getting all hyper about multimedia and the Internet and so on; but when it comes right down to it, people want things on paper. Quark, realizing this, sneaked a few printing features into Immedia—just enough to keep us paper-happy folks content.

Because you're actually authoring your projects in QuarkXPress, you can print whole pages of those projects using XPress's normal printing features. But once you've exported a project, you no longer have XPress's robust print engine behind you. In fact, you've got a rather limited number of printing options. QuarkImmedia lets you trigger four actions related to printing: Print Current Page, Print EPS, Print Text Object, and Page Setup.

Note that the Immedia Viewer assumes that you have a Post-Script printer. This is a pretty significant assumption, of course. If you don't have a PostScript printer, Immedia may print fine, it may spit out an error, or it may not do anything. Worst-case scenario: You'll encounter some kind of "system anomaly" (some people call these "crashes").

Show Print Dialog. The three actions that cause a page to print— Print Current Page, Print EPS, and Print Text Object—all share one feature: the Show Print Dialog checkbox. When this box is checked (it is by default), Immedia shows you the Print dialog box before printing. This feature is useful because it gives the user the options to cancel, to print more than one copy at a time, or to set up other printing options (see Figure 12–1).

Every now and again, however, when you want Immedia to print something fast, you may want to turn off the Show Print Dialog option. When you do this, QuarkImmedia uses the printer driver's default settings.

Print Current Page

Printing from multimedia programs is usually poor quality because you typically get just what you see on your screen: plain old bitmapped graphics, and jaggy text that looks ugly. Well, the folks at Quark didn't want to disappoint you, so they included a feature to give you just this: the Print Current Page action.

When you trigger a Print Current Page action (see Figure 12–2), Immedia prints out exactly what you're looking at on screen. There

Figure 12–1
Print dialog box

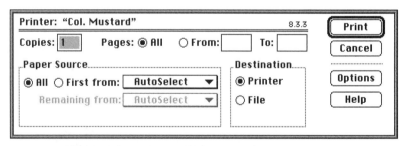

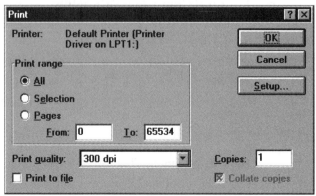

The Print dialog box on Windows

is one hidden feature here, however: if your page won't fit on the paper, Immedia resizes the page proportionally to fit. For instance, a standard 640-by-480-pixel project won't fit on an 8.5-by-11-inch page. Immedia figures out how much it needs to resize, so that you don't have to worry about it.

This is the only printing action that is even somewhat reliable on non-PostScript printers.

Figure 12-2
Print Current Page

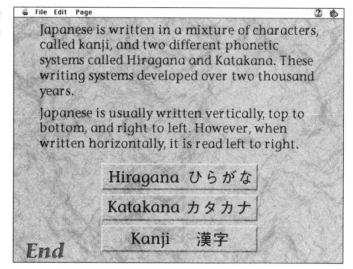

If it looks like this on screen . . .

. . . it'll look like this when printed.

Print EPS

Again, the problem with Print Current Page is that you can only get those ugly, jaggy graphics and text. Wouldn't it be nice to print a nice smooth PostScript file instead? That's what the Print EPS action does. When you select Print EPS from the Action popup menu, Immedia lets you pick an EPS to print from the EPS popup menu (choose Other to pick an EPS from your hard disk; see Figure 12–3). Note that you do not have to use Get Picture to import the EPS into your document first.

You can create an EPS in many different applications, including Adobe Illustrator, Adobe PageMaker, Macromedia FreeHand, or even QuarkXPress. In fact, if you already have content in XPress that you want to print, you can save it as an EPS file (using Save as EPS from the File menu) and then select that file from the EPS popup menu in the Print EPS action.

The problem with Print EPS is file size. EPS files can be large (sometimes really large). And while your document size remains small (because Immedia only creates a link to the EPS), the entire EPS gets embedded when you export the project, making the exported project very big indeed. Granted, the size of an EPS might not be much in comparison to a QuickTime movie or a sound file, but it's something to think about if you need to save space.

One other potential problem: your user must have a PostScript printer. If they don't, either nothing will print out or they'll just get a bunch of garbage.

Print Text Object

The third printing action, Print Text Object, is sort of the best of all worlds: you can get nice clean printouts, but it adds very little to your exported project's file size. The drawback is that you can only print text with very limited formatting and no graphics.

The Print Text Object action prints the text in any text box that you've specified as a Text Box Object on the Object tab of the Quark-Immedia palette (see Chapter 4, *Text*). It can be editable, scrollable, a list, or even just a simple textbox object. There are a few things to keep in mind, however.

Figure 12-3
Print EPS

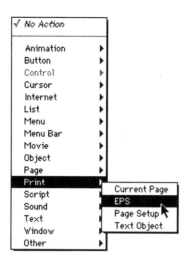

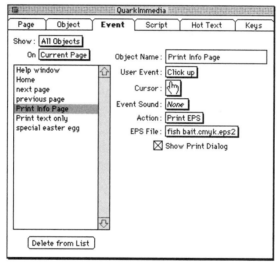

> ▶ When you use Print Text Object, it prints the entire story in the text box, even if it's overset and you can't see some of it.

> ▶ As I pointed out in Chapter 4, *Text,* you have very limited formatting possibilities for text in text box objects. You're pretty much limited to font, size, and the bold, italic, and underline styles. Plus, if your end user doesn't have the same font, the Immedia Viewer replaces it with another font (usually Helvetica). Note that Quark's documentation claims that you can't format the text at all . . . that just ain't the case.

▶ The size of the text box has no bearing at all on how the text is formatted when it prints. Immedia simply fills the printed page with as much text as it can. On a LaserWriter, this means the text prints all the way to a quarter-inch from the edge of the page.

Print Text Object is somewhat undependable on non-PostScript printers. Sometimes it works, but Immedia often doesn't know where the page margins should be, causing longer text lines than you'd expect.

▼ ▼

Tip: Text on Pasteboards. When you place text in an Immedia project, it's usually formatted in such a way that it looks good on screen. That means you'll use easy-to-read fonts at an easy-to-read size, like 14- or 18-point New York or Geneva, with anti-aliasing. This is exactly the opposite of what you want printed out with the Print Text Object action: fonts and sizes that look good on paper, like 11-point Palatino (with no anti-aliasing).

Instead of pointing the Print Text Object action to the text box on your page, consider duplicating the text box and moving the copy out to your pasteboard (see Figure 12–4). You can make the pasteboard copy a text box object, and format the text so that it'll look right when printed. It seems that this would add a lot of extra data to the exported project, but it doesn't, because text in text box objects compresses really well.

▼ ▼

Page Setup

The Page Setup action is one of the simplest actions in QuarkImmedia: it opens the Page Setup dialog box (see Figure 12–5). As you probably know, it's important to look over the Page Setup settings before you print to a new printer or use a new printer driver (the software that runs the printer). For instance, if you switch from a Hewlett-Packard DeskJet to a LaserWriter Pro 630, you need to

Figure 12-4

Put text boxes
on the pasteboard

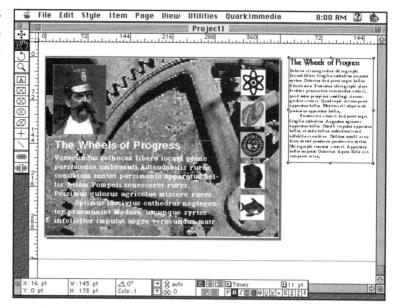

select a different driver in the Chooser dialog box *and* peruse Page
Setup before printing.

People usually put the Page Setup action in one of three places
in their projects.

▶ On the File menu, as a separate menu item. This is where people usually look for a Page Setup or Print action, because this
is the way most programs work.

▶ As a separate button in the project. People can press the Page
Setup button before pressing the Print button. Personally, I
think this is kind of awkward.

Figure 12-5

Page Setup dialog box

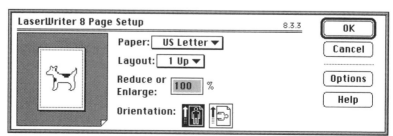

*This dialog box may look different from
yours, depending on what printer driver you're using.*

▶ In a "Printing" script. This kind of script might have two or more actions in it; perhaps the first action would be Page Setup, then another action would print. This way, users are forced to at least glance at the Page Setup dialog box to make sure that it's set up correctly. See Chapter 13, *Scripting*, for more information on building scripts.

If you run this project on a Windows machine (using the Windows viewer), Page Setup opens the default Properties dialog box.

▼ ▼

Three, Two, One . . . Print

While QuarkXPress is world-renowned for its printing capabilities, Immedia probably never will be. That's okay; it was built for multimedia, not as a powerful printing tool. Nonetheless, there are times when getting something off the screen and onto paper is just the ticket, and it's good that Immedia can handle the basics.

In the next chapter, we'll take a look at one of the most important aspects of building multimedia projects: pulling together a number of actions into scripts. With that in place, you'll be ready to construct almost any kind of project you want.

Scripting 13

Have you ever noticed that everyone wants multimedia programs that are scriptable, but that almost no one actually wants to do the scripting? The reason is simple: building scripts in most programs requires an advanced degree, along with 18 years of experience in arcane computer-programming languages. By the time you actually design, write, and debug your first script, you've torn out half your hair and your spouse has called the police, wondering why you haven't been home for three days.

Scripting in Immedia is different. Very different. In fact, I think its scripting system convinced me that Immedia was the multimedia program for me. In this chapter we'll explore this simple yet powerful system, and see why anyone (even I) can be building scripts in no time at all.

▼ ▼

Building a Script

Scripting is like writing a recipe for a casserole—it's a step-by-step procedure made up of actions. You can use a script anytime you want one event to trigger more than one action. A script could say, for example, "Jump to page three, then open this window, then play that movie."

Technically, there's no actual "scripting" involved in Immedia—you don't write any computer code. Instead, Immedia's scripting relies almost entirely on popup menus. Every action you can trigger with a button or hot text can be included in a script. Plus, there are other actions that you can use only in a script.

The Script Tab

In order to build a script, you have to open the Script tab of the QuarkImmedia palette (see Figure 13–1). The left side of the palette controls whole scripts (adding a new script, deleting a script, naming a script, and so on). The right side of the palette controls actions within whatever script you have selected in the script list.

When you first open the Script tab in a new project, there are no scripts yet, so almost everything is grayed out. Here's how you can make your first script.

1. Press New. This adds a script to the script list and lets you change its name in the Script Name field. I suggest naming it something descriptive; after you create three or four (or 40) scripts, it's nice to be able to find the one you want quickly.

2. Each time you create a new script, Immedia adds a place-holder called "No Action" in the script (the "recipe") on the

Figure 13–1
The Script tab

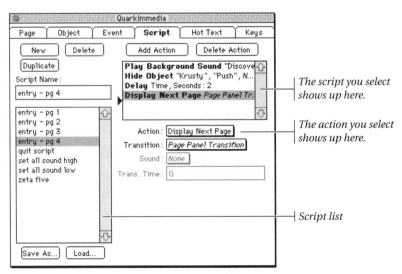

The script you select shows up here.

The action you select shows up here.

Script list

right (see Figure 13–2). Go ahead and change this placeholder into a real action by making a selection from the Action popup menu.

3. To add a second action, press the Add Action button. Immedia displays another "No Action" placeholder and waits for you to specify which action you want.

Figure 13–2
Making a new script

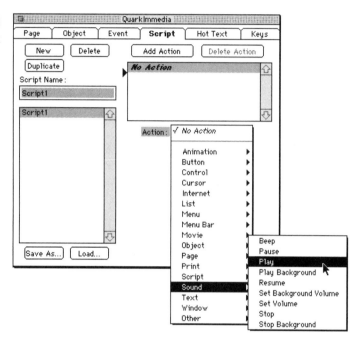

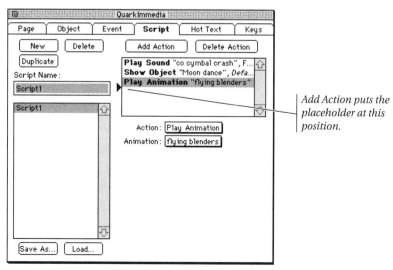

Add Action puts the placeholder at this position.

4. Continue adding actions until you're done. Note that if you want to change the order of the actions, you can drag them within the script.

That's basically it! Of course, there are the super-complicated details, too—to delete an action in a script, for example, you can select it and then press Delete Action.

▾ ▾

Tip: Copying Scripts. When you first start scripting, your scripts will be pretty small. But later you'll find yourself building enormous scripts that do all sorts of cool things. And these larger scripts are going to take some time to build. When you're done with them, you'll think to yourself, "I sure wish I could use this same script in that other project I'm working on." And indeed, you can.

To copy a script from one project to another, select the script from the list on the Script tab of the QuarkImmedia palette, and press the Save As button. This lets you save the script anywhere on your hard drive. Then switch to the other project, press Load, and select your saved script from the disk.

Even better, you can save more than one script at a time by Command-clicking on each script you want to copy. Or if you want to select all the scripts, click on the first one, then Shift-click on the last script (that selects all the scripts between the two). Immedia saves all the scripts in a single file on disk.

▾ ▾

Scripts Calling Scripts

The more complex your scripts, the more you want to break them up into smaller pieces. This helps in debugging problems in the script (we all make mistakes), and it helps in later trying to figure out how you built something last week. Computer programmers call this technique "building procedures" or "building routines." We mere mortals call it "scripts calling scripts."

The concept is easy: one script can trigger another with the Run Script action (see Figure 13–3). Let's say you're designing an order form that lets people fill in various fields, then prints a form for them to mail. The OK button on the final page could trigger a script that calls three others, one at a time.

1. The first script could check to see if all the fields were filled in, and if they weren't, could open a window asking you to fill in the appropriate field.

2. The next script could process the information into something useful, and then print it out.

3. A third script could jump to another page in which the user can quit or go back to the beginning.

This can be run from a single user event: pressing the OK button. There are several benefits to scripts running scripts.

▶ If you need to debug a script (figure out why it's not working the way you expected it to), it's much easier to debug a small piece of a script rather than the whole thing.

▶ You can use the same miniscripts several times in various larger scripts. This saves lots of time.

▶ It's much easier to build a complicated script by breaking it down into smaller pieces, and working on them one at a time.

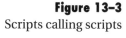

Figure 13-3
Scripts calling scripts

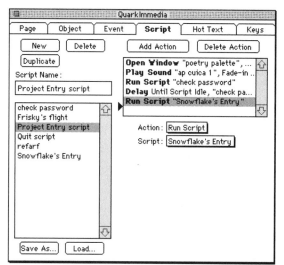

▼ ▼

Running a Script

Once you've got the script built, you've got 90 percent of the work done. Running it is even easier. You can start a script either manually (with a user event, like pressing a button) or automatically (when starting the project or displaying a page). Let's look at each of these options.

Actions

There are four actions that let you control how QuarkImmedia runs scripts: Run Script, Stop Script, Disable Script, and Enable Script. They're as simple as can be, with very few options, and any user event can trigger them (see Figure 13–4). You can even trigger them from within another script.

▶ **Run Script** starts whatever script you specify on the Script popup menu. Note that running a script just starts the script; it doesn't necessarily stop anything else from happening (see "Control and Flow," later in this chapter).

▶ **Stop Script** stops a script that is currently running. If the script isn't running, Immedia ignores this action. You can also change the Select popup menu to All Scripts, which stops every currently running script. Stop Script even stops scripts

Figure 13–4
Script actions

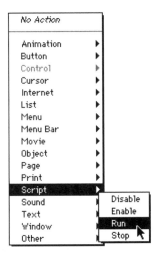

in the middle of an If, While, or Loop action (see "Control Actions," later in this chapter).

▶ **Disable Script and Enable Script.** Scripts, like buttons, can be disabled using the Disable Script action, and then enabled again with Enable Script. When you try to run a script that is disabled, Immedia just ignores the action.

For instance, you might set up a project so that, depending on which button the user presses, one script out of three is enabled and the others are disabled. Later, you could run all three scripts, and Immedia will ignore all but the enabled one.

Page Entry and Page Exit

User event actions aren't the only way to trigger scripts. You can also run a script automatically each time you enter or exit a page, or when you engage a project (see "Project Scripts," below). Here's how to launch a script automatically when you enter or exit a page.

1. Open the Page tab of the Immedia palette (see Figure 13–5).

2. Choose the page to which you want to tie the script.

3. Select the script from either the Page Enter or Page Exit pop-up menu.

Figure 13–5
Scripts on Page Entry or Page Exit

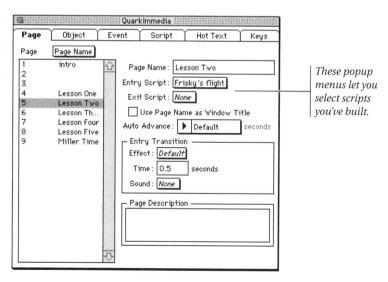

These popup menus let you select scripts you've built.

These automatic scripts run every time you display or leave that page. If you want, you can have a different script set up for every page in your project.

Project Scripts

You can set a script to run automatically at three other times: when the project first starts up, when the user quits the project, and when the project is idle for a length of time. You can find each of these settings on popup menus in the Immedia Preferences dialog box* (see Figure 13–6).

Figure 13–6
Project scripts

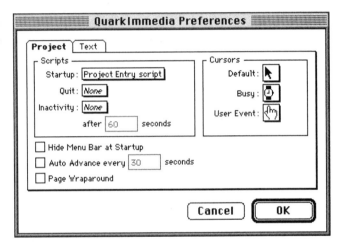

For example, if you want a script to run when the project is first engaged, but not every time the user sees the first page, you can choose the script from the Project Entry popup menu. Or if you want a little splash screen to appear every time you exit the project, you can make that happen by selecting a script from the Quit popup menu (perhaps the script would open a window, delay for three seconds, then close the window and quit).

If you select a script from the Idle popup menu, Immedia only runs it if the project has been sitting idle in an engaged state for a certain length of time (you get to specify how many seconds).

---

*I know why Quark put these popups in the Immedia Preferences dialog box: because that's where you make documentwide settings. Nonetheless, I personally find it nonintuitive, and I often have to think for a moment before remembering where those darn popup menus are.

▼ ▼

Control and Flow

As I said earlier, a script is like a recipe that Immedia follows. Some recipes aren't totally linear, though. For instance, if you're making cookie dough, the recipe might call for the chocolate chips to be added slowly while you mix, then to wait for five minutes, then to either drop the dough onto a cookie sheet or eat it raw (which would *you* do?). Immedia lets you create this kind of script, too, using actions like While, If, and Delay. These actions are only available when you're building scripts.*

Let's look at each of the actions that determine the flow of a script, and then let's move into conditional actions.

Delaying Scripts

Immedia doesn't run only one script or action at a time. For example, if one script calls another script, Immedia won't wait for the first one to finish before the second one starts up. Instead, the Run Script action might be better called "Begin Script"—once the script starts, Immedia goes on to whatever action comes next. Similarly, if a script has two Play Sound actions in a row, it won't wait for the first sound to finish before starting the second.

If you need to pause a script, insert a Delay action (from the Other Action popup menu). When you insert a delay, Immedia won't trigger any more script actions until the conditions for the delay are met (see Figure 13–7). You've got eight options for Delay.

> ▶ **Time.** This is the simplest type of delay: the script just pauses for a certain number of seconds (the value you type in the Seconds field on the Script tab).

> ▶ **Until All Idle.** When you select Until All Idle, Immedia pauses the script until every action, animation, movie, sound, or script has finished.

---

*Actually, as of this writing, some script-oriented actions—such as Delay and Allow User Interaction—are always available. However, these really only work in scripts; there's no good reason to select them at any other time.

Figure 13–7

Delaying progress
in a script

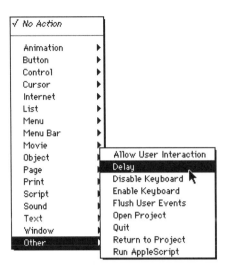

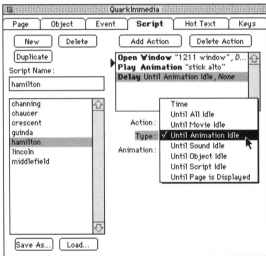

▶ **Until Movie Idle, Until Animation Idle, and Until Sound Idle.**
These three items let you pause for a single animation, sound,
or movie to finish. For instance, Until Sound Idle is very useful when you need your sound to synchronize with actions on
the screen ("Don't go to the next page until this instructional
voice-over ends").

▶ **Until Object Idle.** Either the Until Object Idle option is buggy,
or it's just redundant with the other Delay options. Either way,
I don't use it.

▶ **Until Script Idle.** The Delay Until Script Idle action can be extremely useful when you create scripts that call other scripts. If you place this action in between two Run Script actions, Immedia waits patiently until the first is done before proceeding to the next.

▶ **Until Page is Displayed.** If you're allowing user events during the script (see "Cached User Events," later in this chapter) or if you're running your project over the Internet, you may include the Delay Until Page is Displayed action. This makes the script wait until a particular page (you specify which one) has finished displaying before the script continues. This is also useful if you've got long page transitions.

Control Actions

Let's face it: we live in a world where we constantly make decisions based on our environment. So why should an Immedia project be any different? Fortunately, Immedia lets you make decisions, too, in the form of control actions within scripts. For instance, you can write scripts that say, "While the alert window is open, play a sound," or "If Button A is turned on, and if no scripts are running, then jump to page six; otherwise, jump to page four."

If/End If. The most basic conditional is the If action, which must always be followed in the script—usually after some other action or actions—by an End If action. When you place an If in a script, Immedia checks to see whether the If condition is met; if it is met, then Immedia continues with the actions after the If. If the conditions are not met, then Immedia skips everything between the If and the End If actions (see Figure 13–8). For instance, here's generally how an If/End If script would read.

```
If -- Editable Text Box "A" is Empty
Beep
Open Window -- "Warning"
End If
```

Figure 13-8
If/End If

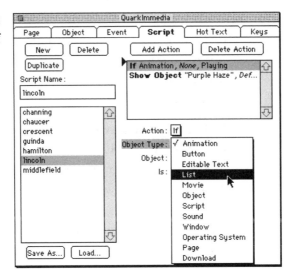

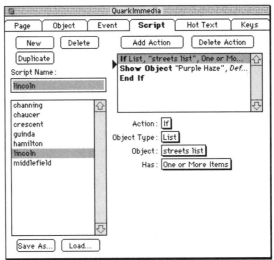

You could put this little If/End If snippit anywhere in a script, or it could be the entire script. If the text box A is not empty when the script runs, then Immedia just jumps over the Beep and Open Window actions.

Table 13-1 shows all the conditions you can check for with an If statement. In every case except for Operating System and Page, you must specify a particular object—that is, you can't say "if any animation is playing" or "if any item in any list is selected."

While most of these conditionals are self-explanatory, Download is an exception. It lets you check to see if an animation, a movie, or a sound has already downloaded from the Internet. We'll take a look at Internet-related issues more in Chapter 15, *The Internet and the World Wide Web.*

▼ ▼

Tip: Nesting "If" Statements. You can also include an "and" statement in your If actions, though unfortunately it's not quite as clean or intuitive as simply using the word "and." You make an "and" statement by nesting conditional actions. For example, you can say "if button A is on *and* if button B is off" with two nested Ifs ("nested" just means that one If/End If group is inside another).

```
If -- button "A" is on
If -- button "B" is off
<insert some action here>
End If
End If
```

Or you could use a While statement.

```
While -- movie "A" is playing
If -- sound "B" is not playing
<insert some action here>
End If
End While
```

Remember that each If must be followed (sooner or later) by an End If, each While must be followed by an End While, and so on.

▼ ▼

Else. Did you hear the phrase "Do it or else" a lot when you were growing up? Well, all your training is finally paying off, because "or else" translates directly into Immedia's control actions. You can insert an Else action in between an If and an End If to make the statement read, "If such-and-such is true, then do this-and-that, *otherwise* do blah-blah-blah."

Object Type	**Condition**
Animation	Playing
	Not Playing
	Paused
	Not Paused
Button	On
	Off
	Enabled
	Disabled
	Hidden
	Not Hidden
Editable Text	Empty
	Not Empty
List	No Items
	One or More Items
	First Item Selected
	Last Item Selected
	Any Item Selected
	No Item Selected
	A Different Item Selected
Movie	Playing
	Not Playing
	Paused
	Not Paused
Object	Enabled
	Disabled
	Hidden
	Not Hidden
	Dragged
	Not Being Dragged
	Under Mouse
	Not Under Mouse
Script	Enabled
	Not Enabled
	Running
	Not Running
Sound	Playing
	Not Playing

Table 13-1
Conditions

Object Type (cont.)	Condition (cont.)
	Paused
	Not Paused
Window	Open
	Not Open
Operating System	Mac OS
	Windows
Page	Current
	Not Current
Download	Animation
	Movie
	Sound

The following miniscript is a toggle switch for hiding or showing an object. If the object is hidden, this script will show it; if it's showing, the script will hide it.

```
If -- Object "A" is Hidden
Show Object "A"
Else
Hide Object "A"
End If
```

▼ ▼

Tip: Nested "Or" Statements. Earlier we looked at how to make an "and" statement. If you want to add an "or" statement like, "If either button A *or* button B is on . . . ," you could build it with an If statement nested inside an If/Else statement.

```
If -- button "A" is on
<insert some action here>
Else
If -- button "B" is on
<insert same action here>
End If
End If
```

▼ ▼

While/End While. You can use the While action to repeat one or more actions, as long as some condition is being met. For instance, perhaps you want to play a beep every five seconds while a window is open, as a reminder to the user to do something (see Figure 13–9).

```
While -- Window "A" is Open
Beep
Delay -- Time: 5 seconds
End While
```

Of course, you always have to follow a While with an End While, so that Immedia knows what actions to repeat.

The While action uses all the same conditionals as the If action, so it's just like saying, "Keep repeating these actions until such-and-such isn't true anymore." You can also break a While/End While action by inserting a Break If statement in the middle of it.

```
While -- Movie "Herbie Goes to Denver" is
        Playing
Set Object Position -- "Yellow Dot" to x
        Offset of 10 points
Delay -- Time: 1 second
Break If -- Button "A" is Off
End While
```

Figure 13–9
While/End While

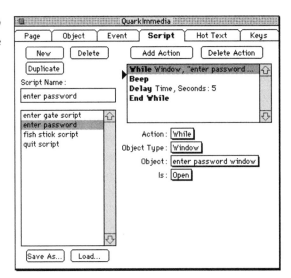

In this script, the Yellow Dot object keeps being repositioned until either the movie ends or the Break If condition is met (the button is turned off).

Note that if the condition of the While statement isn't met at the beginning of the While/End pair, Immedia skips the whole thing.

Loop/End Loop. Both If and While work with conditionals; the actions are only triggered when certain conditions are met. The Loop action, however, *always* triggers the actions, and keeps repeating them until either the entire script is stopped (with a Stop Script action), or a Break If action stops the loop. A loop, like If and While, must be followed by an End Loop action.

```
Loop
If -- Button "A" is On
If -- Button "B" is On
Play Sound -- "Big Bang"
End If
End If
End Loop
```

This script constantly checks to see if both button A and button B are turned on. As soon as they are on, Immedia plays the sound, and it keeps repeating the sound until one or both of the buttons are turned off.

Break If. You can put a Break If action anywhere in a script between a While or Loop action and an End While or End Loop action. This tells Immedia, "If such-and-such is true, then jump out of the Loop or While." It's sort of like a quick exit from the conditionals. Though Break If is just like an If statement itself (see Figure 13–10), you don't have to use an "End Break If" or anything like that.

In this snippet, for instance, the script plays a movie repeatedly until the user turns a button off.

```
Loop -- Button "A" is On
Play Movie -- "Friedman Defeats Godzilla"
Delay -- Until Movie is Idle
```

```
Break If -- Button "A" is Off
End Loop
```

Figure 13-10
Break If

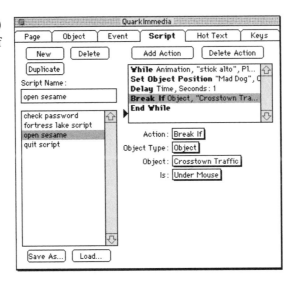

▼ ▼

Tip: Button Variables. Let's say you want someone to visit every page in your project before quitting. How do you know what pages have already been visited? You can store that information by changing the status of buttons, lists, or hidden objects. For example, if there are six pages in the document, you could have six On/Off buttons sitting on the pasteboard somewhere. Because they're on the pasteboard, no one ever sees them in the finished project. Nonetheless, they're still there!

Then give each page an entry script that turns on one of the buttons. Later, when the user presses a Quit button, you can run a script that checks to see if each of the buttons is turned on. If one or more isn't turned on, your script knows that the user hasn't seen one of the pages, and can act accordingly.

Each button can actually store three pieces of information—it can be On or Off, Disabled or Enabled, and Hidden or Not Hidden. So hypothetically, a button could be turned on if someone has visited a page; hidden if they've actually done anything on the page; and disabled if they've pressed a certain button. You could check that single button later for all that information.

You can use objects other than buttons—lists, editable text boxes, and so on—but I find buttons usually the easiest to use for this sort of thing.

▼ ▼

Tip: Saving Variables. In the previous tip, I talked about how you can save variables throughout the project. The problem is that when you quit the project and later start it up again, those variables are all gone. The only way to save variables in an Immedia project is to write them to disk as text using the Write Text File action (see "Reading and Writing Files" in Chapter 4, *Text)*. Needless to say, the Write Text File and Read Text File actions are simplistic, so you have to be clever about how to write and read your information. I'll leave this as an exercise for you, the reader.

▼ ▼

Cached User Events

Immedia blocks all user events in the middle of an action. For example, nothing happens if you click a button while Immedia is displaying a new page. Because Immedia thinks of a script as a single action, it blocks user events until the script has finished. During the time it takes to run the script (or turn the page, load the animation, start the movie, or whatever) you can click all you want, but it won't do anything until Immedia has actually finished the script, or begun the animation or movie.

What happens to all those clicks and keystrokes? Immedia saves them in a cache until it's finished with the action. Then it plays them back, one at a time. This is a double-edged sword; sometimes that's exactly what you want it to do, and sometimes it's a disaster.

If you're viewing a project on the Internet, it's hard to know how long it'll really take to display a new page or play a sound. Many people—especially those folks who grew up on MTV and high-speed modems—have less than an optimal dose of patience, and so they'll jump in and start clicking and typing and trying who-knows-what. Finally, they'll give up and just wait. When the page actually does turn and the user event cache spills open, all hell breaks loose.

Fortunately, Immedia includes two actions that help manage this potential problem: Flush User Events and Allow User Interaction. Either of these can be triggered at any time, but they're really designed to be used in scripts.

Flush User Events

The first action, Flush User Events, clears all the stored-up, unprocessed user events out of the cache. For instance, instead of just using the Open Window action, you might run a little script like this.

```
Open Window "Happy Window"
Delay -- Until All Idle*
Flush User Events
```

That way, if the user clicks 14 times while a window is slowly opening, as soon as the window is fully open, all those clicks are thrown away. Note that the following user events are always processed, no matter what.

▶ Command-period

▶ Escape key on Windows

▶ Stop button on the Internet Controls palette

▼ ▼

Tip: Delaying Flush User Events. Either the Flush User Events action wasn't working quite right in the 1.0 version of the product, or it was implemented in a completely nonintuitive way. If you want to ignore all user events while you slowly display a new page, for instance, you cannot use a script like this.

```
Display Next Page -- Digital Dissolve,
        Time: 2 seconds
Flush User Events
```

---

*I don't know why Immedia won't let you delay until a window is open, but the Until All Idle works just as well in this case.

This won't work because the Flush User Events action is triggered immediately after the page begins transitioning. You also cannot use a script like this.

```
Display Next Page -- Digital Dissolve,
      Time: 2 seconds
Delay -- Until Page 2 is displayed
Flush User Events
```

This one won't work because Immedia thinks a page is displayed as soon as the transition begins, too. Odd, but there you go.

The workaround appears to be to add a tiny amount of time delay. For example, the following script does work.

```
Display Next Page -- Digital Dissolve,
      Time: 2 seconds
Delay -- Time: .25 seconds
Flush User Events
```

It appears as though this works because the Delay Time action won't begin until the page (or window, or object, or whatever) is fully displayed. While I hope they change or fix this action in the next release, adding a short delay seems to solve the problem.

▼ ▼

Allow User Interaction

If you want your user to have the option of pressing buttons, typing, or selecting menus while a script is running, you must include an Allow User Interaction action somewhere. I usually just place it at the top of a script.

```
Allow User Interaction
While -- Button "A" is On
Play Animation -- "Funky Waddle"
End While
```

Allow User Interaction gets complicated when more than one script is running at a time, or when one script calls another script.

▶ If two scripts are running at the same time, they *both* need to have an Allow User Interaction action in them. If the first script does and the second doesn't, Immedia blocks user events until the second script is finished.

▶ The one exception to this is when the second script is started by the first script. Anytime a script that contains an Allow User Interaction action calls another script, that second script automatically inherits the ability to handle user events.

Note that Allow User Interaction only lets you process user events in the middle of a script—not in the middle of an action. Immedia still waits until an action is complete (the page is turned, the movie is loaded, or whatever) before processing an event.

▼ ▼
Simple Scripting

You may not want to believe it, but scripting is at the heart of many multimedia projects. Fortunately, Immedia provides all the ingredients for your scripting recipes, and lays them out in neat popup menus so you don't have to do too much work. It's like Tinker Toys: just piece them together, and little by little you create a masterpiece.

With your scripts in tow, it's time to step into the next chapter: the *pièce de résistance,* the ultimate goal of Immedia projects, exporting your project.

Exporting **14**

I F YOU'VE GOTTEN THIS FAR through the book, you're probably itching to get *out* of QuarkImmedia and use your projects in the real world. Fortunately, as I pointed out in the introduction, you don't have to be in XPress in order to view your project. You can export the project and view it with a separate viewer.

Of course, it's never quite as simple as that. You have options. And options mean you have to make decisions about all sorts of things. Do you want one big file with everything in it? Or a bunch of small files that you an put on an Internet site? Do you want to use compression? And what if you're using the same material for both CD-ROM and the Internet?

In this chapter we take a look at *all* the options.* Don't worry; it's really not as difficult as it sometimes seems.

▼ ▼

QuarkImmedia Usage

QuarkImmedia Usage (under the QuarkImmedia menu) is most important to us when we take steps toward exporting our project,

---

*I have a love/hate relationship with options; I always want more choices, but I have a really tough time choosing one of them!

because it tells us the status of every linked file that we have used in our project.

Remember that Immedia doesn't actually embed media files— QuickTime movies, sounds, animations (sequences), custom cursors, EPS files, or AppleScripts—into your project until you export it. It only maintains a link to those files. Similarly, if you use the Open Project action, Immedia remembers where that project is, but it doesn't embed that entire project. The reason this is so important to remember at export time is because Immedia won't let you export a project that has any "loose ends" in the form of missing or modified animations, movies, and whatnot (see Figure 14–1).

Figure 14–1
Exporting with
loose ends

The Dialog Box

When you select QuarkImmedia Usage from the Immedia menu, you get a list of every linked file you've used while building your project (basically, everything except text and pictures; see Figure 14–2). The dialog box is much like the Picture Usage dialog box; it shows you the path to the file on your hard disk, the location in the project, the type of file, and the file's status.

Name. The path to the file is in the Name column of the dialog box. The first part of the path is the hard drive, then names of the folders separated by colons, then finally the name of the file. However, unless you never learned how to make folders on your hard disk, the file path is almost always way too long and Immedia truncates out the middle parts to make it fit in the column. This makes it less than useful. Oh well. Better than nothing.

Location. The Location column doesn't show you the location on disk; rather, it tells you where you used that file in your project.

Figure 14–2

QuarkImmedia Usage

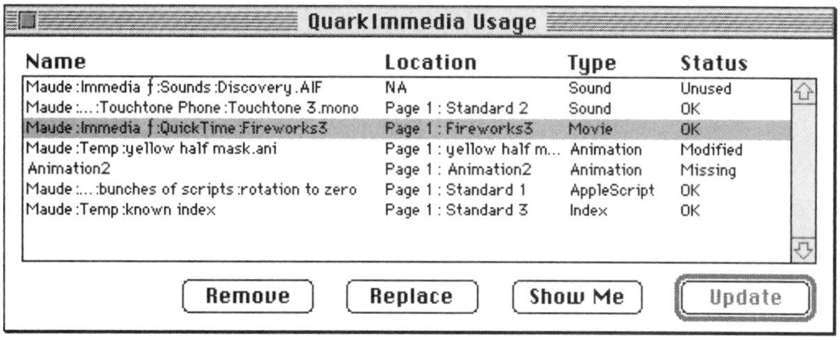

Typically it displays the page number, then the name of the object on the page that uses the linked file. If the file is unused in the project (see "Status," below), the Location appears as "N/A." It's important to note that if you use the same file multiple times in your project, QuarkImmedia Usage only displays the first occurrence.

Type. The Type column is pretty self-explanatory. It just reminds you whether the file is a movie, an animation, a cursor, and so on. Personally, one of my topmost wish-list items is a way to sort and export this list. Wouldn't it be nice to see all the QuickTime movies together? Quark? Are you listening?

Status. The last column in the dialog box displays the status of the link. You can encounter five things here: OK, Modified, Missing, Wrong Type, or Unused.

▸ **OK.** Keeping track of all your linked files can be a trying experience. "OK" lets you know that you're doing a good job. This is what you dream about in this business.

▸ **Modified.** If you import an animation, then later open the animation file and edit it in any way, Immedia tells you here that the file has been modified. In rare cases, this notice may appear even when you haven't changed anything—that usually means that you've been moving files among machines on a network when computer clocks aren't synchronized.

▸ **Missing.** The Missing status is a thing from which nightmares are born. If you move the file, rename the file, delete the file, or rename the file's folder (or any other folder in the file path), that file will show up as Missing. But don't panic yet. If you saw my office, you'd know that I miss files all the time! There are all sorts of things you can do to relink them (I talk about this in the next section).

▶ **Wrong Type.** Every once in a while you'll run into a Wrong Type status. This means that Immedia can find a file that has the right name, but for some reason the type has changed. For instance, let's say you named an animation "Whap!" and then later named a sound file the same thing. If you accidentally erased the animation, Immedia might get confused when it looked for an animation and found the sound instead.

▶ **Unused.** QuarkImmedia doesn't just keep track of the files you are actually using in the project. It also keeps track of all the files you *ever* used. If a button used to play a sound of a lion roar when you pressed it, but you later changed it to a simple click (you know art directors . . . always toning down magnificent effects), Immedia still keeps track of that lion sound. The only way to totally break the link is to use the Remove button (which we'll get to in a moment).

Maintaining Files

The QuarkImmedia Usage dialog box is not just a place to go check out the status of your files. You can also actually maintain the files, too. There are four buttons at the bottom of the dialog box that give you control over these linked files.

Remove. The first button, Remove, simply deletes whatever linked file (or files*) you have selected. Fortunately, Immedia does ask if you are sure you really want to delete each file (some people find this annoying, but it's reassuring to me; I still make mistakes). Removing the file means one of two things. If the linked file is not used in the project (if the Status is listed as Unused), it simply disappears from the usage list. If the file is being used, however, Quark

---

*As in many Macintosh programs, you can select contiguous files in the list by using the Shift key, or discontiguous files by using the Command key.

Immedia pulls it out of the list, and from everywhere you used it throughout the project.

Replace. If you want to replace one movie with another, or one sound with another sound, or whatever, you can select the file (or files) in QuarkImmedia Usage and press the Replace button. Immedia only lets you replace a sound with another sound, an animation with another animation, and so on. Again, this replaces it throughout the entire project; it's a powerful tool, but can mess you up if you don't think about it first.

Show Me. If you select any linked file from the QuarkImmedia Usage dialog box and press the Show Me button, Immedia jumps to whatever object is using that file. For instance, if a button on page five plays a sound, you can select the sound from the list and press Show Me; Immedia jumps to page five and places the button in the upper-left corner of the page.

The problem with Show Me is that it stops at the first instance of the file. If you've used the same animation three times in a project, Show Me only takes you to the first instance. Grrr.

Update. If any of your files are missing, modified, or the wrong type, the Update button is the place to go. If you're familiar with Picture Usage's Update button, you'll feel right at home here, as it does the same thing, depending on the status of the file.

▶ **Modified.** If you update a file listed as Modified, Immedia asks you if you really want to update it. If you agree, Immedia builds a new preview image (for movies, cursors, and animations) on each page on which the file is used.

▶ **Missing.** Updating a file listed as Missing causes Immedia to ask you to find the original file. Note that you don't have to find the original . . . you can select any file of the same type. If you find the same file, Immedia makes a new link to it. If you choose a different file, however, Immedia acts as though you used the Replace button; it replaces every instance of the first file with the new one.

▶ **Wrong Type.** In those rare instances when you bump into the Wrong Type status, Update lets you clear things up. Select the file and click Update, and Immedia lets you choose any file you want, as long as it's the type of file its expecting (movie, animation, sound, and so on).

Curiously enough, you can't update unused files until you actually use them somewhere in your project. But I'm not losing any sleep over *that*.

▼ ▼
Export Settings

Okay, we've checked all the linked files and we're almost ready to export the project . . . but wait. There's one more step we should take first: choose Export Settings from the Immedia menu (see Figure 14–3). Export Settings lets you control many aspects of the export process. Just as you should open Page Setup before you select Print, you should always check Export Settings before exporting.

There are two tabs in the Export Settings dialog box: Compression and General. I talk about Compression later in this chapter, but let's delve into the General settings here.

Paths

The first section of the General Tab is labeled Paths. It's a bit misleading, though—only one path is specified here: the Auxiliary File Path. The other two fields, Project Name and Auxiliary File Name, are for project names.

Project Name. The Immedia Viewer/Browser keeps track of what projects you've looked at recently (the various features of the Viewer are discussed later in this chapter). However, it somehow keeps track by name rather than by URL or file path. The name that appears on the URL History and Bookmark popup menus is usually the name of the original QuarkXPress document from which you exported the Immedia project.

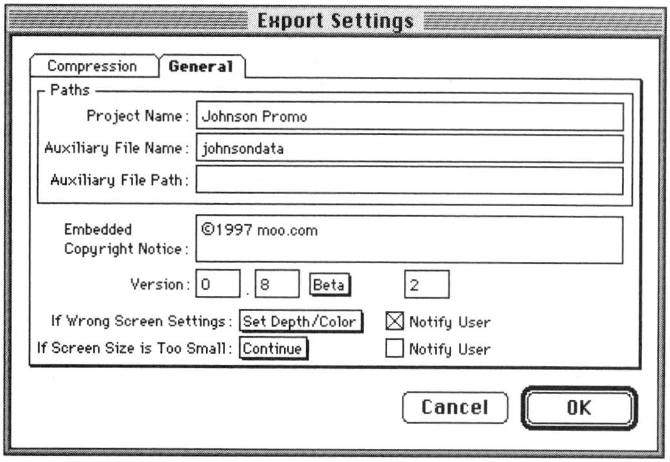

Figure 14–3
Export Settings

You can override that name by entering a new one in the Project Name field of Export Settings. If you're like me, you probably name your documents something like "bizarre job - clientX.qx.imd.3". In this case, it's *really* worth taking the extra four seconds to type a "real name" into the Project Name field.

Auxiliary File Name. When you export your projects in either CD-ROM (two files) or Internet (many files) formats (discussed later in this chapter), Immedia saves the first file (what I call the *master file*) with whatever name you type in the Export dialog box. The other files (called *auxiliary files)* are usually given the same names, followed by 1, 2, 3, 4, and so on.

You can change the base name of the auxiliary files to something else by typing a name into the Auxiliary File Name field in Export Settings. For instance, if you're exporting to CD-ROM, you might want your Project Name to be "Incredible Journey" and the Auxiliary File Name to be "JourneyData". That way, it's very clear which file is which.

Auxiliary File Path. The last section in the Paths area, Auxiliary File Path, lets you tell Immedia where those auxiliary files will be when you go to run the exported project. For example, if your project is set up so that your user copies the master file from the CD-ROM to their hard drive (then runs the project from there), the master file has to be able to locate the auxiliary file or the project won't run. Similarly, some people like putting auxiliary files into a separate "data" folder on the CD. Again, you have to provide Immedia with the file path to that auxiliary file or else it won't know where to look for the file.

While Immedia's documentation says that you should type the file path using slashes, you actually have to use colons (Quark tells me that you'll be able to use either in the next version). It must be complete, starting with the name of the volume (the hard disk or the CD-ROM), then the name of the folder, and so on. For example, a file path for a Macintosh title might be "GreatestHits:Shareware:Data:" (with no quotation marks, of course). Here comes the kicker, though: the entire path name must be less than 32 characters long. Not that I have any strong feelings about this—but this is *insane!* I hope this also gets changed in a soon-to-come version of Immedia.

Note that you only need to type a path in if you're going to put the auxiliary file in a folder different from the one the Immedia project is in. Also, this is currently only relevant for CD-ROM (two files) exports; as of this writing, you *must* put auxiliary files for Internet (many files) exports in the same folder as the project.

Embedded Copyright Notice

The next section in the Export Settings dialog box lets you embed a version number and copyright notice in the exported master file (these are not, at the time of this writing, added to the auxiliary files). Anything you type in the Embedded Copyright Notice field shows up in the Get Info dialog box on the Macintosh (select the master file on the Macintosh Desktop and select Get Info from the File menu; see Figure 14–4).

The more complex the multimedia project, the more important it is to number each of your exports using the Version feature (just under the Embedded Copyright Notice field). You can specify a full version number (like 1, 2, 3, and so on), a mini-release number (like .1, .2, or .49), and even a micro-release number (like "r1", "beta 3", or "pre-alpha 6").

Microsoft Windows. If you move the exported project to a Windows95-based computer, the copyright and version information is

Figure 14-4
Embedded version
and copyright notice

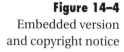

Johnson Demo Info

Johnson Demo

Kind: QuarkImmedia™ Viewer 1.0 docu...
Size: 816K on disk (826,358 bytes used)

Where: Maude: Temp:

Created: Sun, Nov 17, 1992, 12:18 PM
Modified: Sun, Nov 17, 1992, 12:18 PM
Version: 0.08 Beta 2, ©1997 moo.com

Comments:

☐ **Locked**   ☐ **Stationery pad**

supposed to appear in the file's Properties window (the thing you get when you right-mouse-button click on the file). Unfortunately, it doesn't work in the currently shipping version (1.0). If that changes, I'll update you on my Web site (see "Where to Find Me," at the back of this book).

Screen Settings

The last two controls in the Export Settings dialog box let you decide what to do if the monitor on which the user sees the project is different from the one you intended. This is more common than you'd think. For instance, many projects are built on 17- or 21-inch monitors. It's easy to build a project on these screens that won't fit on a standard 640-by-480-pixel screen.

If Wrong Screen Settings. Immedia wants you to run projects on a screen set to 256-color mode. This is just dandy for anyone who has an 8-bit monitor. But more and more people have 16-bit ("thousands of colors") or 24-bit ("millions of colors") monitors. If they run your project while their screen is set to millions of colors, what do you want the Immedia Viewer to do about it? You get a choice on the If Wrong Screen Settings popup menu.

► **Set Depth/Color.** The default setting is Set Depth/Color. This means the Immedia Viewer will actually go in and change the

Monitors setting (on a Macintosh) or the Display setting (in Windows) to 256 Colors before running the project. If you turn on the Notify User option, Immedia gives you a choice between switching or quitting (see Figure 14–5). While it can be a little disconcerting when a program changes your screen settings without first asking you, it doesn't bother me much because when you quit the Viewer changes the setting back to whatever it was (though it only changes back when you quit the Viewer, not the project).

Figure 14–5
Set Depth/Color

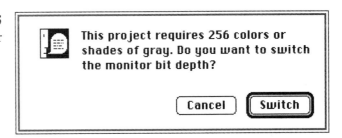

This project requires 256 colors or shades of gray. Do you want to switch the monitor bit depth?

Cancel   Switch

▶ **Continue.** If you choose "Continue" from the popup menu, the Immedia Viewer goes ahead and runs the project in thousands or millions of colors. The problem is that Immedia is optimized to load a single color palette and use just that palette. If you're in 16- or 24-bit color mode, your Immedia projects may run more slowly, especially on older computers.

▶ **Quit.** I can't think of any good reason to choose Quit from this popup menu. When Quit is selected, the Immedia Viewer simply won't run the project at all. In fact, if Quit is selected and you don't turn on Notify User, *nothing* happens (very disconcerting; I don't recommend it at all).

▼ ▼

Tip: Set Depth Affects Engage. It took me a while to realize that if I left the If Wrong Screen Settings option at the default, "Set Depth," Immedia would set the screen depth every time I engaged the project. Very annoying on a 24-bit color monitor. As soon as I switched this to "Continue," it stopped and my tension level subsided.

▼ ▼

If Screen Size is Too Small. The second screen concern is what to do when your project is bigger than the screen. The default setting is Continue, but I like to turn on the Notify User option, too. Otherwise, the user may not understand that what he or she sees isn't the whole picture. If you really don't want people looking at the project without a big enough screen, choose Quit from the popup menu. But, again, have the courtesy of notifying the user if you choose this. Otherwise, the user has no idea why the project won't run.

▼ ▼

Exporting a Project

After checking linked files and the export settings, it's finally time to export your project, jettisoning it into the cold, harsh world. The key, of course, is selecting Export from the Immedia menu (see Figure 14–6). But, wait . . . oh no, there are more options in this dialog box!

If you've gotten this far, you can probably breeze through the three final choices you have to make: Export Format (is this a CD-ROM project, an Internet project, or what?), Embed Viewer (and if so, what kind of Viewer?), and Full Compression During Export.

▼ ▼

Tip: Cleaning Up Your Projects. While there are many habits that have had to be broken in the move from prepress to multimedia, there are

Figure 14–6
Export dialog box

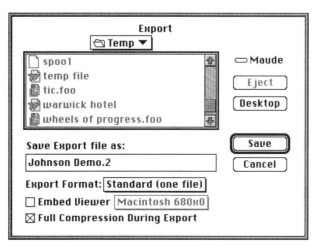

some that remain as important as ever. In prepress, you should always browse your document for hidden files (such as pictures hiding behind white boxes) before printing. Similarly, in Immedia, it's always a good idea to carefully peruse your projects before exporting them. Hidden objects and linked files, whether sitting on the pasteboard or behind other objects, may be exported without you knowing it, resulting in much larger file sizes than expected.

For instance, let's say you're using a QuickTime movie in your project, but when you decide you don't like it, you move it off to the pasteboard. Later, when you export your document, Immedia includes that movie, even though it never appears in the final piece.

Another example: let's say some music plays when you click a button. Later, you move the button to the pasteboard or hide it with a white box. Even though you cannot see the button or the sound, that sound gets exported.

On the other hand, Immedia is smart enough not to export pictures that don't appear in the project. A PICT image in a picture box will *not* get exported if you hide it or put it on the pasteboard, unless there's some action that refers to it (like Slide Object or Show Object or something like that).

▼ ▼

Export Format

Immedia can export your project in three different ways: as a single file, as two files, or as many files (see Figure 14–7). Which you choose depends almost entirely on how you intend people to view the project, but each has important ramifications.

Standard (one file). The first choice on the Export Format popup menu is Standard (one file). This is the default selection, the one that most people end up using at first. The result is a single exported file that contains everything—images, sounds, movies, animations, EPSes, AppleScripts, buttons, and anything else that has crept into your project. This file is suitable for running off your hard drive or a floppy disk. You can put files like this on a CD-ROM or on the Internet, but unless they're small they won't run very efficiently.

Figure 14–7
Export Format

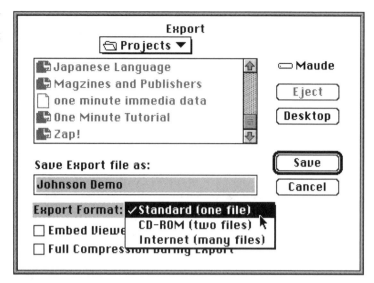

CD-ROM (two files). In general, running the entire exported project from a hard drive as a single file produces the best results. But demanding that someone copy a 200 Mb file from a CD-ROM to their hard drive is asking a little much (even in this day and age of cheap gigabyte hard drives). The larger the project, the more sensible it is to break it into two pieces: a small "master" file that can be copied to the hard drive, and a large auxiliary file that stays on a CD-ROM. That's exactly what you get when you choose CD-ROM (two files) from the Export Format popup menu.

The master file contains just enough information to view the first page of the project, plus a few extra items, so it's pretty small. It also contains a link to the auxiliary file, which stores all the movies, animations, sounds, additional pages, and so on. Note that you should not change the name of the auxiliary file, or else the master file won't be able to find it (see "Export Settings," earlier in this chapter, for information about how to specify the names of the master and auxiliary files).

By the way, if you're distributing your project on CD-ROM, you can also just export as a single file. But in most cases, the project runs more quickly if you break it into two and have the user copy the master file over to the hard drive.

▼ ▼

Tip: Running Over a Network. If you wanted to run your file from a server over a fast network (like Ethernet), it would seem as if saving it as two files is the way to go. Curiously enough, while the two-file export works well for CD-ROM, there doesn't appear to be much benefit to using this method over a network. Don't know why. I'd just use the Internet (many files) or Standard (single file) formats.

▼ ▼

Tip: Same Buttons, Smaller Files. Curiously enough, the master file in CD-ROM and Internet exports includes all the buttons you use in a project, whether they're on page 1 or 51. That means if you use 20 different button designs throughout your project, your master file will be bigger than if you just use the same button 20 times. Buttons aren't that big, but they're big enough to make a difference, especially on exports for the Internet.

▼ ▼

Internet (many files). If you want to place your project on the Internet (or an intranet server), you can save it in the standard, single-file format. But beware: in this format, the Viewer must download the entire project before running it. If your project has multiple pages, or includes sounds, movies, animations, and other linked files, this can take a long time.

Instead, you can choose Internet (many files) from the Export Format popup menu. This builds a single, small master file, just like the one in the two-file format. But it breaks down each project element (movie, animation, page, sound, and so on) into a separate auxiliary file, so you can potentially end up with tens, or even hundreds, of smaller files. The benefit is obvious and immediate: the Viewer has to download the master file to begin with, and then only downloads the additional auxiliary files that it needs, as it needs them (the Viewer caches each auxiliary file locally on the hard drive so you only have to download it once, even if you use it several times in a project).

Again, don't rename any of the auxiliary files, or else the Viewer won't be able to find them.

I discuss putting your projects on the Internet or an intranet in much greater detail in Chapter 15, *The Internet and World Wide Web*.

▼ ▼

Tip: Export Statistics. It's always useful to get a clearer picture of what's going on behind the scenes with Immedia. In the case of exporting your project, you can get a peek backstage by holding down the Option key when pressing the Save button in the Export dialog box. When you do this, Immedia creates an Export Statistics window while it saves the exported project (see Figure 14–8).

There's a screen-redraw bug in Immedia which occasionally hides some of this document when it's done, so you may need to click on its Zoom box to force it to redraw (the Zoom box is that box in the upper-right corner of the window).

Export Statistics works for any export format, but I find it most useful when saving as Internet (many files) because Immedia tells you all sorts of goodies, including how long it thinks each linked file will take to download with a 28.8 Kbps modem, how large each file is, and how much compression it was able to achieve on each file.

Figure 14–8
Export Statistics

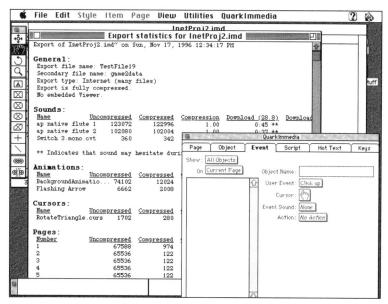

It even tells you if a sound will be likely to pause before playing over the Internet.

You can print the information in the Export Statistics window, copy and paste the pieces you want, or save the whole thing as a text document by choosing Save from the File menu.

▼ ▼

Embed Viewer

You must use the QuarkImmedia Viewer to play an exported project (see "The QuarkImmedia Viewer," later in this chapter). This means that someone who wants to see your project must have the viewer application on their hard drive. However, you can embed the Viewer into your exported projects so that the user won't need to worry about a separate application; it'll be in your project already.

It's easy to embed the Viewer: turn on the Embed Viewer option in the Export dialog box. Note, however, that you can only embed the Viewer for single-file and two-file exports; you cannot embed it in the Internet (many-file) format. That means that you *must* have the separate stand-alone Viewer to see Immedia projects over the Internet.

There are three things to note when embedding the Viewer.

Exporting for CD-ROM. First, if you're exporting in CD-ROM (two files) format, the Viewer gets embedded in the master file.

Viewer size. Next, Immedia is smart about embedding the Viewer. It doesn't embed the entire Viewer—it only embeds as much of the Viewer as is necessary to run that particular project. The stand-alone Viewer program on the Macintosh is currently about 1.1 MB, but when you embed it into an exported project, it can become as small as 420 K.

If you have a QuickTime movie or a sound or just about anything interesting in your project, more of the Viewer is necessary in order to play it, so the file size increases. In most projects, embedding the Viewer adds about 700 K to 950 K to the size of your project.

Viewer type. Finally, it's important to pick the right viewer from the Export Format popup menu (see Figure 14–9). If you choose the wrong type, the project may run slowly or not at all. Note that you cannot embed a Viewer that works on both Macintosh and Windows platforms; the operating systems are just too different.

▶ **Macintosh 680X0** is the lowest common denominator for the Macintosh platform. It will run on older Macintoshes based on the 680X0 chip (like the Quadra 650, the IIci, and so on), as well as Macs based on the PowerPC chip (like the 8100, 9500, and just about every Macintosh made today by Apple, Power Computing, and other manufacturers). The downside is that if you use this embedded Viewer, your projects will run more slowly on a PowerPC-based computer because it has to run in emulation mode (the PowerPC pretends it's a 680X0 chip).

On the plus side, this is the smallest of all the embedded Viewers; if size is a bigger issue than speed, this might be the choice to make.

▶ **Macintosh with PowerPC** gives you a slightly larger embedded Viewer, but it runs much faster on PowerPC computers. The downside is that it *only* runs on PowerPC computers. You cannot run a project with this embedded Viewer on an older machine based on the 680X0 chip.

Figure 14–9
Embedding
the Viewer

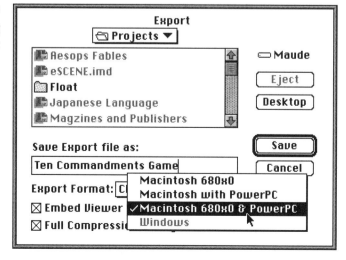

▶ **Macintosh 680X0 & PowerPC** appears at first to be the best of both worlds: you can run this embedded Viewer on computers based on either the 680X0 or the PowerPC chip, and it doesn't have to run in emulation mode on PowerPCs. The big downside to this embedded Viewer is that it's really big (up to 600 K larger than just the 680X0 alone). If an additional half-megabyte isn't that big a deal in the grand scheme of your project, then this is the best choice of all.

▶ **Windows** is the final choice in the Embed Viewer popup menu. While people in the Windows world usually have more options than those who use Macintoshes (different drivers, different hardware configurations, and so on), in this case, the choice is simple: if you want to embed a Viewer that will work in Windows (and only in Windows), choose Windows from the popup menu.

Note that when Immedia first shipped, Quark was not finished developing the Windows Viewer, so "Windows" was grayed out in this popup menu. If it's still grayed out for you, you should get a new QuarkImmedia Data file from Quark (they should send it to you as part of a free upgrade package).

Full Compression During Export

The last checkbox in the Export dialog box is Full Compression During Export. We'll talk about compression in just a moment, so suffice it to say that while Immedia always performs some file compression, when you turn this feature on, Immedia both compresses the file more *and* includes the compression from the Export Settings dialog box. When this option is turned off, Immedia ignores any compression you've specified in Export Settings.

I almost always leave this option turned off while I'm testing out different projects because Immedia exports much faster. Later, when I'm getting serious about fine-tuning a project, I turn it on and get a cup of coffee.

▼ ▼

Tip: Naming Your Files. The name you give your project can have significant repercussions. If you're exporting the project so that it can be used on a computer with Windows 3.1, you should stick to an eight-dot-three file-name format (eight characters, plus the ".imd" extension). Similarly, if you put a project on the Internet, you may need to be sensitive to the limitations of the Web server. Plus, it's a good idea to use the ".imd" suffix so that MIME typing will work properly (see Chapter 15, *The Internet and the World Wide Web*).

In general, no matter where your project is bound, it's a good idea to avoid characters such as periods (except for a suffix), commas, colons, semicolons, dashes, brackets, and slashes.

▼ ▼

Compression

Sometimes it seems like the "bigger is better" mentality will sweep us all away. Bigger corporations, bigger special effects, bigger shoes—it's epidemic. Don't get me wrong; I like big multimedia as much as the next guy—big sounds, big movies, big animations. But the problem with "big" is that, when it comes to computers, big means "slow." To really be efficient, whether you're doing prepress or multimedia, you want to make a big impact with *small* files.

If you include a CD-quality sound effect in your project and then put the exported project on the Internet, you're going to sit there and wait a *long* time for it to play. The better the quality, the bigger the sound file (more data in the file), and the longer it takes to transmit across telephone wires. In fact, you probably couldn't even get away with putting this good a sound in a project playing off a CD-ROM.

However, by sacrificing the quality of the sound, you can boost the quality of the user experience.

Automatic Compression

There are various ways to compress the size of data files such as sound, movies, animations, backgrounds, and so on. QuarkImmedia automatically compresses all your background pictures, text, and flat colored areas. It's so good at compressing these that a full page of text on a colored background can compress down to 20 K, and many pages compress down even smaller.

However, some pages compress more than others. When you turn on Full Compression During Export, Immedia compresses each page down as much as it can.

▼ ▼

Tip: Compression Tricks. QuarkImmedia compresses images using a lossless (loses no image quality) compression scheme that finds groups of pixels with the same color. In Chapter 7, *Sound*, I mentioned the analogy of socks: instead of saying "I've got a blue sock and a blue sock and a blue sock and a blue sock," I can compress the statement down by saying "I've got two pairs of blue socks." It's easy because they're all the same color.

You can take advantage of this kind of compression by using solid colors or colors made up of repeating patterns of pixel color (see Figure 14–10). Similarly, a scanned image converted to Indexed color mode in Photoshop compresses better than one in RGB mode. And if you convert it to Indexed color mode with fewer than 256 colors (8-bit), Immedia can compress it down even further. Making little changes like this can save hundreds of K in file size per page.

Because Immedia looks for these patterns horizontally by row of pixels, you can even save a little space making blends that run vertically rather than horizontally (see Figure 14–11). Better yet, build those blends in Photoshop as indexed color with a patterned dither.

▼ ▼

Export Settings

So far, we've been discussing compressing images and that's all very well. But the largest data files in multimedia aren't the images, they're the sound and QuickTime movies. Fortunately, Immedia can compress these, too. You can control how it compresses sound and video in the Export Settings dialog box (see Figure 14–12).

The Settings For popup menu lets you specify different compression settings for each of the export formats: Standard (one file), CD-ROM (two files), and Internet (many files). This is useful because the settings for an Internet-bound project are usually very different than one bound for your hard drive or a CD-ROM.

Figure 14–10
Solids and patterns
compress well

Solid colors compress the best.

*A color made up of
patterns compresses well.*

*The more "noise," the
worse it compresses.*

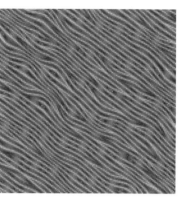

Figure 14–11
Blends and
compression

Horizontal blend: 13.5 K

Vertical blend: 10 K

*Vertical blend built in
Photoshop and saved
in indexed color: 4 K*

Figure 14–12
Compression in
Export Settings

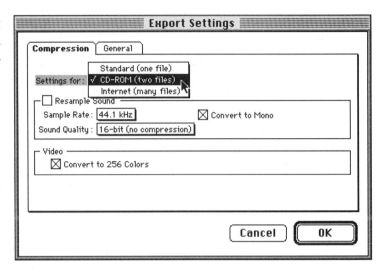

Resample Sound. As I said in Chapter 7, *Sound*, capturing sound at the highest quality, you can affords you the widest flexibility in repurposing that sound. You can always sample down, but you can never recapture detail in the sound. If you import a 44 kHz, 16-bit stereo sound into your Immedia project, you can use the Export Settings dialog box to downsample it to a reasonable value.*

There are three controls in the Export Settings dialog box: Sample Rate, Sound Quality, and Convert to Mono. Immedia only downsamples; that is, it only throws information away. If you import an 8-bit, 22 kHz monaural sound and tell Export Settings to give you 16-bit, 44 kHz, or stereo, Immedia just ignores the command.

▶ **Sample Rate.** Immedia gives you four options in the sample rate (this is also called sound resolution): 44.1 kHz, 22 kHz, 11 kHz, and 5.5 kHz. The lowest value sounds like a mediocre telephone connection, but it's often all you can use if you're trying to stream audio over the Internet. The highest value is CD-quality, but is rarely useful for playback on computers. If you can use 22 kHz sound, you'll end up with a much larger tonal range and, for most music, this really helps. However, if your project will be run on a standard computer without special amplified speakers, 11 kHz may be all you need.

---

*Reasonable is defined as whatever works for you and your user. Some people get hives listening to 11 kHz sound, while to others it sounds just fine.

▶ **Sound Quality.** There is a great difference in distortion and noise between 8-bit and 16-bit sound but, like high-resolution sound, you just don't hear it on many computer systems. On the other hand, it all depends on the kind of music, how it was recorded, and so on. Some sounds can really fall apart when you downsample them to 8-bit; with others, you'd never know the difference.

When preparing for a conference recently, I used low-resolution (8-bit, 11 kHz) sound in my presentation. It sounded okay on the computer at my office, but when it blasted out of the speakers in the conference hall, it sounded horrible! Remember that 16-bit sound is literally twice as much data as 8-bit sound.

▶ **Convert to Mono.** You'd think it would be a no-brainer to convert stereo sound to monaural, especially when you're playing the sound back on a computer with only one speaker. But as it turns out, even this procedure can knock out some important sounds, especially in the higher tonal ranges. Nonetheless, the difference in file size is significant (stereo is twice the size of mono), so even though stereo sound is nicer to listen to when you've got good speakers, this is often the first thing I try when downsampling.

As you can probably tell by my hedging, there is no one solution for audio downsampling. It all depends on the sound or music, the device it'll be played on, and your tolerance for static and noise. There are two sure things, however. First, you have to test out different combinations of these settings for each sound. And second, if you use more than one sound in your project, there's a good chance you'll get a better result doing the resampling in some commercial sound-editing software (like Macromedia SoundEdit 16). That way, you'll be able to really fine-tune each file, getting the best sound in the least amount of data.

Video. QuarkImmedia gives you one and only one control for downsampling video: Convert to 256 Colors. While QuickTime movies that are saved in 24-bit color mode look beautiful, they're really

(really) big. And even movies that are saved in a 256-color palette may be larger than necessary if you're using a custom color palette in your project.

If you turn on the Convert to 256 Colors option, Immedia converts every frame of every QuickTime movie in your project to your project's color palette. This makes the movie look better and run more smoothly on 8-bit color monitors (or when you've turned on the Set Depth/Color option in Export Settings) because the Viewer doesn't have to do the palette conversion on the fly.

▼ ▼
The QuarkImmedia Viewer

Quark made the decision a long time ago that Immedia documents would be written in a format totally different than HTML, Acrobat, or anything else on the market. The result is that the only software that lets you look at these projects is the QuarkImmedia Viewer. You can spend your days shouting about the demise of society and how all programs should be able to open any file format, but it won't get you anywhere. The ugly truth is that you (and everyone you want to show your files to) needs that Viewer, either as a separate application or embedded in the project itself.

When you embed a Viewer into your project (we talked about that earlier in the chapter), none of the Viewer's user interface appears; the project just runs and when you quit the project, the Viewer automatically quits, too. On the other hand, the standalone QuarkImmedia Viewer application (some people call it the "browser") does have a user interface, and that's the subject of this last section. Note that I'm talking about the Viewer both on the Macintosh and in Windows; they work pretty much the same way.

There are four ways to open (or run, or play, or whatever you want to call it) an exported Immedia project. Note that the Viewer can play a project exported in single-file, two-file, or many-file format. That means that if you're authoring for a CD-ROM or the Internet, you don't have to actually burn a CD or put the files on your server in order to try them out.

▶ **Double-click.** The most intuitive way to open a project is simply to double-click on it. If the Viewer application is not currently running, the Macintosh or Windows operating system launches it and then opens the file.

▶ **Drag-open.** I sometimes drag Immedia documents on top of the Immedia Viewer (or, more often, an alias of the Viewer). But because it's exactly the same thing as double-clicking on the project, I don't know why I take the trouble to drag.

▶ **Open.** If you're already in the Viewer, you can open a project from your hard drive, on a CD-ROM, or over your network using the Open command on the Viewer's File menu. If you don't know how to use Open, your problems run deeper than I can solve in this book.

▶ **Open URL.** If your computer is connected to the Internet or to your office's intranet Web server, you can use Open URL from the Viewer's File menu to connect to it (or press Command-L—the same keystroke both Netscape Navigator and Microsoft Internet Explorer use for this feature). The Open URL feature is exactly the same as typing the URL into the Internet Controls palette, except that the dialog box is easier to type in (see Figure 14–13). We'll cover running projects over the Internet, intranets, and the World Wide Web in more depth in Chapter 15, *The Internet and the World Wide Web.*

▼ ▼

Tip: Simulating Transmission Speed. At the last moment before shipping version 1.0, Tim Gill, founder of Quark and father of Immedia, snuck a mind-blowing feature into the Viewer that should become a standard in all Internet authoring tools: simulated transmission speed. If you hold down the Option key when selecting Open from the Viewer's File menu, you're presented with a popup menu labeled Simulated Speed (see Figure 14–14).

There's no benefit here when opening a project exported as Standard (one file) or CD-ROM (two files). But when opening a file exported as Internet (many files), you can select a modem speed

Figure 14–13
QuarkImmedia
Internet Controls

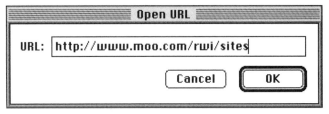

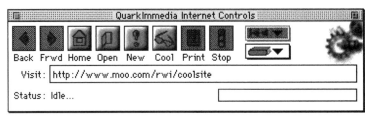

from the Simulated Speed popup menu. This actually gives you a feeling for how the project will play over the Internet without having to upload the files to a server. Talk about saving time! Between this and the Export Statistics feature, Immedia eases the pain when authoring for the Internet.

▼ ▼

Figure 14–14
Simulated Speed

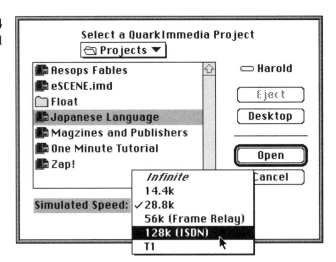

Bookmarks

The QuarkImmedia Viewer's Internet Controls palette lets you save bookmarks of various Immedia sites so you can return to them quickly later on (actually, you can save any kind of URL as a bookmark, including HTML Web sites, FTP sites, and so on . . . but there's no good reason to save anything but Immedia sites here). You can save a bookmark in one of two ways.

▶ You can open the site, then select Add to List from the Bookmarks popup menu on the palette (see Figure 14–15). As of this writing, this isn't working for HTML sites or projects saved to disk.

Figure 14–15
Bookmarks

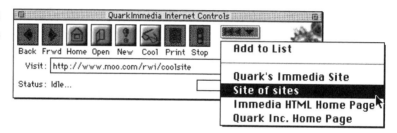

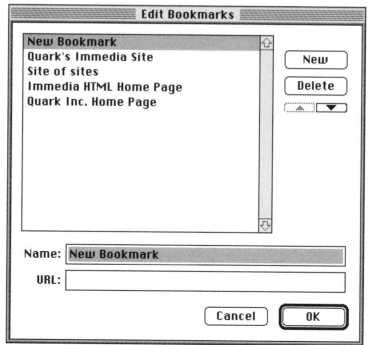

▶ You can select Edit Bookmarks from the Edit menu (or press Command-B). The process is pretty self-explanatory: to create a new bookmark, press the New button, type in a name and a URL, then either click OK or click somewhere in the bookmark list. To change the order of a selected bookmark, use the Up and Down Arrow buttons in the dialog box. You *can* type in URLs to HTML sites or projects on your hard disk here, as long as you use the standard URL format (such as "file://MyHardDrive/project folder/happyproject.imd").

There's no doubt that Immedia's bookmark feature has a long way to go to rival other sorts of browsers. There's no way to collect sites into groups, and there's no way to provide longer descriptions of a site. Nonetheless, it's a step in the right direction, and the more you use bookmarks, the more you find them invaluable.

Preferences

As with most browser applications, you can customize the Quark-Immedia Viewer in several ways via preferences dialog boxes (on the Preferences submenu of the Edit menu; see Figure 14–16). The three preferences dialog boxes are Internet, User, and Security. I encourage you to take the time to visit and customize each of these to your needs. Some features of the Viewer won't even work unless you do.

Figure 14–16
Viewer preferences

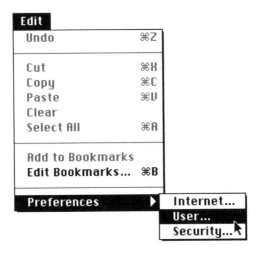

Internet. The first dialog box, Internet Preferences, lets you control several aspects of the Viewer's Internet Control palette as well as how it handles Internet files (see Figure 14–17).

> ▶ **URLs.** First, you can customize the Home, New, and Cool buttons that appear in the palette by typing in the URLs you like most (Quark's are good, but you might find other ones you want to use instead). For instance, my What's Cool site is set to "http://www.moo.com/rwi/coolsite".

Figure 14–17
Internet Preferences

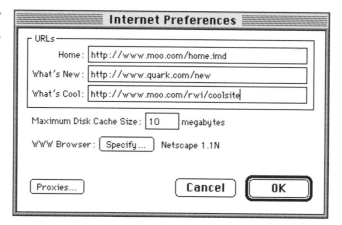

> ▶ **Cache.** The Immedia Viewer keeps a cache of every master and auxiliary file that it encounters when viewing Internet projects, so that when you use the same file again, it doesn't have to download it again. This is obviously a major time savings. The Internet Preferences dialog box lets you specify how large you want this cache to be. I've found little reason to change it from the default 10 MB, though I suppose if you had very limited disk space . . . no, it's probably better for you just to buy a larger hard drive.

> ▶ **WWW Browser.** The third preference in this dialog box is the WWW Browser. As you know, Immedia doesn't create or view HTML files. If you type a URL that points to an HTML file in the Open URL dialog box, or if you use the Open URL action to jump to an HTML site, Immedia won't know what to do with it. However, if you click on the Specify button and guide the Viewer to an HTML-aware browser, such as Netscape

Navigator or Microsoft Internet Explorer, the Viewer will simply hand off any HTML sites to that application. This is called making Navigator or Explorer a "helper app."

▶ **Proxies.** Some businesses have an intermediary computer, called a *firewall*, between the Internet and all the computers on their internal network. These companies have people whose business is to help people like us set up our Web browsers. If your computer is behind a firewall and you want to use the Immedia Viewer to see Immedia sites on the Internet, ask your system administrator for three addresses: HTTP Proxy, FTP Proxy, and SOCKS Host. Then click on the Proxies button in the Internet Preferences dialog box and type these addresses in the appropriate fields (see Figure 14–18).

Figure 14–18
Setting up proxies
for a firewall

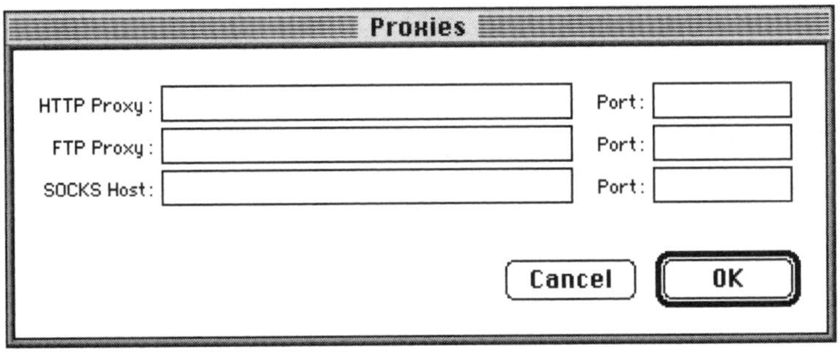

User. Quark is hoping that everyone who has a QuarkImmedia Viewer will open the User Preferences dialog box and fill in their name, e-mail address, mailing address, and so on (see Figure 14–19). The reason: the automatic text entry features in Immedia can read this information and drop it into text boxes (like ordering forms) automatically. If people leave the dialog box blank, then project authors like us can't use those features effectively (see "Editable Text Box Objects" in Chapter 4, *Text)*.

The truth of the matter is that it doesn't really matter much whether you fill out this dialog box. In the future, if you find yourself using on-line Immedia catalogs a lot, having this information in Preferences could save you time when typing your name and

Figure 14–19
User Preferences

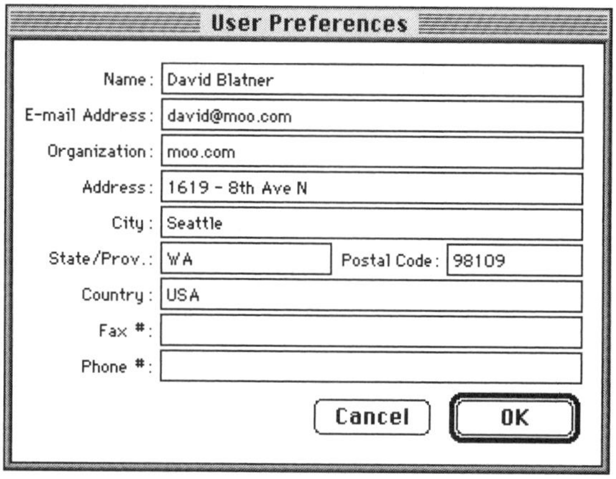

address into text boxes. In the meantime, however, Quark's going to have to figure out how to encourage people to visit this dialog box.

Security. Unless you've been living on another planet for the past couple of years, you've probably heard of something on the Internet called Java. No, Java isn't a new brand of coffee; rather, it's a way to download and run little programs over the Internet. I'm oversimplifying, but basically you can write Java "applets" that reside on a Web server but run on your desktop computer.

The implications of Java are enormous, and one of the first things people started worrying about was security. "If it's running on my computer, maybe it can move my files around or erase them like a virus," people wondered. Fortunately, Java no can do. The whole idea of Java is that it runs within a strictly defined shell; it cannot get outside of that shell to do anything else on your computer.

Now, Immedia really has nothing to do with Java (I hope I wasn't giving the impression that it did). But the fears that people have *do* have something to do with Immedia, because Immedia *can* cause real havoc on a Macintosh—by running AppleScripts. The power of AppleScript is also its weakness: it's not bounded by a shell; it can control anything on your computer, or even on your network.

Fortunately, Quark had the presence of mind to include some security measures in the Immedia Viewer. The Security Preferences dialog box (select Security from the Preferences submenu) contains various options to ensure your safety. The keys are the four check-boxes in this dialog box, which are all on by default.

▶ **Warn if Executing AppleScripts.** AppleScripts are incredibly powerful, and I can't tell you how happy I was when I found that Immedia could run them. But you have to use some common sense when running unfamiliar projects. When this checkbox is on, the Viewer warns you whenever it's about to run an AppleScript (see Figure 14–20). If you're not expecting an AppleScript, you may want to cancel the operation right then and there.

Note that if you're authoring a project that triggers Apple-Scripts, remember that people will probably get this warning. You should prepare them in whatever way you think best.

Figure 14–20
Warning of
AppleScripts

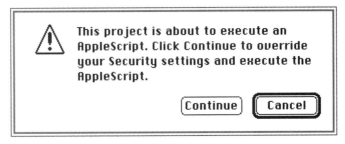

▶ **Warn if Printing EPS.** AppleScripts aren't the only thing that can cause trouble. There are some little-known ways to write a virus into an EPS file that causes havoc with your printer. So here, too, the Viewer warns you whenever the project tries to print a document across the Internet. Remember, as in life, the chances that someone will sabotage you are pretty slim.

▶ **Warn on Submit Page.** In the next chapter, we'll see how Immedia lets you send information from a project over the Internet to a Web server, using the Submit Page action. Some people (I'm among them) get a little nervous when it comes to my personal information getting moved around without my knowing it. Fortunately, the Viewer warns me before the project sends anything. Unfortunately, upon getting this warning, there's no way to find out *what* is being submitted, so you have to either agree to the action (override the security measures) or cancel it altogether.

► **Restrict all Reads/Writes to Scratch Directory.** The last checkbox in the Security Preferences dialog box ensures that if a project reads from or writes to your disk (using the Read File or Write File actions), it will only do so in a particular folder. To specify the folder, click on the Scratch Directory button in the dialog box. If you don't specify a folder, Immedia won't let you read or write from an Internet project at all. Typically, it's safe to create a special folder for this sort of thing or just specify the same folder as your copy of the Immedia Viewer.

The final preference in the Security Preferences dialog box, Apply Security Options, lets you control when the Viewer will warn you or control reading and writing. It's interesting that this defaults to Internet Projects Only because that implies that there's no danger from projects running over an internal network or from a CD-ROM. If you're the nervous sort, you might want to change this to Always (although I think you'll find it a bigger pain than it's worth).

▼ ▼

From Disk to Diskless

Once your project is exported and it leaves behind the sheltered confines of QuarkXPress and QuarkImmedia, it moves into a whole new stage of life. Multimedia projects, unlike printed pages, typically require testing and tech support. If you're fabulously lucky, everything in your project will work perfectly, and you'll have to export only once. If you're a mere mortal, however, you'll probably find yourself exporting a number of times, with each cycle becoming successively better.

And at some point, the heavens will open up, your name will be praised from on high as "getting it just right," and then your boss will walk in and say, "Now we need to put your project on the Internet." At that point, don't despair—instead, read the next chapter.

The Internet and World Wide Web

B ACK IN THE 1970S, MY STEPFATHER would tell me stories of the Internet—where it had come from and how computer scientists like himself were using it. Pretty cool, I thought, but it didn't really apply to me. Years later, before hardly anyone had heard of it, he told me about a new thing called the World Wide Web, and how it was going to be big . . . really big. Suffice it to say, he's a better visionary than me—I just smiled and nodded and failed to make the connection. Of course, now the Internet and Web have become a deluge of biblical proportions, and every day they're changing our lives in new ways.

Quark, knowing a good thing when it sees one, included Internet capabilities in QuarkImmedia. But what does that mean, exactly? How does Immedia work with the Internet? And how is it different than anything else on the Web? To understand QuarkImmedia's place in all this, we have to take a short detour through some definitions.

Internet versus Intranet

The Internet connects computers that are all over the world, using particular standards of computer-talk (protocols). Almost any computer can be connected to the Internet if it can "talk the talk and walk the walk." However, these protocols aren't just limited to computers on the Internet; any bunch of computers can talk to each other using the very same "language." With this in mind, more and more people are building *intranets* in their offices.

An intranet is a network of computers that talk to each other using the same standards as those on the Internet (TCP/IP), but that are not necessarily connected to the worldwide Internet.* Typically, that means a local area network (LAN) connected with Ethernet (that's what I've got in my office).

The great benefit of an intranet is bandwidth—you can move around Web pages, or e-mail, or whatever, at high speeds because you're not limited to slow modems or telephone lines. When we start talking about transmission speed and file size and so on, you'll see why Immedia projects, while often barely workable on the Internet, are ideal for intranets.

Whenever I say "Internet" in this chapter, you can probably apply that to intranets, too.

World Wide Web versus Internet

People talk about "the Web" and the Internet (or the "information superhighway") interchangeably these days, but they are not the same at all. The Internet is like the telephone lines that span the world—it's an underlying system that links computers together. And just as people move all kinds of information over telephone lines (such as voice, fax, and data), people can move all sorts of stuff over the Internet.

The Web is only one type of thing that can be moved over the Internet. Other "types of things" are e-mail, FTP (file transfer protocol), and newsgroups. Each of these use the "telephone lines" of the Internet, but each in a different way.

As Adam Engst, author of the *Internet Starter Kit* (a must-have if you're working on the Internet) points out, "At its base, the Web is a method for sharing information." How you share that information is up to you.

---

*Some intranets have gateways to the Internet—perhaps a single computer that acts like a liaison between the two systems.

HTML versus Everyone Else

If you use Netscape Navigator or Microsoft Internet Explorer, you've undoubtedly been looking at World Wide Web pages that are built using HTML. HTML is a markup language that tells a Web browser how to display text and graphics—what font, size, style, and so on. The good news is that HTML is just text, so it transfers across modems and telephone lines quickly. The bad news is that HTML is pretty limited in what it can display.

There's no doubt that you can design a beautiful page in HTML; it's just that if you're used to designing for the printed page, you're going to feel frustrated making pages in the ultra-structured world of HTML (see Figure 15–1). Fortunately for us, HTML isn't the only game in town.

QuarkImmedia does not use HTML. It doesn't export HTML. The Immedia Viewer doesn't even try to interpret HTML. Immedia is a whole different ball game. The great benefit of Immedia pages over HTML is that you can design your page any way you want. And, as we saw in the last chapter, anything you can put in an Immedia project, you can export for the Internet.

But wait, there's more! You can actually build actions into your projects that take advantage of an Internet connection, from jumping among locations on the Internet, to importing text from the Internet into your project, to sending information from your project to a file on your Web server. We'll see how in this chapter.

There are several potential downsides to putting Immedia projects on the Internet, however. First, hardly anyone has a QuarkImmedia Viewer yet. Next, many Immedia projects are just too big to reasonably transmit at Internet speeds.

Adobe Acrobat versus Immedia. Some of you have seen (or even created) Acrobat Portable Document Format (PDF) files for the Internet. Acrobat PDF is another non-HTML format that lets you display complex designs on screen. You can build an Acrobat PDF* from just about any program, from PageMaker to XPress to Microsoft Word to

---

*Not to be confused with PDF files that come with QuarkXPress, which are Printer Description Files.

Figure 15-1

HTML and others

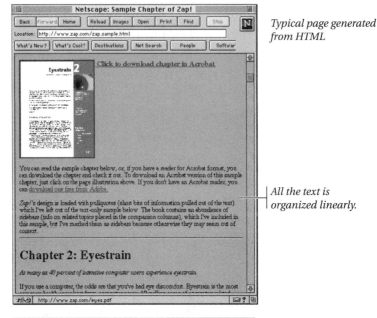

Typical page generated from HTML

All the text is organized linearly.

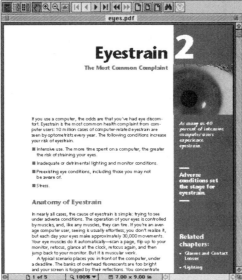

Typical Adobe Acrobat file

Illustrator. In fact, Acrobat was originally designed so that you could make a brochure or a newsletter or other destined-for-print piece and then send it—in PDF format—to someone else who doesn't have the same software or fonts as you.

Until recently, in order to view Acrobat PDF files over the Internet, you had to download the entire PDF file, then view it with the

Figure 15–1 (cont.)
HTML and others
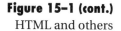

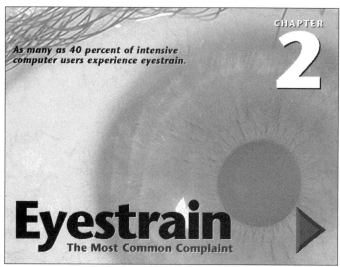

An Immedia page on the Internet

Acrobat reader. Now, Adobe has developed a plug-in that allows you to view Acrobat PDF files over the Internet using Netscape Navigator or Microsoft Internet Explorer—the file actually appears right in the browser's window.

Some people have argued that Acrobat is easier to use than the Immedia Viewer because of this plug-in architecture. Forgive my standing on a soapbox for a moment, but this just isn't true.

► While there isn't currently a plug-in for Immedia projects, you can set up Navigator and Internet Explorer to automatically hand off Immedia projects to the Immedia Viewer (see "Immedia as a Helper Application," later in this chapter). It takes exactly the same amount of work to do this as to properly set up the Acrobat plug-in.

► The Acrobat plug-in actually launches the Acrobat Reader in the background and uses it as a "helper application" to the browser. In other words, Immedia and Acrobat handle their Internet files in the same way, except Acrobat files appear in the browser's window rather than their own.

► Immedia projects cannot currently appear in the browser window because the browser's window is too limiting. As you know, an Immedia document can take up the entire screen, including the menu bar.

▶ Unless Acrobat 3.0 and the plug-in were installed on your computer when you bought it, you have to download the software (it's over 4 MB, which takes over a half-hour to download at fast modem speeds). Immedia's Viewer is just over 1 MB. (Of course, if you have this book, you already have it.)

There's no doubt that Acrobat is useful for some things and has some great features. For instance, you can zoom in or out within a PDF, and the fonts and graphics remain smooth. If the PDF is bigger than your screen, you can pan around it using a grabber hand tool. You can even print a PDF without having to embed a separate EPS. Immedia allows none of this.

However, Immedia offers other features that Acrobat doesn't have, such as animation, custom cursors, custom menus, and so on. Immedia was designed from the ground up to create on-screen, interactive, multimedia projects.

Viewing Immedia Projects On-line

I hate to be redundant, but just in case you've skipped ahead in the book and haven't heard me say this eight times before: You must use the QuarkImmedia Viewer to view *any* Immedia project, whether it's on your hard drive or on the Internet. While you can embed the viewer for projects on disk (even on CD-ROMs), you can't do this for files viewed over the Internet.

The Viewer is on the CD-ROM in the back of the book. It's free, so you can distribute to anyone you want. Of course, you cannot legally distribute the QuarkImmedia XTension (the authoring tool).

There are several Internet-related preferences that you should set before using the Viewer to play projects over the Internet, including Scratch Disk and Security Preferences. I discussed those back in "The QuarkImmedia Viewer," in Chapter 14, *Exporting*, so I won't bother here.

▼ ▼

Tip: Sequential Downloading. The Viewer has several features that are particular to playing projects over the Internet, including the ability to download pages in the background during times of inactivity. Any time the user doesn't do anything for several seconds, Immedia starts downloading subsequent pages in the project (the progress bar won't move, but you can see the little gears in the Internet Control Palette chug away). For example, if you stop to read a bunch of text on page three, Immedia starts downloading page four in the background. That way, it takes hardly any time at all when you jump to page four.

No, there's currently no way to tell Immedia to download anything other than the next page in the project. But knowing about this feature may help you streamline your project.

▼ ▼

Immedia as a Helper Application

When you're surfing along the information superhighway, you don't want to get stopped suddenly just because your browser doesn't know what to do with some file. Web browsers can't be expected to know every sound file format, every movie file format, and every graphic file format out on the Internet—there are just too many of them! So sometimes the browser can ask for help from another program, kind of like calling in a specialist. This other program is called a helper application.

As I said earlier, HTML browsers can't view Immedia projects, and the Immedia Viewer doesn't understand HTML. Fortunately, your browser and your Immedia Viewer can act as helper applications to each other. When your Web browser stumbles on an Immedia project, it can automatically launch your Immedia Viewer. And if you jump to an HTML site while in the Immedia Viewer, it launches your Web browser.

Setting up the Viewer. I pointed out how to make your Web browser a helper application to the Immedia Viewer back in Chapter 14,
Exporting, but I'll do a quick recap here.

1. Open the Immedia Viewer and select Internet from the Preferences submenu (under the Edit menu; see Figure 15–2).

2. Click on the WWW Browser button.

3. Find your Web browser on your hard drive. For instance,
   select Netscape Navigator, Microsoft Internet Explorer, Mosa-
   ic, or any other HTML-aware browser.

That's it! Whenever the Immedia Viewer senses that it's downloading HTML rather than an Immedia project, it'll hand it off to
that browser automatically.

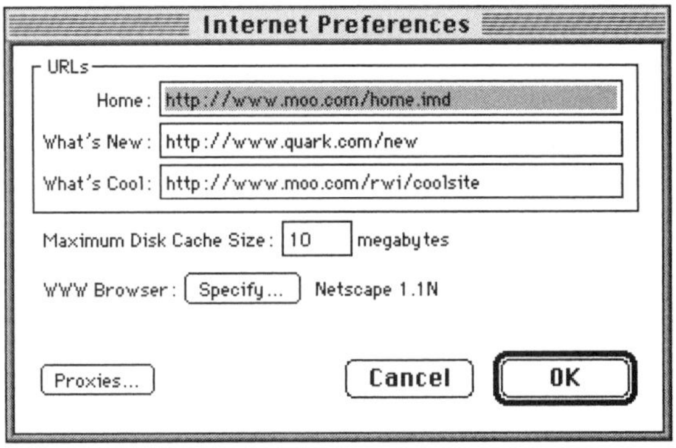

Figure 15–2
Selecting a
Web browser

Tip: Using the Right Suffix. In the following two sections, I discuss
setting up Netscape Navigator and Microsoft Internet Explorer so
that they'll pass off Immedia projects to the QuarkImmedia Viewer.
However, note that this usually only works when the project has an
.imd at the end of its name. For instance, Navigator and Explorer
should be able to hand off "myproject.imd" fine, but have trouble
with "myproject.export" (of course, you can still open the site from
within the Viewer). I continue to be frustrated by this (I think you
should be able to call your projects anything you want), but them's
the rules.

Setting Up Netscape Navigator

Telling Netscape Navigator to use the Immedia Viewer as a helper application is a little more difficult than vice versa, unfortunately. But it's not too bad.

1. Select Preferences or General Preferences from the Options menu (different versions of Navigator have different feature names, but they all do the same thing; see Figure 15–3).

2. Choose Helpers or Helper Applications from the General Preferences dialog box. Scroll through the list of helper applications to see if there is already one for QuarkImmedia files. If there is, you can skip the rest of this.

Figure 15–3
Helper applications in Navigator

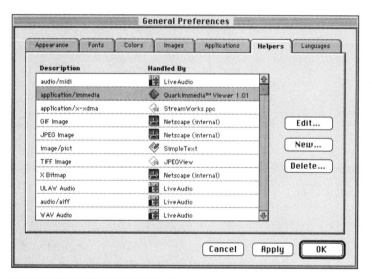

3. Press the New button. This tells Navigator to create a new Helper Application type.

4. Type "application" in the MIME type field, "Immedia" in the subtype field, and "imd" in the Extensions field.

5. Press the Browse button and go find the QuarkImmedia Viewer. This way, Netscape knows which application to launch when it sees an Immedia project.

6. Choose Launch from the Action radio buttons and make sure the File Type popup menu is set to ODOC. (If this popup menu is set to TEXT or is blank, check out "Tip: Rebuilding the Desktop," below.)

You're set. Note that this only works if your Web server (whichever computer on the Internet actually has the Immedia project that you're viewing) is configured properly, as well (see "Setting up Your Server," later in this chapter).

▼ ▼

Tip: Rebuilding the Desktop. I had a dickens of a time trying to get *ODOC* to appear on my File Type popup menu until, out of desperation, I rebuilt my Mac's desktop file. This invisible file stores all the information about what kind of applications you have, what their file types are, and what their icons look like (plus lots of other stuff). For some reason, it occasionally gets all higgledy-piggledy (that's the technical term for it), and you need to rebuild it. You can do this by restarting your machine and holding down the Command and Option keys until you see a dialog box asking if you're sure you want to rebuild the desktop files.

▼ ▼

Setting Up Microsoft Internet Explorer

There are lots of HTML-savvy Web browsers out there, but most people use Netscape Navigator. Almost everyone who doesn't use Navigator uses Microsoft's Internet Explorer. You set up the Quark-Immedia Viewer as a helper application to Internet Explorer in just about the same way as for Navigator.

1. Choose Options from the Edit menu, then click on the Helpers tab (see Figure 15–4).

2. Press New to open the Configure File Type dialog box.

Figure 15–4

Helper applications in Internet Explorer

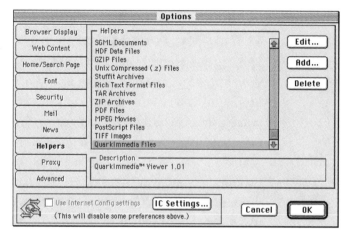

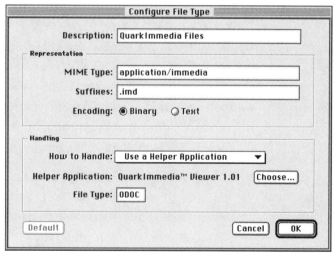

3. You can use any description you like; for example, you might type in "QuarkImmedia Projects".

4. Type application/Immedia for the MIME type, and set Suffixes to ".imd". Encoding should be set to Binary.

5. Click on the Choose button and find the QuarkImmedia Viewer on your hard disk. The How to Handle popup menu should change to Use a Helper Application.

6. Type "ODOC" in the File Type field.

As I noted above, you still must make sure that the Web server you're using (the one that has the Immedia documents saved on it) is configured properly, too.

Setting Up Your Server

There is talk around Quark HQ that you must configure your Web server properly for QuarkImmedia projects or else they won't play properly. However, this doesn't appear to be the case. At least, there doesn't seem to be any reason to configure the Web server if you're opening the projects from within the Immedia Viewer.

If you want to open your projects from within Navigator or Explorer, you may or may not need to have the server configured properly. I'd say don't worry about it unless you find that you, or your users, run into troubles.

▼ ▼

Tip: Default Web Site Pages. You know how you can use Navigator or Explorer to jump to a URL like "www.zap.com"? You don't have to specify a particular file on that Web server because the server software is configured to use a default page (one that the server uses whenever you don't specify any other file). You can make an Immedia project be your default web page using one of two methods.

▶ You can create a little HTML file called "index.html" (most Web servers are configured so that "index.html" is the default Web page). The HTML file should include code that forces the Web Browser to jump automatically to another file. The proper code should sit in the HEAD section of the HTML, like this.

```
<HTML>
<HEAD>
<META HTTP-EQUIV="Refresh" CONTENT="0;
URL=http://www.company-
name.com/project.imd">
</HEAD>
</HTML>
```

▶ If you have control of the Web server, you can configure it so that your Immedia project is the default page.

▼ ▼

Configuring the server. There are a lot of Web browsers floating around out there, but I only discuss Navigator and Explorer. There are even more Web servers, which causes me to be even more vague when talking about how to set your server up to handle Immedia documents. You (or your server's administrator) need to create two new MIME types in the server's configuration file.

1. The first is of MIME type *application/Immedia* and has an extension *.imd*. If your server is on a Macintosh, you might be able to specify a file type and creator. If so, this first MIME type has a file type of *ODOC* and a creator code of *QORN*.

2. The second MIME type is also *application/Immedia*, but there is no extension. If you can, set the file type to *OPRT* and the creator code to *QORN*.

That's all there is to it. If you had problems before when opening projects from within Netscape Navigator or Microsoft Internet Explorer (and you've set up your projects and the Web browser in the way I discussed earlier), the troubles should be cleared up now.

▼ ▼

Actions

Okay, so you're all set for surfing the 'Net with the Immedia Viewer and your Web browser. But let's focus again on the authoring side of Immedia. You've got a host of Internet-related actions to play with in Immedia, from jumping to a new URL to submitting forms to a CGI script on your Web server (see Figure 15–5). Let's take a look at each of these actions and how you might want to use them.

▼ ▼

Tip: Breaking Out Internet Actions. Each of the Internet-related actions *only* work when you are in the QuarkImmedia Viewer and

Figure 15–5

Internet-related actions

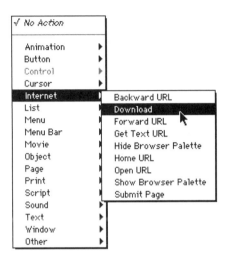

are connected to the Internet. That means you can't test these actions by engaging the project within QuarkXPress. You must export the file and open it in the Viewer. (Yes, it's a major pain in the left buttock, but it makes sense if you think about it.)

The problem is that your file might be enormous and it could take a long time to export it. If you had to do this every time you wanted to test an Internet-related action, you'd be taking too many trips to the coffee machine and you wouldn't be able to stop shaking from all the caffeine. The solution is to break out the Internet-related actions into a separate project that exports quickly. Once you get it working the way you want it, copy all the pieces back into your big project. It's an annoyance, but it can really save you a lot of time.

▼ ▼

Show/Hide Browser Palette. Back in Chapter 14, *Exporting*, we learned that the Immedia Viewer has one palette: QuarkImmedia Internet Controls. This palette, no matter how useful, tends to get in the way of your project at the worst times. Plus, sometimes the palette is open even when you run the project from the hard disk or a CD-ROM. Fortunately, you can hide the palette with the Hide Browser Palette action. Later, when you want to show it again, use the Show Browser Palette action.

If you're expecting that your project will be run from a CD-ROM or a disk, you might include the Hide Browser Palette action in your entry script (see Chapter 13, *Scripting*); the user probably won't miss the palette.

Download. Transmitting files over the Internet can be a long, drawn-out process, even if you have a high-speed connection (I get into this in more detail in "Transmission," later in this chapter). The Immedia Viewer downloads animations and QuickTime movies as soon as you display the page they're on. The result: when you run that project over the Internet, everything moves along smoothly until you display a page with a movie or animation; then you sit and watch the progress bar crawl across the Internet Controls Palette.

Similarly, the Viewer tries to download the sound as it's playing (this is called *streaming*), but as we saw in Chapter 7, *Sound*, sound files are often too large to stream successfully; the result is jerky, stuttering sound.

You can force the Viewer to download a sound, a movie, or an animation before the program actually needs it with the Download action. For example, you might use a Download action to download a sound in a Page Entry script. That page would take longer to appear (because the Viewer would be busy downloading the sound file), but the sound on that page would then run without an initial pause or stuttering.

▼ ▼

Tip: Communicate Your Download. I find many people get annoyed every time the Viewer pauses to download a file, because they don't realize what's going on; they just think the project has frozen or something. I sometimes write a short script that opens a window that reads "Please Hold — Downloading", and then proceeds to download one or more files with the Download action. At the end of the script, I close the window and let the user proceed.

There are all sorts of variations on this theme. For instance, it's easy to include a countdown or a status bar in the window that tells you how many files are going to be/have been downloaded.

▼ ▼

Build Your Own Browser

You don't have to rely on the QuarkImmedia Internet Controls palette to jump from one URL to another.* You can build buttons or hot spots in your Immedia projects that perform the same task as several of the palette's buttons. So, if you don't like the palette's interface, build your own!

Open URL. The Open URL action is similar to the Open Project action (see "Other Actions" in Chapter 3, *Building Projects*) in that it closes the current project and opens a new one. However, it's different in three ways.

> ▶ Open Project only opens files on a disk. To open a file on the Internet, you must use Open URL instead. Open URL can open both disk and Internet projects.

> ▶ You can use Open URL to open an HTML file (the Viewer launches your Web browser to view it).

> ▶ When you set up the Open Project action, you have to specify a particular file to open. Open URL is dynamic; you can choose a URL from any list or an Editable text box. For example, your user could type a URL into a text box and the Open URL action could jump to that site.

The Open URL action asks for four things (see Figure 15–6).

1. First, you must choose where the URL is—choose either Enter URL or Text Object from the Method popup menu.

2. If you chose Enter URL, then you must type one in the URL field. If you chose Text Object, then select one from the Text Object popup menu (this can be any text box given a name and set to Text Object on the Object tab of the QuarkImmedia palette; see Chapter 4, *Text*).

---

*URL stands for Uniform Resource Locator. It's like a street address; it tells the Viewer exactly where to find the site. For instance, the URL *http://www.quark.com/immedia.imd* tells the Viewer there is a file called "immedia" on the server www.quark.com.

Figure 15–6
Open URL

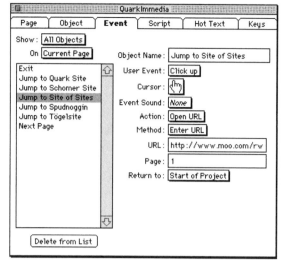

3. Choose the page on which you want to enter the project, and type it into the Page field. If you want to jump right to the third page of that project, type 3. Of course, Immedia ignores this if the URL turns out to not be an Immedia project (if it were an HTML site, for example).

4. What should happen if or when the user returns to this project—for example, if they press Back on the Internet Control palette, or if that project triggers a Return to Project action? You can choose either Current Page or Start of Project from the Return To popup menu. Current Page returns to whatever page you were on when the Open URL action was triggered. Start of Project takes you all the way back to the first page of the project. Again, if the URL isn't an Immedia project, Immedia ignores this setting.

▼ ▼

Tip: Projects on FTP Sites. You can put a QuarkImmedia Project on an FTP server if you want. To jump to that site, use a URL like "ftp://projectname". However, QuarkImmedia won't let you upload or download files to an FTP site; you'll have to use an FTP-aware program like Fetch or Anarchie for that.

▼ ▼

Tip: Sending E-mail. Rumor has it that Quark will include the ability to send e-mail directly from a project in a later version of Immedia. In the meantime, however, here's a clever workaround: use the Open URL action, but instead of a URL beginning with "http://" use one that starts with "mailto:", such as *mailto:david@moo.com*. When you trigger this action, QuarkImmedia launches your Web browser and brings up its Send E-mail dialog box with the proper e-mail address already filled in.

▼ ▼

Forward/Backward URL. The Forward URL and Backward URL actions do exactly the same thing as pressing the Forward and Backward buttons on the Internet Controls palette. Let's say you have a series of projects that are linked together using the Open URL action. If you ran the first project, jumped to the second, then jumped to the third, Backward URL would take you back to the second project. If you then triggered a Forward URL, it would move back to the third project.

Backward URL is actually the same as the Return to Project action (from the Other popout menu in the Action menu), and you can use them interchangeably.

Home URL. If you're building projects for an intranet—one in which you can set up all the Viewers the way you want—then the Home URL makes sense; otherwise, I can't imagine when you'd use it. The Home URL action jumps to whatever URL is specified in the Home field of the Viewer's Internet Preferences dialog box (see Figure 15–7). But why would you jump home unless you knew what site was home? Again, in an intranet, you could get everyone to set their Home URL to a common, central site. Maybe then you'd put a little "home" icon on all your project pages which, when pressed, would take you to that site.

By the way, I have no idea why you can't trigger actions for the Internet Control palette's other buttons, New and Cool. That's just life, I guess.

Figure 15–7
Home URL

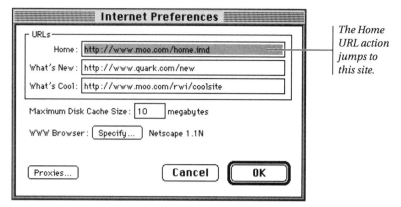

The Home URL action jumps to this site.

▼ ▼

Tip: Distributing Preferences. As I said above, the Home URL action makes sense if you can control the Home setting in the Viewer's Internet Preferences dialog box. If you're setting up an intranet on your network, you can do this easily. No, you don't have to open each person's Viewer and make the change yourself. Just make the change on your computer, then copy your QuarkImmedia Preferences file (in the Preferences folder in your System Folder) into everybody else's Preferences folder. When you distribute the Preferences file, you distribute the preferences, too.

▼ ▼

Moving Information Around

Immedia has two other Internet-related actions: Get Text URL and Submit Page. The first lets you pull information off the Internet and into your project. The second does the opposite, letting you take stuff from your project and send it to a server on the Internet.

Get Text URL

I've got a QuarkImmedia project on my site that lists where and when I'm speaking at conferences (www.moo.com/rwi/schedule). My schedule changes pretty often, and I don't want to be bothered with re-exporting this project all the time. Instead, that project automatically imports and formats a text file that contains the information; I just keep that text file up-to-date and everything works like clockwork.

You can get your projects to import text from the Internet using the Get Text URL action (see Figure 15–8).

1. As with the Open URL action, you must first choose where the URL is going to come from by choosing either Enter URL or Text Object from the Method popup menu.

2. Next, if you chose Enter URL, you have to type the text file's URL into the URL field. If you chose Text Object, you have to specify which text object contains the URL for the text file. Again, this can be any text box object, whether it's Editable, Scrollable, or even a List (see Chapter 4, *Text*).

3. Finally, you have to tell Immedia where you want the text to go after it pulls it in. This, too, must be a text box object (any kind will do).

When you trigger the Get Text URL action, the Immedia Viewer looks for the text file with the URL you've specified, grabs the text from it, and writes it into a text box on your page.

▼ ▼

Tip: Formatting ASCII Text. The Get Text URL only brings in plain ASCII text. That means no fonts, no styling, no service. However, because the text flows into a text box object, you can apply some formatting to the incoming text (this follows the basic rules of text box objects that are discussed in Chapter 4, *Text*).

▶ Font

▶ Size

▶ Style (bold, italic, bold italic, and underline only)

▶ Color

▶ Shade

You can even specify a Text Inset for the text box (choose Modify from the Item menu, or press Command-M). However, just about

Figure 15-8
Get Text URL

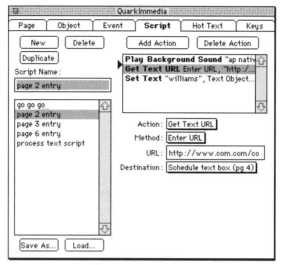

any other formatting is ignored, including Leading, Space Before/After, Vertical Alignment, and multiple columns. If you want space between paragraphs, you need to type an extra carriage return. If you want an indent, type a tab or five spaces. Your formatting won't be beautiful, but it's still better than what you could do with HTML.

By the way, you don't have to have any text in your text box in order to apply this formatting. However, if it makes you feel better, type in some dummy text, format it, then delete it. Remember that you cannot have some text formatted one way and other text formatted another way—Immedia formats all the incoming text the same way.

Note that if the person looking at your project doesn't have the font you chose, the Viewer picks a different typeface. It's supposed to use the font you've specified in the QuarkImmedia Preferences dialog box (see "Formatting" in Chapter 4, *Text*) but, as of this writing, it doesn't work correctly. It's probably best to stick with fonts that you know people will have.

▼ ▼

Tip: Hybrid Projects. Notice that I said that the actions in this chapter rely on your audience having an Internet connection, not that the projects themselves necessarily have to be on the Internet. One of the most clever uses of Immedia is a hybrid project: part on a CD-ROM or a hard drive, and part on the Internet.

► You could distribute a small project on a floppy disk which, when run, would access data on the Internet.

► A CD-ROM designed for the Pippin or some other low-cost device might contain a project filled with movies, sounds, and other bandwidth-hogging data. But the *text* for the project could sit on a Web server somewhere and only get downloaded with the appropriate password.

► You could even fill a CD-ROM with QuickTime movies, sounds, and animations, then put on the Internet the project that calls each of those.*

The trick to all of these scenarios is cleverly using the Get Text URL and Submit Page actions (I'll discuss the latter in just a moment) to move information back and forth over the Internet. I've shown an example of this in the "Internet project" on the Real World QuarkImmedia CD-ROM.

▼ ▼

Submit Page

Submit Page lets you send text to your Web server. For instance, let's say you have a form in your project with which people can request more information on a product. Once they fill in the form (name, address, phone number, and whatnot), they can press a button and it gets mailed off across the Internet to your Web server. Your Web server accepts and processes this information—it could save it on disk, e-mail it to some other address, or add it to a database. That's all controlled by programming CGI (Common Gateway Interface) scripts for the server and is outside the scope of this book.

---

*In case you want to do this, the secret is to export the file in the CD-ROM (two files) format, and make sure Auxiliary File Path is set up correctly in Export Settings (see Chapter 14, *Exporting*).

Unfortunately, reality is about nine hundred times more complicated that this little description. The problem isn't with Immedia, it's with Web servers. There are so many different types of servers and configurations out there that there is no one-size-fits-all description for how to work with the Submit Page action (no matter how easy Quark's documentation makes it sound).

Nonetheless, I'll take a stab at describing how the action works, and then how you can make it work for you.

Get versus Post. Different Web servers act differently, so Submit Page lets you use either Get or Post when submitting text (choose one from the Query Type popup menu; see Figure 15–9). You should check with your server administrator to see which you should use. Note that Get only lets you send 256 characters at a time, while Post lets you send as much text as you want.

Method. The Submit Page action sends your Web server information about every changeable item on a single page (see "What Gets Sent," below). But which page? You must choose Current Page, Page Number, or Page Name from the Method popup menu. I've experienced some odd, unexpected results when using Current Page, so I try to use Page Name whenever possible.

Figure 15–9
Submit Page

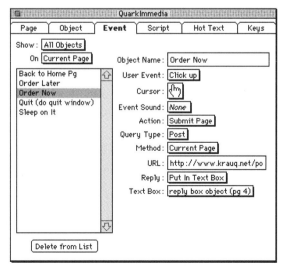

▼ ▼

Tip: Submitting from a Window. The Submit Page action won't let you submit the contents of a window. One workaround is to build a script that copies the contents of each text box into a text box on a different page. Then, use the Submit Page action to send the contents of that page. You don't even have to ever display that page; it can just be used as a dummy repository page.

▼ ▼

URL. Next, you must type a valid URL in to the URL field. This should be the URL of a CGI script on your Web server. The CGI should accept the text that is handed to it and respond in some way. Again, writing CGIs is outside the scope of this book. However, I've placed some handy pointers about CGIs and the Submit Page action in general on my Immedia Web site (see "Where to Find Me" at the back of this book).

Reply. CGI scripts typically respond to a Get or Post action by sending back something; most CGI scripts that are on Web servers today send back an HTML document that a Web browser can display. The QuarkImmedia Viewer can't currently display HTML, so this is pretty useless. You can, however, write a CGI script that returns text suitable for placing in a text box object. You can use the Reply popup menu to specify in which text box object you want the CGI's reply to be placed.

For instance, the CGI script could send a reply that reads "Your form has been successfully submitted. Thank you." and you could place it in a text box object in a window on your screen.

What Gets Sent. As I said above, the QuarkImmedia Viewer sends information about every changeable item on a page when you trigger a Submit Page action.

▶ The contents of each Editable text box object (including lists)

▶ The currently-selected item in popup menu objects

▶ The current state of all On/Off buttons

▶ The current "on" button in a button group

Web servers generally use a number of special characters—such as spaces, returns, tabs, equal signs, and ampersands—as control characters, so Immedia automatically replaces these characters with their hexadecimal-equivalent and gives them a percent sign prefix. For example, all space characters become *%20*, carriage returns becomes *%0D*, and so on.

Each item is submitted in the form *<item name>=<object contents>*. For example, if your user types "Sally" into an Editable text object called "name", the Submit Page action would send *name=Sally*. Similarly, if the user selects "West Coast" from a popup menu that you have named "Region" (in the Object tab), the Submit Page action sends *Region=West%20Coast*. If a button you've named "Get More Info" was turned on, the Submit Page action would send *Get%20More%20Info=on*.

Finally, all the items are submitted in one long string, separated by ampersands. So, the above text, popup menu, and button would get sent like this:

name=Sally&Region=West%20Coast&Get%20More%20Info=on

Popup menus always seem to be listed first in the string, followed by each of the other items in the order they appear in your project (from the top-most item to the bottom-most item; see "Object Layering," in Chapter 3, *Building Projects)*.

Your CGI script must somehow make sense of this mess and perform the task it was built to do.

▼ ▼

Transmission

Remember when television sets took 10 or 20 seconds (or more) to warm up? It never bothered me until I saw a newer model at a friend's house that provided a picture only a moment after being turned on. Now, how annoyed would you be if, while watching TV, you had to wait 10 or 20 seconds every time you changed the channel? What if you had to wait a minute or more?

Multimedia is a form of communication, but communication doesn't work when the person on the receiving end gets tired of waiting and turns off the computer. Currently, almost everything on the Internet falls into the "change the channel and wait" category and, frankly, most of it isn't worth the patience we give it.

Switching versus Transmission

The delay you experience when jumping from one URL to another can be broken down into two parts: switching time and transmission time. You can do very little about switching time. It's as though your computer is calling an operator, asking for a number, waiting for the operator to switch you to that number, and, finally, waiting for the person on the other end to pick up the phone. Yes, switching time is shorter for people with faster connections to the Internet (or those on an intranet). But that's only because their computers can talk to the "operators" faster.

When you break it down, data transmission time is what almost always causes the bottlenecks, the slowdowns, the annoying, still silences that make you feel like you're standing in a bread line, wishing that you'd never gotten hooked on this Internet thing. There is a debate raging in the Internet world revolving around how many graphics to put on your page. Text transmits across telephone lines very quickly. However, bitmapped graphics, sound, and movies, even when compressed (I'll be talking about compression in just a moment), are ungainly things that can take a long time to transmit.

Unfortunately, there's little to QuarkImmedia projects *other* than graphics, sound, and movies. Every page is a bitmapped graphic. Most of the text is rasterized into bitmapped graphics. Windows are all graphics, as are animations. So, while you can put any Immedia project on the Internet, you'd better think carefully about it first.

The first question you need to ask yourself when considering putting a project on the Internet is, "Who's my audience?" This question really breaks down into "What does my audience want?" and "How fast is their Internet connection?"

What they want. I rarely "surf the 'Net" looking for sites that look really cool. When I'm on the Internet, I'm usually looking for information, and I don't want to piddle around waiting for it. If your audience is using your project to get information, don't hamper them with anything unnecessary. Yes, Immedia gives you the tools to create your pages any way you want, but that won't mean diddly if people get bored, stop the transmission, and never see the page at all.

Internet connections. Bandwidth is like the diameter of a water pipe; the larger the bandwidth, the more data can move through it every second. Data (text, graphics, sounds, and so on) is the water that needs to move through the pipes. Time-sensitive data (stuff like movies, animations, and sound that rely on being played at a certain rate, without interruption) doesn't handle low bandwidth very well, so you get stutters, pauses, and generally poor performance. Non-time-sensitive data (like a page full of text, or a picture of the Queen) deals with low bandwidth by simply taking a long time to transmit before displaying.

If your audience is viewing your project from a hard drive, you have almost total free rein over what you put in your projects, because the bandwidth from a hard drive is enormous. Most of the world's CD-ROM drives are still relatively slow, so their effective bandwidth is much smaller than a hard drive. Intranets based on Ethernet are fast, but even Ethernet may have difficulty with Quick-Time movies and some larger sound files.

And if your audience plays your project over the Internet, you've got to be really careful because bandwidth over the Internet is really tight. A T1 line is a very fast, dedicated connection to the Internet, but it's still only about a sixth the speed of Ethernet. ISDN is about a sixth the speed of T1, and the vast majority of people who connect to the Internet use 28.8 Kbps or 14.4 Kbps modems, which are, at best, half the speed of ISDN.

Building an Immedia project suitable for transmitting over a 14.4 Kbps modem is . . . well, challenging. Faster dial-up modems (28.8 Kbps) can handle really basic projects. People with ISDN will still wince at projects that contain QuickTime movies, and so on . . . .

Server speed. Your audience could be viewing your project with a super-fast connection, but if your project is sitting on a slow Web server, or a Web server that has a slow connection to the Internet, it'll still run at a crawl. Unless it's your server, you may not have any control over this. Nonetheless, it's an important factor to keep in mind.

▼ ▼

Keeping Things Speedy

As I said earlier, bandwidth and size of data are the two major factors in how well a project performs over the Internet (or from a CD-ROM, for that matter). You, as a multimedia author, have very little control over your audience's bandwidth, but you've got lots of control over the data you provide them. Throughout the book I discuss methods to compress and simplify data so that takes less space on disk and transmits quickly. Here's a quick recap of the major issues.

Non-time-sensitive data. A great deal of your project is made up of non-time-sensitive data such as text, graphics, EPS files, and buttons. In order for these pieces to transmit quickly, they must be as simple as possible. Anti-aliasing text makes your page look better but compress less than leaving it aliased. Better yet, if you turn the text box into a text box object, the text compresses way down . . . at the expense of most of your character and paragraph formatting.

The more complex your graphics, the less they'll compress—a solid-color background may take up 3 K, while a scanned photograph might take up over 100 K.

A button is just two or more graphics, right? That means when you view a page that has a button, Immedia has to download two, three, four, or six different pictures. Of course, the more complex the button (more colors, more shades, fewer patterns, and so on), the less it compresses and the longer it'll take to download.

Time-sensitive data. Time-sensitive data, like QuickTime movies, animation sequences, and sounds are the biggest concern when bandwidth becomes limited, because when the information does not show up on time, the Immedia Viewer has to either pause or skip frames. Nobody likes the result.

Animations follow the same compression rules as graphics: smaller images, fewer colors, more solid or patterned areas. Sound and movies, on the other hand, are significantly more complex to work with and often require additional software to downsample successfully.

Keep It Simple

The most important rule in building projects for the Internet (and some may argue *any* multimedia project) is "Keep it simple." Yes, the world loves splash, but your projects won't splash if they move so slowly that they cure insomnia—they'll bellyflop. So keep it simple *and* keep it moving.

The Real World QuarkImmedia CD-ROM

I HAVE ALWAYS RELIED UPON THE KINDNESS of strangers. I'm not much of an illustrator, so to get the job done I often buy clip art drawn by other people. And, although I know enough about sound and animation to be dangerous, I often don't have time to sit down and build custom sound files or animations, so I use commercial clip media, at least for prototyping my projects.

Because I rely on clip media so much, when I started collecting files to put on the *Real World QuarkImmedia* CD-ROM at the back of this book, I knew that I needed to include as much clip media—animations, cursors, buttons, movies, and sounds—as I could. My hope is that you can rely upon the folks who built this stuff, especially while you get up to speed with building your own QuarkImmedia projects.

But that's not all I put on the CD-ROM. I've tried to fill the disc with programs and projects to help you learn this program and get your work done. The contents of the *Real World QuarkImmedia* CD-ROM break down into 10 sections.

▶ Sample projects

▶ QuarkXPress and QuarkImmedia demos

- ▶ PickUpSpot XTension

- ▶ Animations

- ▶ Backgrounds and Stills

- ▶ Buttons

- ▶ Cursors

- ▶ QuickTime Movies

- ▶ Sounds

- ▶ Utilities and demos

In this chapter, I delve into each of these areas, describing in broad strokes what you can expect to find on the disc, and how you might want to use it.

What Can You Give to Other People?

While some files on this disc are shareware or freeware, the majority of the *Real World QuarkImmedia* CD-ROM is for your use only. You bought the book, so you get the goodies. It's tempting to share this stuff because you got it "free," but you shouldn't.

Specifically, please don't give away any of the clip media files (movies, animations, cursors, buttons, background images, and so on), and please don't distribute any of the QuarkImmedia projects.

On the other hand, there are some files (notably demos of programs and freeware/shareware utilities) that you can give to any of your friends or relations. Throughout this chapter, I'll tell you when it's okay to distribute something. When in doubt, look for a ReadMe file on the disc for more information.

Shareware programs. Some application developers have included their software on this disc as shareware. That means that if you use any of these programs more than a couple of times, you're honor-bound to send the software developer money. Buying this book does not help the developer put food on their table . . . your registering the program does.

Most shareware utilities or XTensions come with a ReadMe file that tells you where to send your money (you can often register the software electronically). When you do, you may get a better, cooler, more updated version of the software. Or you might receive a good deal on future upgrades and other products they sell. And sometimes you just feel better about yourself for helping support a programmer who invested a lot of hard work in creating the software.

Copyright stuff. Please note that every item on the *Real World QuarkImmedia* CD-ROM is copyrighted by someone. Although you have permission to use or change some of these pieces for projects you make, you almost certainly don't have the right to sell the files themselves. For instance, you can customize one of the buttons and then put it in a project that you sell, but you cannot sell the button itself. Again, I discuss this more later in this chapter, but you should also check for ReadMe files when in doubt.

▼ ▼

Sample Projects

In previous chapters, I've mentioned several QuarkImmedia projects as examples you might look at to learn how to create some sort of effect—from AppleScripts to custom menus. These projects and more are in the Projects folder on the disc. Some of these projects are accompanied by their source files (the original XPress documents) and may even include some of the media (sounds, button libraries, and so on) used to make them.

I encourage you not only to play with the projects, but also to explore the source files to see how they were built. There's rarely a "right" way to make an Immedia project, so don't take the methods you see as anything more than a helpful guide in learning how to use this program.

The Viewer. While a few of these projects are "standalone" (the Viewer has been embedded), most of them require the QuarkImmedia Viewer to play. If you do not have the Viewer on your hard

drive already, double-clicking on the project will launch the Viewer
from the CD-ROM. This is okay, but the projects usually play more
smoothly if you first drag one of the Viewers onto your hard drive.
You can find a QuarkImmedia Viewer in the QuarkImmedia Demo
folder on the disc.

The projects. Here's a quick description of each project in the Projects folder, and why you might find it interesting.

> ► **Aesop's Fables.** The Aesop's Fables project demonstrates one
> method of building custom menus. It also shows you several
> techniques for displaying text on your pages when you've got
> more text than can fit on a single screen.

> ► **AppleScripts.** In Chapter 3, *Building Projects*, I mentioned
> that QuarkImmedia can trigger system-level AppleScripts on
> a Macintosh with the Run AppleScript action. You can do all
> kinds of things with AppleScripts, including controlling File-
> Maker Pro, QuarkXPress, Photoshop, the Finder, and more. In
> this project, I demonstrate just a few simple AppleScripts
> that control your Mac's sound volume and that build docu-
> ments in QuarkXPress. I've also included a little "don't touch
> me" script written by AppleScript-meister Sal Soghoian. Don't
> worry, its effect may surprise you, but it's never hurt anyone.

> ► **Conditional project.** Jason Carncross built a little project that
> helps teach how to use conditionals when building scripts
> (see Chapter 13, *Scripting)*. First look at the project and see
> what it does. Next, open the QuarkXPress document called
> "Colors No Scripts" and see if you can add scripts that make
> this project do the same as the exported project. If you want
> to see how he did it, take a look at the "Colors" document. But
> remember, there's more than one way to skin a peach.

> ► **eSCENE.** Jeff Carlson is the editor of *eSCENE*, an anthology of
> the best short stories published on the Internet, and he
> designed this project as a promotional piece for the Web site.
> While you can't see the original XPress document, it's fun to
> just explore the site and try to figure out what he did. (Hint:

almost everything in the project is built using Hide Object and Show Object.) If you have an Internet connection, you can also link to his HTML Web page, where you can see (and read) some cool stuff.

▶ **Internet Project.** I wrote the Internet Project as a test of two things. First, I wanted to build a simple hide-and-seek game. Second, I wanted to incorporate several of the Internet actions. When you first launch this project, the Viewer reads a single word from a text file on the Internet and then places it somewhere in the game (the word will change from time to time). When you succeed on the first level, the project jumps to the second level in the game. However, the second level of the game is on the Internet!

▶ **Japan Language.** I love Japan, though I don't know much Japanese. Here's a little project that Debra Carlson and I built that teaches a little about the Japanese language and demonstrates some fun effects, such as text appearing over a picture, and using foreign-language text on screen.

▶ **Mags and Pubs.** QuarkImmedia is a great way to build interfaces to a database of information. In the Mags and Pubs project, I've organized a database of desktop-publishing-related publishers and magazines that Thad McIlroy compiled. What's fun is that I could use the same project to display all kinds of information. Note the button group on the second page (you can only have one button—Magazines *or* Publishers—selected at a time. This project also shows how you can use the Find Text and Add List Items Using Search actions in your projects.

▶ **NecessaryColors.** Fewer colors in your project means that Immedia can compress your projects more, and the smaller the file the faster it'll run, especially over the Internet. The NecessaryColors project is really basic: it displays three indexed-color images at various bit depths so you can see the differences in image quality.

▶ **One-Minute Tutorial.** The "One-Minute Tutorial" in Chapter 2, *QuarkImmedia Basics,* should get you up and running with the program. But if you're the kind of person who learns best by seeing, run through the One-Minute Tutorial project on the disc. I show you, using QuickTime movies built with Vision Software's CameraMan, how to assign actions to objects on your page.

▶ **Peter Tögel.** Peter Tögel works at Quark and seems to have way too much time on his hands. He's included four Immedia projects on this CD-ROM: Balloon, Easter Egg, Helicop, and Rage. Three of the projects are games; the fourth, Rage, is an on-line version of a church newsletter. I find the Easter Egg project almost impossible to figure out without looking at the source XPress document first (and even then it's difficult). The other games are fun, though.

▶ **Quark.** You may have seen Quark's series of prototype CDs. They've built some really beautiful projects, and I wanted to make sure I included at least two of them. Here, then, are Connect with QuarkImmedia and Sword Quest. The first was built by Quark's multimedia department and is a blatant commercial plug for their product—but I love the animation and sound! The second, Sword Quest, is a very impressive Myst-like game built by Quark employee Jason Carncross. Just exploring the Sword Quest world he's built is fun, but solving the puzzles is even better.

▶ **QX Tips & Tricks.** I've been presenting QuarkXPress Tips and Tricks courses at conferences for years, and people keep asking me when I'm going to put some of them into a multimedia presentation. The answer is "right now." Of course, this project only shows two tips . . . . Nonetheless, it demonstrates another way to use QuarkImmedia as a training tool.

▶ **Spudnoggin.** One of the things you'll find when working with QuarkImmedia is that you'll start building silly projects just for the fun of it. Trevor Alyn (another Quark employee) built the Spudnoggin project and put it on the Internet for all to see.

I couldn't help myself—I had to include it here (with his permission, of course).

▶ **Transitions.** In Chapter 3, *Building Projects,* I discussed the 18 default transitions and all the custom transitions you could build. Transitions are much easier to show than to write about, so I built the Transitions project. I used Show Object and Hide Object to show 27 different transitions. Special design note: I forgot to build a Quit button—but Command-Q always works, of course.

▶ **Zap!** Don Seller's book *Zap! How Your Computer Can Hurt You and What You Can Do About It* is the most complete computer health book on the market. He gave me the file for a chapter of the book and I built this project for him. Even though the book was produced in PageMaker, it only took me about a day to convert the chapter into a QuarkImmedia project.

▶ **Jump to URLs.** Where can you find more projects to look at? Where can you find other tools that help you in your multimedia ordeals? If your computer is connected to the Internet (either with a SLIP, a PPP, or another kind of TCP connection), the Jump to URLs project lets you open several projects on the Internet, including my "coolsite" and "Site of Sites" projects.

▼ ▼

QuarkXPress and QuarkImmedia

If you already own QuarkXPress or QuarkImmedia, you can skip this section (and the folder on the disc). If you don't own the programs, the QuarkImmedia Demo folder lets you take them for a test drive.

1. There are four copies of QuarkXPress and QuarkImmedia on the *Real World QuarkImmedia* CD-ROM. Your first step is to find the right one for you. If you use a Macintosh based on a 680X0 chip (like a Quadra or a Centris), open the Macintosh Demo folder. If you use a Mac based on a PowerPC chip (like

any of the PowerMacs and the newer Performa models), open the Power Macintosh Demo folder.

2. Next, you must choose between the English and International English copies of QuarkXPress and QuarkImmedia. If you use an American system, use the English program; if you use any other English-language system (like Australian or British), you should use the International English copy. If you use any other language, check with Quark to get the appropriate files. (I'd have included more languages on the disc, but these were the only ones that were ready when we went to press.)

3. You can't run QuarkXPress from the CD-ROM, so you must copy the whole folder (the folder of whichever copy of XPress works on your machine) onto your hard drive.

System extensions. QuarkImmedia requires several system extensions to run, including QuickTime 2.1 (or later) and Sound Manager 3.1 (or later). Unfortunately, I cannot include these files on the CD-ROM.* These files come standard in the system software these days, so you may have them already (they'd be in the Extensions folder in your System Folder). Otherwise, you may be able to download them from Apple's Web site.

▼ ▼

Tip: Get Your XTensions Here. Quark has released lots of free XTensions over the past few years, including ones with exotic names like Bobzilla, Thing-a-ma-Bob, and Jabberwocky. If you don't have these cool XTensions already, here's your chance. They're all in a folder called Quark XTensions, inside each of the QuarkXPress folders on the disc. Most of them include ReadMe files that describe what they do and how they do it.

▼ ▼

---

*If you've ever dealt with Apple's legal department, you know why.

▼ ▼

PickUpSpot XT

One of the most trying aspects of building multimedia projects is working with custom color palettes. How, for instance, can you get a color from a Photoshop color palette into your list of colors in QuarkXPress? PickUpSpot is an XTension written by Roy Lovejoy of Adept Solutions. His solution to the problem is certainly adept indeed. When you have PickUpSpot loaded (put the PickUpSpot XT file in the XTension folder in your QuarkXPress folder, and then launch XPress), you can copy any color from a PICT or TIFF image into your XPress color list.

Here's how you can use this cool XTension.

1. If you haven't saved the custom color palette to your hard drive from Photoshop, do it now.

2. Open Photoshop's Swatches palette and choose Load Swatches from the palette's popout menu. Choose the custom color palette from your hard drive.

3. Increase the size of the Swatches palette until you can see all 256 colors.

4. Take a screen capture of the screen (press Command-Shift-3). This saves exactly what you see on screen to your startup disk as a PICT file, usually named Picture0 or Picture1.

5. Import this PICT file into a QuarkXPress picture box; make sure you can see the picture of the Swatches palette.

6. Open the PickUpSpot palette (choose PickUpSpot from the Utilities menu; if it's not there, you may not have loaded the XTension in the correct folder).

7. With the picture box selected, click on the picture of the dog in the palette (see Figure 16–1; that's Spot . . . get it?).

Figure 16–1
PickUpSpot XTension

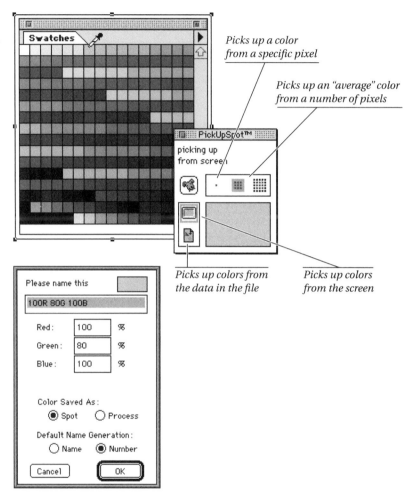

Picks up a color
from a specific pixel

Picks up an "average" color
from a number of pixels

Picks up colors from
the data in the file

Picks up colors
from the screen

8. Click on the color in the picture that you want added to your XPress color list. PickUpSpot asks you how you want the color named and saved, and then adds it for you lickety-split.

It's commercial software. Note that PickUpSpot is commercial software that retails for almost $100. However, the developer is extending a special offer to you because you bought this book: for you, the software is "shareware." If you like it and use it more than once or twice, you are honor-bound to send $40 to Adept Solutions (their postal and e-mail addresses are in the ReadMe file on the disc). Make sure you include a note saying that you got the XTension from the CD-ROM in this book.

This XTension is network copy-protected, so you can't use it on more than one machine on your network. If you want to buy more copies for other people on your network, contact the publisher, and I'm sure they'll try to give you a good deal.

▼ ▼

Clip Media

You may have worked with clip art before; clip media is the same thing except that it's for multimedia. Every clip media file on the *Real World QuarkImmedia* CD-ROM is royalty free, so you can use it in any of your projects without additional cost. Most of the files come from commercial clip media distributors; they've included their stuff in the hopes that you'll like it so much that you'll buy their products. Please check out the ReadMe files in each of the folders for more information.

I've also included lots of clip media files that I (and my cohorts) have built for your enjoyment. As I noted earlier in the chapter, this stuff may be royalty-free, but please don't distribute the clip media files to other people for them to use.

Animations

Need a cool animation to liven up your project? All the animations in the Animations folder have been saved in QuarkImmedia's animation file format, so you just have to import them into a picture box and you'll be raring to go (see Chapter 8, *Animations)*.

The only commercial company represented here is PhotoDisc, which publishes some of the best royalty-free photographs in the business. When you buy their animation packages, the animations come as PICS or animated GIFs; we've converted six of them to Immedia's animation format for you.

The other animations in this folder were built by Jeff Carlson of Never Enough Coffee creations using Strata StudioPro. Some of these are meant to loop, such as the A, the Bell, the Earth, and the Cube animations. Others can be used as animated buttons, such as the Toggle Switch and the Door animations.

Backgrounds and Stills

A white background is a boring background. It's easy to spice up your presentations and projects with a cool background texture. I've included a number of images and textures that can be used as backgrounds, though some are more flexible than others. For instance, the images from Image Farm and Jawai Screen Caffeine Pro are PICTs you can use as backgrounds. The images from Image Club Graphic's WebMorsels and Cartesia's MapArt samples are clip art page elements that you may want to add to a background.

Artbeats. I don't want to gush too much, but I love Artbeats's products. The CD-ROM products they create contain some of the most beautiful artwork on the market, including Marbled Paper, Leather and Fabric, Wood and Paper, and Marble and Granite. I've included a number of files from their discs, including some really excellent seamless tiles (you can open these in Photoshop to build background textures as large as you want), and some sample buttons from the Marble and Granite CD.

I've also included a sample of Artbeats's WebTools product, a cooperative effort between Artbeats and stat™media. The commercial product contains over 600 MB of buttons, sounds, tiles, animations, and background images. This sample lets you look at many of these files, but only lets you save a few to your hard disk.

Backgrounds and buttons. The same Jason Carncross who built Sword Quest and the Conditional project has contributed dozens of background images that he's built, plus a Photoshop file filled with some interesting buttons and interface elements you can customize and use for your own projects.

Buttons

I don't know why, but I love cool buttons (see Chapter 6, *Buttons)*. I've included over 100 fully functional buttons that I've made, and from commercial products like Jawai's Screen Caffeine Pro, Image Club Graphic's WebMorsels, and Artbeats's WebTools CD-ROM.

Some are already in button libraries that you can open directly in QuarkImmedia. And while some of the commercial buttons include source files in Photoshop, too (so you can customize them to your needs), others are only source files, and you'll have to build the Immedia buttons with the old cut-and-paste method.

Real World QuarkImmedia buttons. The Real World QuarkImmedia folder inside the Button folder contains dozens of buttons that I've built and placed in button libraries (I've also included their source Photoshop files). The libraries are placed inside a hierarchical folder structure that may seem complex, but was intended to make it easy to find the button you want when you want it.

▶ The Round and Round Indent buttons are broken down into aliased and anti-aliased groups. You can use the anti-aliased buttons when the button is on a white (or very light) background; otherwise, you should use the aliased buttons. I've also included the Photoshop, Illustrator, and Adobe Dimensions documents that I used to build these buttons; that way, you can customize them to your heart's delight.

▶ The Square and RoundSquare buttons are only available as source Illustrator and Photoshop files.

▶ The buttons in the Dialog Box button library fit into standard Macintosh dialog boxes. They include checkboxes, radio buttons, and buttons labeled OK, Yes, No, Save, and so on.

▶ The Keys button library contains a number of rectangular and square buttons to fit any occasion.

Cursors

Custom cursors can be a fun addition to any project. Plus, a custom cursor is often useful for telling a user what to do. For instance, the pointing finger cursors in Sword Quest leave no question as to what will happen when you press the mouse button.

I've included 18 custom cursors of my own—from phases of the moon to a slowly turning square—in the Cursors folder, which should get you started in making your own. While most of my cursors are black and white, remember that a cursor can contain up to 256 different colors (see Chapter 10, *Cursors*).

QuickTime Movies

I discussed how to play QuickTime movies in Chapter 9, *QuickTime Movies*. However, many people don't have QuickTime movies just lying about, so I've included a handful of them on the CD-ROM.

▶ **Four Palms.** Four Palms is one of the foremost clip-movie distributors in the multimedia market. They've let me include six QuickTime movies of people at work and play, but they've got discs that cover a number of subjects, including planes, trains, and automobiles.

▶ **PaceWorks.** PaceWorks publishes a very cool product called Dancer which lets you build animations quickly and painlessly (it even has features that help you synchronize your animations with music). I wanted to include a full demo of the product, but we weren't able to get it in time. Instead, I'm including a single QuickTime movie that was built using Dancer. Check out the ReadMe file for more information on the program and how to get a demo of it.

▶ **Plastic Thought.** The folks at Plastic Thought have let me use 10 movies of various rotating objects from their 3D Active and ActiveArt WebEdition collections. Some of these are kind of funky (like the toy airplane or the DNA strand). Others are pretty practical (like a rotating floppy disk or the open book). All of them are on a black background. If you're a 3D maven, you'll be happy to note that we've also included the 3DMF and DXF files for each of these objects. If you know how, you can use these files to render the images any way you want.

▶ **Specular.** The last folder in the QuickTime movie folder contains four cool movies that were built using products from Specular International, like Infini-D. These really weren't designed as clip media at all; they're just fun to look at.

Sounds

Compiling all the sounds (there are almost 90 different sound files on the disc) was a lot of fun. I've included both special effect sounds (like bike bells, frog sounds, and submarine sonar blips) and music (everything from rock to classical to new age).

Note that some of the music clips are saved in the QuickTime General MIDI format, so you'll have to play them like a movie (see Chapter 7, *Sound,* and Chapter 9, *QuickTime Movies).* QuickTime MIDI requires a Macintosh with the QuickTime Musical Instruments file loaded (in the Extension folder in the System Folder) in order to sound right.

The sounds on the *Real World QuarkImmedia* CD-ROM come from five commercial developers.

▶ **Artbeats.** These special effect sounds are from the Artbeats WebTools disc.

▶ **Desktop Media.** These loops and musical interludes were composed by Nelson Kole for Desktop Media. There are two types of sounds here: Loops and Page Transitions. Note that Desktop Media wants you to use the sounds on this disc only in projects for your own use (not those that you do for clients). Of course, if you later decide to buy the sounds directly from them, you can use them in any of your projects.

▶ **Jawai Interactive.** I'm including one whole song from Jawai Interactive's JavaBeat CD-ROM in both AIFF and QuickTime MIDI format. The song (about 11 MB in AIFF format) is then broken down into each of its component parts (violins, cellos, and so on). It's kind of fun to listen once to the whole song, then listen to each of the shorter elements of the song.

▶ **Libman Music.** The RoarShox CD-ROM is chock full of fun sounds that they insist are designed for playing on the Internet. Why stop at that? These sounds are cool for a number of multimedia applications. I'm particularly impressed by the QuickTime MIDI files. Most of these sounds are short and built to loop, for hours of endless sound. Note that some of the AIFF and QuickTime MIDI sounds are the same—for example, "AirPipes" and "AirPipes.midi Movie." Try playing both of them; then take a look at the difference in their file size!

▶ **The Hollywood Edge.** Hollywood Edge has hundreds of special effects sounds. However, they're still getting used to the new world of multimedia, so they only offer the sounds on audio CDs. I've included 26 sounds from one of their discs (I saved them as AIFF files from the audio CD using FWB's CD-ROM Toolkit). Some of these sounds are silly (like boings and clangs); others make great background noise (like "Department Store Noise" and "Heavy Rain"); but I find them all really useful when building projects.

▼ ▼
Utilities and Demos

QuarkImmedia does not exist in a vacuum. Sure, you can do a lot just with Immedia, but why not make life easier for yourself and use other programs and utilities for what *they're* good for? For example, you probably already use Adobe Photoshop to make many of the graphic elements in your projects (if not, you probably should). How do you make buttons? You can build them in Photoshop by hand (I describe some methods in Chapter 6, *Buttons)*, but it's so much easier to make 3D-looking buttons when you've got a Photoshop plug-in like PhotoTools or WildRiverSSK.

In this section I discuss a few additional tools that you can use to make your life a happier place. Each of these are in the Utilities and Demos folder on the *Real World QuarkImmedia* CD-ROM. Some are full-working versions, while others are just demos. They all have ReadMe files (although with some you have to install the software on your hard drive in order to find the ReadMe).

Specular 3D Web Workshop. When I first saw Specular's 3D Web Workshop, they were pushing it as a tool for building elements of HTML pages for the Internet. But I regarded it as something different: to me, it simply makes 72 dpi images, and anything that makes 72 dpi images can be used for QuarkImmedia projects. I'm including a demo version of 3D Web Workshop, which gives you a taste of the product. Even though you need PageMill or an HTML-compat-ible Web browser to see a lot of what they've done, while you're play-ing with the program, don't think HTML . . . think "I could use these images and animations in Immedia."

Adobe Acrobat Reader. Since many of the developers put their ReadMe files or documentation on the disc in Acrobat PDF format, I've included the Acrobat Reader (version 2.1). This is freeware, and will let you view almost all Acrobat files. See Chapter 14, *Exporting*, for a discussion of Acrobat versus Immedia.

Dejal SndConverter Pro. SndConverter Pro 2.3 is a sound-editing utility from Dejal Userware. It lets you convert batches of sound from one format to another (like AIFF to SND), downsample sounds, reduce a sound's bit depth, and filter sound names. This is a shareware program (after you use it for a while, it starts to shut off features until you send in a registration fee).

Equilibrium DeBabelizer. As I noted back in Chapter 3, *Building Projects*, no discussion of multimedia would be complete without a word or two on Equilibrium's DeBabelizer. This software is, unfor-tunately, quite complicated to learn at first; but it's worth it and, once you get a few basics, it all makes some sort of twisted sense.

I've included two versions of DeBabelizer on the disc at the back of the book. The first, DeBabelizer 1.6.5 Demo, is a demonstration version of the full-featured product. You can see everything that the program does, but you cannot save or print any work that you do in it, and all the batch conversion features are disabled.

The second version, DeBabelizer Lite LE, is a "limited edition" version of the "Lite" version of DeBabelizer. The Lite version is a file translation program (it doesn't include any of DeBabelizer's cool col-or palette tools, scripting, or image processing tools). However, while the full Lite version handles over 60 different file formats, this limited edition only translates among GIF, TIFF, BMP, and PICT. That's fine with me; those are the file types I use most often! For example, I use this to convert GIF files to PICT files, so that I can import them into my Immedia projects.

Note that the demo version of DeBabelizer also comes with a bunch of demo versions of Photoshop filters from various developers (the full version of DeBabelizer lets you run the same filter on a batch of images).

Quid Pro Quo. More and more people want to create Immedia projects for the Internet, but there's another option: building projects for *intra*nets (see Chapter 15, *The Internet and the World Wide Web).* There are many shareware and freeware (and commercial) Web servers out there that let you build an intranet, but the one I've been using is called Quid Pro Quo (it used to be called WebCenter).

Of course, you can use a Web server for other things than building an intranet. I often launch Quid Pro Quo on my own Macintosh and use it to test CGI scripts before I put them on a Web server connected to the Internet. It's just so much faster! If the idea of a Web server makes you nervous, try this one out . . . it's as easy as double-clicking (although reading the documentation helps, too).

Note that Quid Pro Quo is constantly being updated. If you need a newer version, you can find it at http://www.slaphappy.com.

Movie Cleaner Lite. Terran Interactive's Movie Cleaner Pro is used every day by many professionals working with QuickTime movies. It lets you optimize and compress QuickTime movies for distribution on CD-ROM or the Internet. The version on the *Real World QuarkImmedia* disc is the Lite version; it lets you use some tools, but you can't tweak the movies with any of the advanced features.

DataStream WildRiverSSK. You may have heard about the Sucking Fish plug-in filters for Adobe Photoshop. These filters were freeware and the one that most people used most often was called DekoBoko, which let you build beveled rectangular buttons quickly. Well, Datastream worked with the developer of DekoBoko to create a new package of Photoshop plug-ins called WildRiverSSK. DekoBoko is in this package, but it's much better and easier to use than it used to be. WildRiverSSK also includes other filters that help you create incredible effects, like fire and rain, drop shadows, and embosses.

I've included the demo version of WildRiverSSK on the disc. However, this demo version is really just a severely limited version: you can only use the DekoBoko filter, and you can only use it on a single color. Nonetheless, it's worth taking a look at if you have to make a lot of buttons.

Extensis PhotoTools. Extensis has created a set of plug-ins for Photoshop that are really great and really easy to use. I find myself using PhotoTools constantly when building buttons for my QuarkImmedia projects, though it does more than just bevel selections. For instance, one of the filters in the package, PhotoText, lets you edit text in a WYSIWYG mode inside Photoshop, so you can adjust the font, size, kerning, color, and so on. Another filter lets you create glow effects.

I've included a demo version of PhotoTools on the CD-ROM. Extensis has been very generous with their demo package—it works fully for 30 days, during which you'll get a very good sense of everything it does.

Extensis QX Tools. Extensis, knowing some good technology when they see it, bundled up the bevel, glow, and drop shadow technology that they developed for PhotoTools and turned it into a Quark XTension. This means you can create buttons and other effects right in your QuarkXPress picture boxes without having to go to the trouble of opening Photoshop or switching between applications.

But the Photoshop-like effects are only one part of the QX-Tools package (see Figure 16–2). There are 14 other XTensions in the package. Some are cooler than others, in my estimation, but there are some that you just should not be without—like the QX-Layers palette that lets you put different objects on different layers, or the QX-Scale palette that lets you scale multiple objects on your page at the same time. If you don't already have an XTension package that does these things, take a look at QX-Tools.

The QX-Tools demo on the *Real World QuarkImmedia* CD-ROM works the same way as the PhotoTools demo—it works fully for 30 days, then it gracefully turns itself off (unless you've gone and bought by then).

Figure 16–2
Creating buttons
with QX-Tools

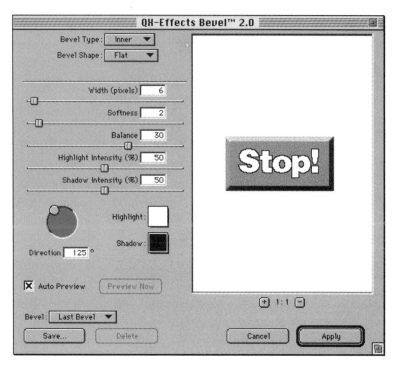

Figure 16–2
Creating buttons
with QX-Tools

▼ ▼

Playing Around

There's almost 500 MB of clip media, programs, demos, sample projects, and source files on the *Real World QuarkImmedia* CD-ROM, enough to keep you busy for a long while. I hope that this chapter has given you a good idea of the sorts of things you can expect to find, and where you can expect to find them at 11 p.m. the night before a big deadline.

The most important lesson of this chapter, and indeed the whole book, is simply "play with the stuff." By playing with the programs, trying out ideas, and looking at other people's work, you will learn QuarkImmedia inside and out in no time. Enjoy!

Colophon

IF I'VE LEARNED ANYTHING over the years, it's that the process is often just as important as the final product. And so, while all you're holding is a printed and bound book, let me give you some insight into the process behind it.

Equipment. One of the questions that I'm most often asked is, "What kind of computer do you use?" In the interests of full disclosure, I use a Macintosh PowerBook 5300c, a Quadra 640, and a PowerMac 8100. I have a Linotype-Hell Saphir scanner, a Radius 17-inch monitor, and 144 MB of RAM (among the three machines).

Software. This book was written almost entirely in Microsoft Word and laid out using QuarkXPress. Illustrations were built using Beale Street Group's ScreenShot utility and Adobe Photoshop. While this book describes QuarkImmedia version 1.01, much of the book was originally written using pre-release "beta" versions of the product (an adventure in itself).

Design and production. The design of this book relied heavily on the book designs of Olav Martin Kvern and Glenn Fleishman. Body text is set in Adobe Utopia 10/15, heads are in the Adobe Futura family.

Finally, the book was imageset and printed by R.R. Donnelly & Sons on 50-pound Athens Opaque Smooth paper.

Where to Find Me

A S WE GO TO PRESS, QuarkImmedia 1.0 has only been shipping for a very short time, and if I know anything about Quark's process, the product will probably be revised several times in the coming months. Because there's no way that Peachpit Press will let me revise and reprint the book that often, I'm going to publish new information about Immedia on my Web site.

But here's the deal: I'll keep writing, but I want to hear back from you, too. I want to hear how you're using QuarkImmedia and what kinds of projects you're building. I want to hear about any Web sites you've built in Immedia. And I want to hear about all the fun tips, tricks, and clever workarounds that you're discovering as you use this new program. And I'm certainly open to hearing constructive criticism about how to make this book better, too.

How to Reach Me

David Blatner
1619 – 8th Ave North
Seattle, WA 98109 USA
fax: (206) 285-0308
e-mail: david@moo.com
Web site: www.moo.com

Where to Find Book Updates

With an HTML Web browser:

www.moo.com/rwi/updates.html

With the QuarkImmedia Viewer:

www.moo.com/rwi/updates.imd

How to Reach Peachpit Press

Peachpit Press

2414 Sixth St.

Berkeley, CA 94710 USA

(510) 548-4393

fax: (510) 548-5991

e-mail: tell@peachpit.com

Web site: www.peachpit.com

How to Reach Quark Technical Support

Quark, Inc.

1800 Grant St.

Denver, CO 80203 USA

(303) 894-8899

fax: (303) 894-3398

Technical support via e-mail:

QuarkXPress for the Macintosh: mactech@quark.com

QuarkXPress for Windows: wintech@quark.com

QuarkImmedia: qimmediasupport@quark.com

America Online forums: keyword QUARK

CompuServe forums: GO QUARK

Web site: www.quark.com

Index

More from Peachpit Press

Designing Multimedia

Lisa Lopuck

If you're interested in being part of the booming field of multimedia, this beautifully illustrated volume shows you how. Its concept-to-product approach is highly visual: with stunning, full-color samples of actual multimedia projects. Title structure, user interface, software dynamics, and many other factors that affect design decisions are explained in detail. *$34.95 (144 pages)*

The QuarkXPress Book, Fourth Edition for Macintosh

David Blatner and Eric Taub

If you're serious about QuarkXPress, this is the book to have. It's the highest rated, most comprehensive, and bestselling QuarkXPress book ever published. Now totally updated and rewritten to cover version 3.3, it includes a handy tear-out card showing keystroke shortcuts. Includes XTensions, EfiColor, and AppleEvent scripting. Winner of the Benjamin Franklin Award, Computer Book Category, and runner-up for the Publish Readers' Choice Award, Mac Book Category. *$29.95 (778 pages)*

QuarkXPress Tips & Tricks, 2nd Edition

David Blatner, Phil Gaskill, and Eric Taub

The smartest, most useful shortcuts from *The QuarkXPress Book*—plus many more—are packed into this book. You'll find answers to common questions as well as insights on techniques that will show you how to become a QuarkXPress power user. Includes a CD-ROM with useful XTensions and demos. *$34.95 (448 pages, w/CD-ROM)*

Real World Scanning and Halftones

David Blatner and Steve Roth

Master the digital halftone process—from scanning images, to tweaking them on your computer, to imagesetting them. Learn about optical character recognition, gamma control, sharpening, PostScript halftones, Photo CD, and image-manipulating applications like Photoshop and PhotoStyler. *$24.95 (296 pages)*

Real World Photoshop 3

David Blatner and Bruce Fraser

If you're looking for straight answers about real production issues Photoshop users deal with on a daily basis, this book can help. It explains in simple language the essential concepts and techniques for producing great-looking documents quickly and efficiently, covering in depth the key Photoshop tools. It's richly illustrated with scores of photographs (color and black-and-white) and many line drawings and screenshots. *$39.95 (600 pages)*

The Photoshop 3 Wow! Book, Macintosh Edition

Linnea Dayton, Jack Davis

A worldwide bestseller! Full color throughout, this book shows exactly how professional artists employ Photoshop 3 to manipulate scanned images and create an astonishing array of special effects. Each chapter deconstructs an actual piece of art, showing step by step how it was created. Most examples were created for real-world commercial uses. There's also a section showing the effects of scores of filters from Adobe, MetaTools, and other vendors. The companion CD contains Photo CD images and a variety of filters and utilities. Winner of a 1995 Computer Press Award. *$39.95 (288 pages w/CD-ROM)*

Order Form

USA 800-283-9444 • 510-548-4393 • FAX 510-548-5991
CANADA 800-387-8028 • 416-447-1779 • FAX 800-456-0536 OR 416-443-0948

Qty	Title	Price	Total
	SUBTOTAL		
	ADD APPLICABLE SALES TAX*		
	SHIPPING		
	TOTAL		

Shipping is by UPS ground: $4 for first item, $1 each add'l.

*We are required to pay sales tax in all states with the exceptions of AK, DE, MT, NH, and OR. Please include appropriate sales tax if you live in any state not mentioned above.

Customer Information

NAME

COMPANY

STREET ADDRESS

CITY   STATE   ZIP

PHONE (   )   FAX (   )
[REQUIRED FOR CREDIT CARD ORDERS]

Payment Method

☐ CHECK ENCLOSED   ☐ VISA   ☐ MASTERCARD   ☐ AMEX

CREDIT CARD #   EXP. DATE

COMPANY PURCHASE ORDER #

Tell Us What You Think

PLEASE TELL US WHAT YOU THOUGHT OF THIS BOOK: TITLE:

WHAT OTHER BOOKS WOULD YOU LIKE US TO PUBLISH?

PEACHPIT PRESS • 2414 Sixth Street • Berkeley, CA 94710